REINVENTING
HIGHER EDUCATION

REINVENTING HIGHER EDUCATION

The Promise of Innovation

Ben Wildavsky, Andrew P. Kelly,
and Kevin Carey

Editors

HARVARD EDUCATION PRESS
CAMBRIDGE, MASSACHUSETTS

Second Printing, 2012

Library of Congress Control Number 2010942139

Paperback ISBN 978-1-934742-87-7
Library Edition ISBN 978-1-934742-88-4

Published by Harvard Education Press,
an imprint of the Harvard Education Publishing Group

Harvard Education Press
8 Story Street
Cambridge, MA 02138

Cover Design: Sarah Henderson
The typefaces used in this book are Minion, Helvetica Neue, and Knockout

Contents

Acknowledgments

IN THE FALL OF 2009, we set out to explore a fundamental question about innovation in higher education: why, in spite of a steady increase in the enrollment of nontraditional students, a steep decline in tenured faculty positions, and revolutionary developments in technology that have touched nearly every other part of society, do most universities still operate much as they did fifty years ago? We quickly found that there had been relatively little systematic research on efforts to innovate or increase productivity within higher education, the environments in which reformers and entrepreneurs operate, or the hazards that may accompany the implementation of new ideas.

To fill this gap, we commissioned eight pieces of new research from a group of eminent researchers and policy analysts. We asked them to examine the potential for innovation in higher education, to explore how to reshape aspects of the traditional postsecondary system, and to analyze the pitfalls that may accompany these reform efforts. We would like to thank the authors for their fine contributions, and for being such active and engaged participants throughout the process.

The collection of essays included here was first presented at a research conference at the American Enterprise Institute (AEI) in June 2010. We thank the following discussants for their invaluable feedback and assistance in shaping these early drafts at that conference: William Kirwan, chancellor of the University System of Maryland; Suzanne Walsh, senior program officer at the Bill & Melinda Gates Foundation; Jack Schuster, senior research fellow and professor emeritus at Claremont Graduate University; Candace Thille, director of the Open Learning Initiative at Carnegie Mellon University; Charlene Nunley, professor at University of Maryland University College; Andrew Rosen, chairman and CEO of Kaplan, Inc.; and Richard Miller, professor and president Franklin W. Olin College of Engineering.

Of course, we are grateful for the unwavering support provided by the Kauffman Foundation, the American Enterprise Institute, and Education Sector. We express our deepest gratitude for financial support for this project from the Bill & Melinda Gates Foundation. Thanks are also due to the wonderful staff at AEI, whose hard work in coordinating the conference as well as compiling and editing the contributions herein we could not have done without. In particular, we would like to thank Raphael Gang and Olivia Meeks for their diligent efforts, as well as Whitney Downs, Daniel Lautzenheiser, and Jenna Schuette for their vital assistance. Finally, we are deeply indebted to the terrific team at Harvard Education Press, most notably Doug Clayton, executive director of the Harvard Education Publishing Group, and editorial and production manager Marcy Barnes, who consistently supported and enriched our efforts to make this volume a reality.

Introduction

Ben Wildavsky, Andrew P. Kelly,
and Kevin Carey

AMERICANS ARE ASKING much of their colleges and universities. A slew of public and philanthropic leaders, including President Obama, have called for a dramatic increase in the number of citizens earning college degrees. Observers of globalization point to the need for U.S. universities to keep up with the rest of the world in today's highly competitive educational marketplace.

But far from being poised to meet the challenge, the U.S. higher education system seems more beleaguered every day. State law makers have withdrawn billions of dollars in public funding. Tenure-track jobs are becoming increasingly scarce. While technology has transformed much of society, many public and private nonprofit institutions seem permanently set in ways that were established decades or even centuries ago. The only part of college not mired in tradition is the price.

The result is growing frustration with and within a part of society that has long enjoyed great esteem. Chasing after more dollars in an austere fiscal environment and funneling resources into the same old system won't solve this problem. Higher education has to change. It needs more innovation.

This notion cuts against the common perception of American higher education as the best and most diverse system of postsecondary learning the world has ever seen. It's true that the United States has the lion's share

1

of the world's great research universities and a fabulous array of institutions from which to choose: public and private, religious and nondenominational, single-gender and minority-serving, urban and rural, gigantic and small. With so much excellence and variation, the argument goes, who could reasonably ask for more?

But these impressions can be deceiving. Beneath a relatively thin layer of world-class research universities and elite liberal arts colleges lies a system that has too often proved shockingly bad at helping most undergraduates earn credentials.

More students than in recent decades are now starting college—about seven in ten high school graduates, up from 50 percent in 1970. But barely half graduate on time, and many don't graduate at all. Results for low-income students, first-generation college goers, and the growing population of minority students are even worse. The majority of black and Latino students who enroll at four-year colleges as first-time, full-time freshmen fail to earn a bachelor's degree within six years. For nontraditional students, the odds are even more daunting. Only 7.3 percent of single parents who enroll in college hoping to earn a bachelor's degree get one within six years. Forty-six percent drop out, with the rest still struggling in college or settling for a lower-value credential. For students who delay going to college after high school, the equivalent success rate is 13.7 percent. For students who work full-time, 10.7 percent. For students whose parents don't help them financially, 7.7 percent.

Higher education has swelled with nontraditional students in recent decades, but the system has not evolved to serve them in effective, nontraditional ways. That's why some 38 million working-age adults report their highest level of education as "some college, no degree." This represents a massive loss of human potential at a time when the nation's social fabric and economic vitality increasingly depend on a well-educated citizenry.

Meanwhile, the scant available information about college student learning suggests that too many graduates leave school lacking the ability to think, analyze, and communicate. According to *Academically Adrift: Limited Learning on College Campuses*, a much-noted recent book by sociologists Richard Arum and Josipa Roksa, fully 45 percent of undergraduates show no statistically significant gains in critical thinking, complex reasoning, or written communications during their first two years of college. Over four years, further research by the authors found, more than one-third of students show no real learning gains. "[L]arge numbers of U.S. college students can be accurately described as academically adrift," Arum and Roksa wrote in the *Chronicle of Higher Education*. "They might graduate, but they are failing to develop the higher-order cognitive skills that it is widely assumed college students should master."[1]

This kind of slipshod quality control may once have been tolerable; as long as a few people were smart enough to found the businesses and lead the institutions that serve the wider society, the rest could manage. With revolutionary advances in communication and transportation knitting human societies together worldwide and other countries quickly ramping up degree production, the United States no longer has that luxury. Social and economic trends within the country have led to a new imperative in American educational opportunity: all comers should have the chance to gain some postsecondary experience. And every student willing to work hard enough for a degree should be able to earn one, and learn something in the bargain.

The higher education system also betrays an innovation deficit in another way: a steady decline in productivity driven by a combination of static or declining output paired with skyrocketing prices. According to the nonprofit College Board, tuition and fees for students studying in state at public universities increased by an average of 5.6 percent annually over the last decade, after adjusting for inflation. This marks the acceleration of a three-decades-long trend of college prices increasing steadily in good economic times and bad, and faster than inflation, family income, or even the health-care costs that are famously jeopardizing America's long-term solvency. While the net price of college (after accounting for financial aid) has not grown as quickly, thanks to significant federal investments in financial aid, the bleak federal budget outlook makes it unlikely that future tuition hikes will be similarly offset.

And while colleges differ from one another in some respects, they are remarkably similar in others. With few exceptions, they offer the same degrees in the same way, counting the number of hours students are taught and adding them up to two- and four-year credentials. They hire people with similar pedigrees and organize them into the standard apparatus of academic departments. Teaching, tenure, and titling policies vary little from place to place. They field athletic teams, joust in obscure journals, and complain about overpaid administrators in much the same way, everywhere. All of this adds up to long-term stagnation and a profound lack of imagination about the possibilities of change.

We are not the first to make these observations. In recent years, a growing chorus of critiques has come from inside and outside the academy. After decades of taking a mostly hands-off approach, federal policy makers began questioning the core work of higher education during the second term of President George W. Bush. U.S. Secretary of Education Margaret Spellings convened a distinguished panel of experts, many with deep roots in the academy, to conduct a top-to-bottom examination of the nation's colleges and universities. Their findings were disconcerting:

> What we have learned over the last year makes clear that American higher education has become what, in the business world, would be called a mature enterprise: increasingly risk-averse, at times self-satisfied, and unduly expensive. It is an enterprise that has yet to address the fundamental issues of how academic programs and institutions must be transformed to serve the changing needs of a knowledge economy. It has yet to successfully confront the impact of globalization, rapidly evolving technologies, an increasingly diverse and aging population, and an evolving marketplace characterized by new needs and new paradigms.[2]

Higher education leaders may have expected a respite with the election of President Obama in 2008. Instead, the president's first address to Congress declared that our higher education system was inadequate, having fallen behind competitor nations in helping adults earn credentials. His subsequent proposals have broken new ground in suggesting that Uncle Sam should step outside the traditional role of funding student financial aid and university-based research to pursue a more aggressive strategy of funding efforts that seek to improve degree completion—and demanding accountability for results in return for federal funds.

Meanwhile, a host of books and scholarly works have examined the flaws of higher education. *College*, Ernest Boyer's prescient 1988 survey of the undergraduate experience, identified many of the fundamental weaknesses in the system. Most went unaddressed. Nearly two decades later, a higher education leader of similar stature sounded the same notes. In his 2007 volume *Our Underachieving Colleges*, former Harvard president Derek Bok wrote that "colleges and universities, for all the benefits they bring, accomplish far less for their students than they should." Others soon followed. Robert Zemsky's *Making Reform Work: The Case for Transforming American Higher Education* asserts that higher education's ingrown unwillingness to change must be dislodged by fundamental, not incremental, change. Mark Taylor's *Crisis on Campus*, released in 2010, calls for the wholesale revamping of venerable institutions like academic departments and faculty tenure. "The Universities in Trouble," Andrew DelBanco's well-regarded 2009 higher education critique in the *New York Review of Books*, also raised a loud alarm.

While varied and frequently uncompromising, these criticisms are still situated within the higher education system itself. They aim to right the ship, but they do not question the fundamental form of the ship or the need for it to progress in the same general direction. Their solutions, moreover, depend on the willingness of long-established institutions to reform themselves. Other critics are less wedded to the ideal of the university as we now understand it. In one way or another, they all see the raging information technology revolution as the key to a whole new world of higher learning.

This, too, is not virgin territory. Diana Oblinger and Sean Rush's *The Learning Revolution: The Challenge of Information Technology in the Academy* was published in 1996, in the very early days of the Internet revolution.

In its wake, the enthusiasm surrounding the dot-com boom prompted many observers to forecast the destruction of brick-and-mortar colleges on a time line that is rapidly approaching present day. These predictions of the traditional university's demise proved premature. But in applying the "disruptive innovation" paradigm to education in their 2008 book *Disrupting Class: How Disruptive Innovation Will Change the Way the World Learns*, Clayton Christensen and his coauthors argued that education is still likely to experience the kind of earthshaking changes in cost, control, and mode of delivery that technology has visited on industries ranging from semiconductors and automobiles to music, publishing, banking, and journalism. Institutional resistance and barriers to change embedded in public policy may slow the pace of change, they assert, but the trend will move only in one direction. Journalist Anya Kamenetz's recent book *DIY U: Edupunks, Edupreneurs, and the Coming Transformation of Higher Education* projects these developments forward to an approaching world in which higher learning shifts fundamentally from an institution-centered model to one that is mobile, flexible, technology empowered, and student centered. For most students, she contends, this world will bear little resemblance to the higher education experience that has persisted in various forms for the better part of the last five hundred years.

We believe that the most important questions of higher education innovation will, for the foreseeable future, reflect both the institutional and disruptive perspectives. Colleges and universities still enjoy massive levels of social and financial capital. The duties they perform and the values they represent cannot and should not be easily discarded. At the same time, it would require willful blindness to assume that institutions created and sustained by the production and distribution of knowledge will escape transformation by technologies that have radically altered the cost and speed of storing, moving, and analyzing information. Institutions built from ancient stone (or even brick and concrete) tend to see their ways of working as written in similarly permanent material. This has been a safe bet for a long time. It is no longer so.

There is a danger, of course, in assuming that all change is virtuous and all traditions are outdated. We ought not fetishize the new. Innovation is a slippery concept, one that is often used principally to flatter the self-styled pioneer.

But as the chapters in this volume demonstrate, higher education as a whole is inhospitable to innovation, properly understood. The depth of that understanding is also inadequate. To date, there has been relatively little systematic research on the prevalence and potential of innovation in American higher education. There are promising examples to be found, of course, and we highlight many of them here. But reformers' ideas about how to reorient higher education are still on the margins of discourse within the dominant traditional sector. Without a comprehensive set of policies to better understand and create more fertile ground for new ideas, today's pressing problems will become tomorrow's irresolvable crises.

The chapters in this book are roughly organized into three thematically related sections. The first assesses current barriers to higher education innovation and how to surmount them. The second examines how changes that have already occurred in the sector are altering the way professors and students interact with institutions in a variety of settings, including traditional research universities, community colleges, and growing for-profit institutions. The third looks to the future in examining higher education institutions that are just coming into existence—or, through the power of information technology, are not institutions in the traditional sense of the word at all.

Dominic Brewer and William Tierney of the University of Southern California begin by sketching the innovation landscape as it exists today. While research practices have steadily evolved, they note, teaching has largely stayed the same. That's because colleges lack incentives to teach differently, or well. Large government subsidies insulate public institutions from market competition, and the enrollment-based nature of those subsidies creates few incentives for colleges to help students learn and earn degrees. Government regulators act as a brake on competition by limiting entrance to the market. By forcing new institutions to adopt the organizational norms of old institutions, accreditors foster risk aversion and standardization. Powerful higher education lobbying organizations help preserve the status quo.

Veteran higher education journalist Jon Marcus goes back even further, to pre-Revolutionary America, to document how higher education has always been slow to change. True innovations, Marcus contends, rarely come voluntarily from within established institutions. Major technological and social change originating outside the academy can do the trick, as with women's suffrage, civil rights, and the rise of the Internet. Otherwise, it takes new colleges to advance new ideas. Marcus provides a case study of one such institution, Harrisburg University of Science and Technology in Pennsylvania, which has taken a rare fresh sheet of institutional canvas and thrown out many of the conventions that are sacrosanct elsewhere.

Former Stanford University vice president William Massy tackles an enduring higher education myth: that colleges are doomed to inefficiency due to their labor-intensive business model. In fact, Massy finds, colleges can increase performance and lower costs just like everyone else, using new organizational models and the power of information technology. The well-regarded National Center for Academic Transformation (NCAT), for example, has cut spending and increased learning in hundreds of introductory college courses nationwide. Like Marcus, Massy finds that new institutions are far more open to innovation than old ones.

Economist Ronald Ehrenberg, director of the Cornell Higher Education Research Institute, focuses on one such convention: faculty tenure. This is a case where fundamental change is happening not by sudden flash of inspiration but by the steady erosion of tenure-track jobs. Ehrenberg analyzes (somewhat ruefully) the many cultural, financial, and institutional causes of this phenomenon and offers predictions for how information technology and new career models could provide better alternatives to the current mix of tenure lottery winners and exploited adjunct instructors.

Paul Osterman, economist at the MIT Sloan School of Management, follows by looking inside the neglected two-year sector, which enrolls nearly half of all new students but receives a far smaller portion of public funding, media attention, and scrutiny from scholars. Osterman notes that the best community colleges—lean, student-focused, and connected to the workforce—are a prime source of innovative practices that other colleges could emulate. At the same time, the two-year sector as a whole has deep problems, with barely more than one-third of all students graduating or transferring to a four-year school. Only by sharpening community colleges' often incoherent missions and matching new resources with accountability for results, Osterman says, will best practices become widespread.

But as Guilbert Hentschke of the University of Southern California observes, most new universities, like Harrisburg University and the University of Minnesota–Rochester, are not traditional public or nonprofit institutions. The real action is in the fast-growing for-profit sector, which is absorbing a larger percentage of college students and federal financial aid revenue every year. While acknowledging the problem of abuses in the for-profit industry, Hentschke finds the sector as a whole to be a hotbed of new organizational models and business practices. For-profits are far more growth-oriented than traditional institutions at a time when national leaders are calling for a major expansion in college attainment. They're also more sensitive to market demand than traditional colleges, which tend to teach what they want to teach rather than what students and employers need. The key, Hentschke argues, is to marry these virtues to improved consumer protection and greater quality control.

In the future, such policies will increasingly be focused on colleges that exist primarily or even exclusively online. Peter Stokes—vice president and chief research officer at the technology-focused consulting firm Eduventures—examines the hype and reality of higher education on the Internet, a medium where more than one-quarter of all college students are now learning. The roots of online learning are in distance education, early examples of which date to the eighteenth century. But the Internet has brought online higher education to the point, Stokes argues, where it could be a disruptive innovation that alters the college landscape in the same way that technology has dramatically transformed the music, publishing, banking, travel, and newspaper industries.

Finally, Kevin Carey provides a case study of the University of Minnesota–Rochester (UMR) and describes how this brand-new public university highlights the possibilities of innovation and reform. As in the case of Harrisburg University, described by Marcus, the administrators of UMR took the opportunity of starting from scratch to discard many long-cherished practices and create a focused, dynamic institution that makes full use of technology. Massy also cites UMR as an organization that puts the lie to the notion that low higher-education productivity is a chronic condition. UMR provides undergraduates with far more in the way of direct teaching and staff resources than the typical university at a fraction of the cost. Carey argues that if lawmakers in Minnesota can overcome the failure of imagination and bureaucratic hurdles cited by many of the chapter authors, other state leaders can do so as well, seeding a new generation of innovative institutions.

In sum, the authors describe a traditional higher education system in which innovation occurs in fits and starts, dependent on the whims of individual actors or the rare opportunity afforded by the creation of new institutions. Public and private nonprofit colleges lack strong enough incentives to overcome the forces of traditionalism and innovate at scale, and so they don't. Meanwhile, the burgeoning for-profit sector is spinning out new definitions of higher education at a rapid rate, but these innovations are often overlooked in debates about their profit motive. What the nation lacks is higher education innovation harnessed to public purpose: institutions rooted in a commitment to knowledge creation and student learning but open and eager to embrace better ways of realizing those goals. This volume provides a glimpse of what that future could look like. But there is much to accomplish in order to get from here to there.

1

Barriers to Innovation in U.S. Higher Education

Dominic J. Brewer and William G. Tierney

Virtually every major innovation of recent decades builds on the work of the university community . . . Countless innovations revolutionizing American life and the American economy have emerged from a university setting. Here we come to a paradox. Though the university community is a major force of innovation in our society, it is curiously resistant—even hostile—to innovations attempted within the university.[1]

HIGHER EDUCATION IS WIDELY lauded as an American success story.[2] Over four thousand public and private postsecondary institutions enroll some twenty-five million students.[3] During the past century, the sector has expanded greatly, providing educational opportunities for an increasingly diverse population and offering a plethora of courses of study, from certificates to doctorates in hundreds of subjects. New providers have emerged that are tailored to shifting student demands.[4] Universities continue to produce breakthrough scientific discoveries and inventions such that the research university remains a central driver for creative vibrancy across urban and regional areas.[5]

Yet despite this backdrop, there is increasing concern that the nation's colleges and universities are ill equipped to adapt to a rapidly changing environment and that traditional institutions are resistant to enabling new providers to enter the marketplace.[6] Even today, the nation no longer leads other industrialized countries in terms of participation and graduation rates.[7] Whereas the country's colleges and universities were once thought of as key components of America's ability to compete in the marketplace, "The public perceives higher education to lack any ability to affect change and finds that most institutions are anything but innovative."[8]

Major challenges associated with demographic shifts, a changing economy, and a declining fiscal base present U.S. higher education with an imperative for major change.[9] First, demographic trends have put pressure on institutional capacity. Population growth, although slower than in past decades, continues to mean more potential students for the sector. Unless the number of seats grows, the fraction of the population attending college will decrease. Further, the population subgroups with the largest growth are those that have traditionally been underserved by postsecondary institutions, posing a challenge to institutions to expand access.[10] Second, the economic value of attending college has risen markedly over the past three decades.[11] Economic returns to schooling beyond a high school diploma have risen since the 1970s: the median income for a worker with a bachelor's degree is about double that of his or her high school counterpart, and the average college graduate will earn over a million dollars more during his or her lifetime than the average high school graduate.[12] As importantly, the income of those without a postsecondary degree has decreased significantly over the last two decades. A thriving postsecondary sector with plentiful capacity to meet the needs of a rapidly changing labor market is important for both individual and societal well-being.

Third, the overall state of the economy, growing fiscal demands from other sectors (including prisons, health and welfare, and K–12 education), and resistance to tax increases have led to a declining fiscal base to support the higher education sector. For example, California's per-student funding for the University of California (UC) has fallen 40 percent since 1990; while the state contributed $15,860 per student in 1990, that figure has recently fallen to $9,650 per student in constant dollars. The result is that, whereas the state used to pay 78 percent of the total cost of education, its contribution has decreased to close to 50 percent.[13] The decline in the state's willingness to support public higher education has come at the same time that states are attempting to deal with consecutive years of historic budget deficits. As a result, each postsecondary segment has been forced to scale back on the number of students it is able to educate, to freeze faculty and staff hiring, and to raise tuition. In the longer term, the aging of the overall population will continue to shrink the proportion of working adult taxpayers whose taxes fund postsecondary education. This picture is similar across many states and will only get worse in the years ahead. Taken together, these forces threaten to limit the ability of institutions to provide educational opportunities for an ever-growing population.[14] Further, tuition has increased faster than inflation, without a comparable increase in quality or results. The sector has been marked by rapidly increasing costs, a fact that has not been lost on policy makers and consumers.[15] The Spellings Commission, for example, noted the ever-increasing costs of postsecondary education with concern and was extremely critical of the sector's overall lack of transparency and its inability to develop common learning outcomes that might be measured.[16]

Given these realities, the sector will have to change and adapt to new constraints and demands or risk being overtaken by a rapidly expanding for-profit sector. Although innovation is taking place within existing providers and through the entry of new providers, it has not dramatically increased the system's capacity to educate more students or driven down costs. Innovation appears to be too little and too slow, particularly when compared to other industries that have improved productivity via the introduction of technology or through strategies like outsourcing or the use of temporary workers who reduce labor costs. In most colleges and universities, the fundamental core technology of teaching and learning remains virtually unchanged. Throughout the twentieth century, colleges and universities essentially have utilized two modes of teaching—the seminar model where an instructor teaches by the Socratic method, or the lecture model with a "sage on the stage." With these teaching formats, the only way to increase capacity is through the reduction in the number of small seminars, an increase in the number of students in the lecture classes, or the addition of more professors. Only relatively recently have low-cost computing and communications technologies made it possible to imagine fundamentally different ways of learning by breaking the constraints of physical space and time.[17] The use of technology to rethink the core business of teaching and learning is occurring primarily on the margins of the sector.

In this chapter, we examine how and why innovation occurs in U.S. higher education, focusing on the barriers that impede both the magnitude and the pace of change. We note that although progress has been made in the past decade in developing innovative instructional delivery mechanisms, progress is slow and confined to relatively few institutions. Many institutions face minimal competitive pressure, significant (but decreasing) state subsidies, and cumbersome internal and external governance structures that resist innovation. Further, accreditation diminishes the potential impact of for-profit institutions by erecting barriers to entry, and there are few systematic mechanisms for testing and disseminating proven innovations across the sector.[18] We suspect that the increasing fiscal and competitive pressure on traditional colleges and universities will force many to change, and that some institutions that resist change—wistfully hoping for a return to the good old days—may find themselves out of business altogether. We suggest that the federal and state regulatory and funding environments, which shape much of the postsecondary sector's behavior, need to change significantly. Existing organizations need strong incentives to change, encouraged purposively through a smarter—and more innovative—government role. Just as a regulatory environment can stymie new entrants and breed lethargic institutions, it also may provide incentives that spur innovation. Our purpose here, then, is not to advocate for innovation for innovation's sake. Rather, a moral imperative exists in higher education. Yes, higher education needs to be more competitive and more cost conscious. But, ultimately, a more innovative postsecondary industry will increase access to higher education, create a better educated workforce, and enable more individuals to participate fully in the democratic public sphere.

WHAT IS INNOVATION?

Innovation is a new method, custom, or device—a change in the way of doing things. It is generally understood as the *successful* introduction of a new thing or method.[19] Innovation can be "supply pushed" through the availability of new technological possibilities in production, or "demand led" based on market or societal needs. In for-profit industries, firms are under continuous pressure to drive down the unit costs of production and to drive profitability up via the continuous refinement of production processes, internal systems, marketing strategies, and the like. The profit motive, and the pressure to innovate that it can encourage, is still quite rare in postsecondary education. Total postsecondary enrollment in the United States was over twenty-five million during the 2007 to 2008 academic year. Of this total, 91.5 percent of the students enrolled in nonprofit or public institutions and 8.5 percent in for-profit colleges and universities.[20] However, the desire to maximize outputs—the goal of accomplishing more (serving more students, generating more research, and so on)—at lowest cost exists, albeit with somewhat mediated incentives to do so. This picture is complicated by the fact that productivity is not directly measured in higher education. Measures of value-added to student learning, for example, are not widely used, nor are institutions typically held accountable (by the state or by markets) for the outcomes of higher education like degrees or higher earnings.

Innovation is linked to creativity, risk taking, and experimentation, attributes that are often lacking in large, public or nonprofit organizations. In the private sector, for example, it has been estimated that only 10 percent of all innovations are actually successful; trial and error are essential. For systematic learning, a research and development (R&D) process, along with evaluation, is required for positive innovation to take hold and spread, and for negative innovation to be abandoned. Innovation requires a willingness to fail, a capacity on the part of institutional leaders to engage in risk taking, an organizational reward structure that encourages such behavior, and a regulatory framework that supports it. Innovations may occur for a host of reasons, and they occur whether supported by, or in spite of, the environment in which they take place.[21]

Although research universities have the production of new knowledge as a major component of their work, they are a relatively small part of the postsecondary sector. Teaching and learning, however, are key functions of every type of postsecondary institution. Whereas research infrastructure—how one conducts research, with whom, its funding, its transfer, and the like—has gone through enormous transformation over the last century, the same cannot be said of teaching and learning. There has been modest change in the core technology of higher education over the centuries—from a labor-intensive tutorial system to the mass lecture halls characteristic of the postwar enrollment boom to forms of online learning. Most examples of innovation—team teaching, first-year seminar, international experiences, service learning, undergraduate research, and writing across the curriculum—are not radical departures from the status quo. Indeed, if one transported John Dewey from when he first started teaching in the early twentieth century to a classroom of today, he most likely would recognize the basic components and infrastructure; the same could not be said if Emile Durkheim investigated how researchers now conduct research.

In order for successful innovations to drive gains in productivity, they not only must be created, but must be adopted by others. Colleges and universities have opportunities to adopt improved techniques in many areas of operation, but they do not all adopt new methods instantaneously. In their study of thirty innovations, Malcolm Getz, John Siegfried, and Kathryn Anderson found (based on a survey of 238 institutions) that higher education takes three times as long to adopt innovations as the average in for-profit industries. They found that "the overall impression is that relatively few measured attributes of colleges and universities are related to the time at which innovations are adopted."[22] Interestingly, curricular and classroom innovations were particularly slow to spread. The core production process that dominates on campuses, namely, professors interacting directly with students, is expensive and difficult to scale. The result has been what we see as sustaining changes, rather than disruptive changes.[23] Rather than hire tenure-track faculty, institutions are now prone to hire part-time or contingent faculty. Rather than have a class of two hundred fifty students with ten teaching assistants, universities increase class size to three hundred students and halve the teaching assistants. Rather than offer a potpourri of classes, institutions decrease class offerings. To maintain the same expectations of faculty is impossible; to increase class size and reduce teaching assistants make a weak pedagogical option weaker; to reduce class offerings while still maintaining that students need to take the same courses makes graduation with a bachelor's degree within a four-year time horizon less likely. These actions are essentially geared toward maintaining the current system rather than creating a more viable system based on new realities.

Labor-intensive industries like higher education are particularly difficult to make more productive. In the 1960s, economist William Baumol noted that in labor-intensive industries, it is difficult to change output without altering staffing.[24] This phenomenon of rising costs without increases in output has been labeled Baumol's "cost disease." His prime example was the string quartet, which produces the same music from the time it is first assembled until the players all retire, yet experiences higher costs as the players demand salary increases to keep up with the wages that others earn.[25] There are compelling indicators that higher education suffers from this malaise: "Some economists have argued that the potential for productivity growth in higher education itself, as in many other service industries, is limited."[26] However, it is not the case that innovation in a labor-intensive industry such as higher education is impossible; evidence from a range of service industries suggests several cures for the disease may exist.[27] Research suggests that service industries have accomplished productivity growth through a range of changes that have taken advantage of new technology, more flexible use of labor, changes to organizational structure, and changes to the external operating environment.

Perhaps the most obvious source of potential productivity enhancement is information technology (IT). Estimates suggest that roughly a quarter of service-industry labor productivity growth can be attributed to investments in IT. IT helps industries track outputs, monitor operations, communicate with customers, and react to shifts in external demands. Service industries such as communications, wholesale trade, retail trade, and finance have dramatically redesigned their delivery systems around IT advancements. Despite some limited incorporation of technology into internal university systems (such as library services, payroll, e-mail), higher education has only just begun to introduce technology into direct instructional services for students. Most colleges and universities have resisted making production process changes, relegating technology to supplementary uses such as course support. In many cases, this has resulted in an increase in staff; for example, the number of library staff people has remained constant, at the same time that IT personnel have increased significantly.[28] Frequently, individuals are performing similar functions, but in different media—one in print and the other in cyberspace. Other technological advances such as computer-based design, modeling, and robotic production prevalent in other innovative sectors can be applied only to back-office functions in colleges and universities.

A second source of innovation in service industries has been the rethinking of labor strategies, including greater differentiation of job roles, creative compensation and retention strategies, and use of less permanent workers. Unlike many service industries where workers increasingly specialize and professional staff perform noncore high-level tasks, colleges and universities continue to rely largely on the professor as a general practitioner who knows what students need to learn and who carries out many leadership and administrative roles. Many organizations, public and private, consciously manage their workforces in reference to the broader labor market by trying to retain individuals who have specialized skills, resulting in salaries that are highly differentiated. There are also examples in the public sector—for instance, the military—where there are limits on the number of people at the high points in the pay scale, clear promotion processes, and dismissal of ineffective employees. Some elements of this meritocracy, including compensation tied to productivity, exist in higher education, particularly in private institutions and in the competition for top research talent in the nation's elite research institutions. However, until recently, the vast majority of institutions whose primary mission is teaching retain a civil service-like structure with uniform salary scales. What *is* occurring, however, is a significant increase in the hiring of part- and/or full-time nontenure-track faculty to do the teaching that tenure-track faculty have traditionally done. The difference between this trend and the changes taking place in private-sector hiring, however, is that hiring in the private sector frequently occurs according to strategic design, whereas in traditional higher education, this kind of hiring is done to fill gaps and needs. Even though there has been a growth in contingent faculty, tenured professors continue to meet with students a couple of times a week on residential campuses, just as they did decades ago.[29] Institutions in the for-profit sector, however, have institutionalized new strategies for recruitment, training, and compensation.[30]

A third, related strategy for increased productivity involves reengineering of key processes and the elimination of others. Some firms have abandoned in-house production of key components and assigned them to independent contractors. Others have reassigned key tasks to different layers of production or shifted them to the consumer. Postsecondary institutions have moved in this direction only to a limited degree and frequently with a great deal of controversy. The outsourcing of labor such as custodial services to private contractors has been of greatest concern to students and faculty at public institutions where equitable labor standards are a key concern. In general, the most significant changes have been in secondary activities such as dining and food services. Reduced costs and equitable contracts in private universities have resulted in the public sector tentatively moving in the same direction. Those who have proven most adept at increasing efficiency are the newest entrants to the postsecondary market—for-profit colleges and universities. Between 2007 and 2008, for example, public four-year institutions added very little capacity (18.8 percent of total new enrollment) and are now maxed out, given ineffective business practices. At the same time, for-profits have been responsible for 33.5 percent of the total growth with only 8.5 percent of total enrollment.

Fourth, private-sector services have tended to become more focused, divesting themselves of businesses that took them away from their core. In many cases, this divestiture has increased the productivity of both the parent firm and the ones spun off, eliminating inefficiencies caused by corporate bureaucracy and internal cross-subsidies. U.S. colleges and universities have more often moved in the opposite direction and are plagued with mission creep: teaching institutions sought to add doctoral programs; liberal arts colleges added professional degrees; community colleges attempted workforce preparation, college transfer, and adult continuing education simultaneously; second-tier athletics departments built facilities to become NCAA Division I; rising universities added teaching hospitals, and so on.[31] When one looks at the history of higher education in the twentieth century, the norm is to see institutions that sought to become more complex institutions rather than distinctive institutions with a singular focus. Thus, teachers colleges evolved into state colleges that offered multiple degrees and then changed to universities that offered master's degrees and, in many instances, doctoral degrees. Concomitant changes in the expectations of the faculty—from one of primarily concentrating on teaching to one of doing more research than teaching—and increases in student costs, such as room and board, were the outcome of this evolutionary process. The overall result was a movement away from a singular focus on the organization's raison d'être—student learning.

Finally, research suggests that the regulatory environment in which an industry operates can have effects on its ability to increase productivity and innovate. Studies of the retail, communications, and banking sectors indicate that deregulation has been associated with increases in productivity.[32] Limits on labor use, information exchange, and service-delivery models may restrict productivity; removing them can generate greater competition and development of new products, and spur the entry of new talent into a sector. On the other hand, reckless deregulation may remove important protections for consumers and workers, and result in the destructive failure of institutions. Striking the right balance among regulation, incentives, and accountability is the key task of policy makers. The framework that undergirds the postsecondary sector has undergone relatively little change over the past several decades. As with the other sources of productivity growth in labor-intensive industries we identified earlier, U.S. higher education has only just begun to take advantage of some of these trends. In the next section, we explore some of the barriers that appear to limit innovation and expand on our discussion about the environment in which postsecondary institutions operate.

BARRIERS TO INNOVATION

Though many widely bemoan the lack of innovation in higher education, there is relatively little systematic research on the topic. In part, until recently, people around the world have considered American higher education the best in the world, so there has been little incentive to rethink conventional practices and structural arrangements. Further, it is virtually impossible to test competing explanations for why or how innovation takes place in the sector. Extrapolating from research in other industries provides some clues. And higher education commentators and researchers have suggested possible explanations, albeit often indirectly. On a basic level, however, innovation occurs when the incentives to innovate are strong and conversely is less likely when the incentives are weak. Hence, if new technologies generate significant cost savings without a deleterious effect on product quality, institutions have a large incentive to adopt them, to generate either higher profits or a surplus that they can spend in other ways (on fancier buildings, administrator perks, reduced workloads for some faculty, and so on).

Not surprisingly, these incentives, opportunities, and costs vary across the array of institutions in the postsecondary sector. Many colleges and universities must be responsive to student needs because their revenues depend on enrollments—notably for-profit privates and nonelite privates that have neither a large endowment to subsidize operations nor prestige to guarantee hungry applicants willing to pay sky-high prices. The result is that these types of institutions may be quite willing to innovate. Public institutions where funding is only loosely tied to student numbers, and even more loosely linked to actual results, are liable to have weaker incentives to innovate. Hence, innovation is likely to vary by several characteristics, including type of institution, institution size, market niche, and resources. Incentives are partly driven by economics and partly by politics and policy. The faculty, boards, administrators, accreditors, legislators, and others can help drive or stifle change. Just as importantly, the environment in which the organization operates also needs to reward, or at least not sanction, innovation and experimentation.

Federal and State Funding Mechanisms

Arguably, the mechanisms by which federal and state governments fund higher education represent a major barrier to innovation, both for new entrants of any type and for existing public institutions. Funding flows from federal and state governments to all kinds of institutions through research funding, direct institutional subsidies, and student financial aid. Research funding via the National Science Foundation (NSF) and the National Institutes of Health (NIH), among others, is significant. Research funding, although critical for the well-being of the country, is unlikely to influence more than one hundred of the country's elite institutions. Though the success of the research enterprise is crucial to America's ultimate productivity, our focus here is more on the vast panoply of institutions that are more typically affected by the other factors we have discussed than by the federal (and sometimes state) funding of research.

The public subsidy of public postsecondary institutions is typically provided to state university systems directly. Although typically granted some governing autonomy, institutions are publicly financed and operated; employees are state workers, funding is loosely tied to student enrollments, and money is provided directly out of state general-fund tax revenues. In this environment, few incentives for innovation are built into financing formulas. When the funding for an institution is certain from year to year, the need to reform is not acute. More recently, states have cut funding in order to balance their budgets, without any plan for systematic reform or organizational experimentation.

In contrast to postsecondary education, in K–12 systems, many states have purposively enabled alternatives to the status quo, such as charter, pilot, and magnet schools. The idea that public educational institutions must be both publically funded *and* publicly operated has clearly been breached.[33] Although the outcomes of K–12 charters are in question, a similar approach has not permeated public higher education. There is no public charter university in any state. Over a decade ago, then-Chancellor Barry Munitz invited the California State University (CSU) campuses to become a charter university where they would have increased autonomy and reduced regulation; not a single administration or faculty group wanted to move away from what was then perceived as the security of state funding and operation. Indeed, when California decided to expand its campuses for the UC and the CSU systems, the institutional leaders and faculties chose to create institutions that were far more similar than different from what currently existed. The newest public institutions in California—for example, CSU Channel Islands and UC Merced—offer traditional programs in traditional formats. The workloads of tenure-track faculty are equivalent to their counterparts in the other institutions, there are similar numbers of part-time faculty, and the teaching and learning format is equivalent to what one finds on every other campus. Even the geography of the campuses also seeks to recreate what students have elsewhere.

Student debt levels, particularly among students who attend for-profit institutions, have recently become a target for federal regulators, in part because of the housing crisis. Some in the government believe that students who graduate from a for-profit institution have often assumed too large a debt load because they do not understand what they agreed to when they first enrolled (rather than smart student choices based on relevant curriculum, flexible schedule, or career placement services). Insofar as the housing crisis occurred partly because low- to moderate-income individuals took out loans that they could not afford, the U.S. Department of Education has struggled to come up with ways it might ensure that students do not find themselves in a fiscal situation that is equally untenable. Currently, the department is considering a policy that will tie debt load to future earnings. The levels vary, but one possible scenario is that a for-profit institution cannot allow a student to take on a (ten-year) loan that is more than 8 percent of anticipated, median gross income; in other words, if a student has a loan of approximately $30,000, then he or she would need to be able to anticipate earning $60,000 in the first job. Although the attempt is well intentioned—to assure that consumers recognize the amount of financial obligation they are assuming when they attend a postsecondary institution—the ability of the government to estimate future earnings in this manner is weak at best, and ironically the rule would apply only to for-profit institutions. Presumably, philosophy majors who graduate from a public university might have similar, if not greater, issues with regard to debt load relative to earnings potential, but the traditional institutions are exempt from this proposed regulation.

Federal and State Regulation

Funding and regulation have tended to go hand in hand, although conceptually they are separable. On the one hand, the state has funded public institutions in a manner that has discouraged innovation, and on the other hand, it has tightened oversight such that it dampens experimentation. The regulatory environment for postsecondary providers is made up of three primary layers. First, the federal government provides a significant amount of student aid through Title IV of the Higher Education Act of 1965 and related legislation, and this aid comes with regulatory strings attached. Second, states have regulatory control of their public institutions and, to a certain extent, private and for-profit colleges and universities. Third, accreditation occurs via regions and professions.

Various policies have acted as a brake on allowing new entrants into the market. Although each state recognizes that it needs to increase participation in the postsecondary sector in order to improve its economic well-being, most states have made no plans whatsoever to work with private and for-profit institutions in a manner that would enable them to increase capacity and help the state achieve increased participation. Some states, such as Missouri, have even moved in the opposite direction and proposed eliminating state financial aid to students who attend nonpublic institutions. Legislation often arises that seeks to prevent for-profit providers from offering courses in a state, thereby forcing students to attend the public system or established private colleges and universities. Online learning, for example, has become particularly problematic insofar as the learning may cross state borders; some states have tried to put limits on these sorts of innovations by not allowing the online provider to offer transfer credit to other state institutions. Accrediting associations also try to make online providers gain licensure in every state where they operate; the expense of jumping through this regulatory hoop in multiple states is prohibitive. Some states also restrict the forms of financial aid students are allowed to apply for if they attend a for-profit institution. Other states insist that only accredited institutions offer doctoral-level courses. California recently passed Assembly Bill 48, which reinforced the regulation of for-profit institutions after the previous bill had lapsed, but the new bill pleased no one. Those who sought stricter controls were dismayed that the state does not have greater oversight of institutions that seem to engage in unscrupulous practices. The for-profits were disappointed that they were again being subject to reporting requirements that are not required of the rest of the postsecondary system.

The federal government also plays a significant role in blocking new entrants to the market and restricting their growth. The Department of Education has sought to play a larger role that some claim inhibits the expansion of the for-profit sector.[34] The dispute largely centers on financial aid and student debt loads. The federal government has long been troubled by for-profit institutions that enroll students for courses and succeed in obtaining federal financial aid for the students (and tuition revenue for the institution) but have many students default on their loans, graduate with a very high debt load, and/or fail to attain the jobs that the students thought they were guaranteed. To combat the rise in student loan defaults, some states have instituted policies requiring that institutions obtain accreditation, while others have established punitive measures if an institution's default rate is determined to be too high. Failure to adhere to or meet the standards established by such policies results in penalties ranging from fines to forced closure. Such policies seek to ensure that fly-by-night companies do not bilk the taxpayer; while one cannot argue that unscrupulous practices should not be eliminated, these policies have the unfortunate consequence of tainting the entire industry in a manner that does not occur when scandals take place in the private nonprofit or public sector. Just because a public university in Louisiana, for example, may be found to violate the privacy rights of students does not suggest that all public universities in California act in a similar manner. Nevertheless, these restrictive policies have limited the entry and expansion of for-profit institutions, which rely on tuition revenue as their primary means of capital.

Until recently, for all of the other postsecondary institutions, the federal and state governments and the accrediting agencies have been interrelated and played a critical role in shaping the ability of existing institutions to innovate or new providers to enter the market. Another component of Title IV, for example, has stipulated how many online courses an institution may offer and still be eligible to receive federal student aid. Further, eligibility is also contingent on the percentage of the overall operating budget that comes from student aid. That is, if a private or for-profit institution has no resources other than student aid, it will be ineligible for federal support. Institutions also have to be accredited in order to be eligible for student aid. If an institution is ineligible, then a student may not apply for federal financial aid, which in turn prohibits the individual from acquiring state aid. States will prohibit the transfer of credits from an unaccredited institution to an accredited institution; states also may have regulatory control over who is able to offer courses. The result is that for-profit institutions and, to an increasing degree, private colleges and universities pay a great deal of attention to federal and state legislation. The new push by President Barack Obama to increase participation in postsecondary education has come under a great deal of scrutiny with regard to what role, if any, the government sees for nonpublic providers.

Finally, a major concern of for-profit institutions is that the data the federal government collects do not accurately portray their students. National databases provide broad brushstrokes with regard to crucial issues such as retention, completion rates, default rates, debt burden, and a host of other issues, but they do not realistically reflect the students who attend a for-profit institution. Currently, the Integrated Postsecondary Education Data System (IPEDS) at the National Center for Education Statistics accounts for less than 50 percent of all students in four-year institutions and an even lower percentage of two-year students, because of the way they track and count students. IPEDS does not account for the graduation rates of incoming transfer students or of part-time students. The result is that IPEDS does not analyze over 50 percent of the total student population. Instead, the portrait is often of students who are duped by unscrupulous admissions agents in for-profit institutions. Such a portrait results in stultifying policies and legislation that creates an organizational straitjacket that stifles innovation.

Accreditation and Nongovernmental Associations

Accreditation was a well-intentioned and useful idea that initially provided careful oversight without unnecessarily stifling innovation. One only need look at any developing country to see the problem that accreditation sought to overcome. In much of Latin America, for example, anyone may open a college or university. In Central America, the phrases *universidades garajes* or *universidades patito* are used to signify that if someone has a garage, then he or she is able to advertise that a new university has opened and offer classes to the unsuspecting public.[35] From this perspective, accreditation can function like the U.S. Food and Drug Administration, warning the public about the health of a particular drug (or institution). Accreditation has the potential to regulate an industry and keep out providers that offer substandard services.

Accreditation in the United States has also helped some struggling institutions make themselves into reputable organizations. The tribal college movement, for example, started in the 1960s with federal legislation as a way to enable Native Americans to open community colleges on Indian reservations. Frequently, with a small staff and a miniscule budget, administrators had the best of intentions—to educate individuals in areas where unemployment rose as high as 70 percent—but they had no idea how to go about creating a viable institution. Accrediting bodies worked with the institutions on many levels—from creating a curriculum to professionalizing administrators—to ensure that these new institutions eventually met minimal standards for accreditation.

While such attempts may have been useful in the past, a great deal of literature highlights how standardization affects innovation.[36] Accreditation can be seen as a normalizing agent; in some instances, such standardization can be useful to protect against consumer fraud and to help struggling institutions develop. Setting standards for outcomes, for example, is helpful, but accrediting agencies also tend to have specific expectations about the processes that must be employed to meet those outcomes. The challenge, however, comes about when new entrants wish to enter a market. These new entrants are capable of developing on their own and believe that they have a product equivalent to or better than those institutions that are currently accredited. Accreditation fosters risk aversion and standardization, but by definition, aspiring new institutions are start-up companies that must be risk takers and are often offering something new and different. Accreditation is a model that wants institutions to conform to norms, while new providers, like those in the for-profit world, work against those norms.

Online courses, for example, challenge educators to think in new ways about learning and pose a challenge to traditional accreditation. Courses that begin every other week or are not based on credits but instead on what a student learns differ from what one may find in traditional two- and four-year institutions. The process by which students find their way to a for-profit institution and the tactics employed to gain financial aid for those students will be a dramatic departure from the norm. These differences may not all be bad, but the tension emerges when the dominant institutional norms are process based rather than outcome based. That is, if a traditional education is where one achieves a degree after the accumulation of a set number of credits over a set time horizon, then those providers who suggest alternative processes will find barriers thrown in their way until they meet the norms that have been created. However, if one were to focus on outcomes—what does a student learn, what is the satisfaction level of future employers, and so forth—then processes can be dramatically different from one another. Accreditation, however, is more process focused, where a template of possible processes exists, and if one does not adhere to those processes, they will not receive accreditation. As we noted earlier, the lack of accreditation for an organization can be a death knell insofar as the students will be unable to access federal and state grants and loans. So long as accreditation continues to focus on process rather than outcomes, innovations in program design, competency-based credits, and online delivery may not take root, which will preclude innovative providers from setting up shop.

Like all trade associations, the higher education lobby exists to preserve the missions of its various constituencies, whether the American Council on Education (ACE) for traditional institutions, the American Association of University Professors (AAUP) for the faculty, the Association of Governing Boards (AGB) for trustees, or the Association of Public and Land-grant Universities (APLU) and the Association of American Colleges and Universities (AAC&U) for public institutions. Given their emphasis on preservation, these groups are unlikely to push for innovation or the entrance of new providers; on the contrary, their job is often to fight any changes that seek to alter current arrangements. They have been particularly successful acting as gatekeepers that keep new entrants out. ACE, for example, has a history of working actively against the interests of for-profit institutions; the AAUP has worked with their member campuses on legislation that would privilege institutions that employ full-time faculty as opposed to contingent labor.

Of course, any set of organizations with common interests has an incentive to create groups that lobby to advance and protect those interests. Indeed, the for-profit colleges and universities have an association, the Association of Private Sector Colleges and Universities (APSCU), which was particularly effective during the Bush administration. Regardless, when one looks at the alphabet soup of higher education associations in and around One Dupont Circle in Washington, D.C., one cannot help but conclude that their emphasis is largely on maintaining the status quo. For example, the publications from ACE over the last decade do not suggest that significant changes are either imperative or even necessary in the way higher education is structured or functions. The underlying assumption is that the system works relatively well, and innovation is relatively unimportant compared to the ability to expand the current structures that characterize the status quo.

Faculty Governance and Contracts

At the turn of the twentieth century, no one looked to the United States for primacy in higher education. Elite institutions existed in Europe, primarily Germany and England, and America's colleges and universities were largely considered intellectual backwaters, many of them small, private, religious institutions. They could fire and hire faculty at will, and faculty governance did not exist except in a handful of institutions such as Harvard and Yale. During the ensuing century, the dynamic changed. The United States now has a preponderance of institutions rated the best in the world in whatever international ranking systems you choose. Tenure for faculty developed in the United States and, with it, structures of shared governance. One can reasonably argue that throughout much of the twentieth century, a great deal of innovation has occurred in the presence of tenure and academic governance (which themselves were innovations in an earlier era) and, further, that quality institutions have emerged in a manner unexpected in 1900. While we certainly make no claims of a causal relationship between faculty tenure, for example, and institutional quality, we also would be foolish to argue the opposite: that tenure ensures institutional stagnation and loss of quality.

Rather, we suggest that the parameters of innovation are subject to shifting determinants, and what may be an innovative structure or practice at one moment may appear rigid and sclerotic at another. By the end of the first decade of the twenty-first century, American higher education has arrived at a moment when institutions hire more part-time and nontenure-track faculty than tenure-track faculty, but the panoply still gear their reward structures toward tenure. Similarly, as faculty compensation contracts have shrunk and some institutions expect faculty expect to do additional work, governance has become more akin to labor negotiations than to discussions about how to improve academic offerings. Budget cuts in states such as California, for example, are a useful illustration of the current state of faculty governance. Over the last several years, California has cut the budgets of its state higher education systems and raised student tuition. The result has been reduced services for students, some sizable reductions in faculty pay via furloughs, and hiring freezes. Not surprisingly, a great deal of faculty energy has been concentrated on how to handle the budget cuts, but the recommendations underscore how traditional institutions have moved away from innovation. Faculty have called for greater transparency in the budget and demanded that the state restore full funding. Nowhere are there recommendations that faculty should teach more—an obvious cost reduction—or that institutions could eliminate program duplication. Indeed, if full funding were restored to public higher education in California, one suspects that the legislators, regents, administrators, and faculty would breathe a collective sigh of relief and go back to business as usual. The faculty and their contractual and governing obligations, then, are not so much a roadblock to reform; instead, the manner in which these contractual and governing obligations are interpreted preclude faculty decision makers from developing innovative ideas that might improve the teaching and learning capacity of the institution.

Private universities have tenure-track faculty and an elaborate governance system; for-profit institutions do not. Both types of institutions, however, are more experimental and innovative than their public counterparts. The point is not only that such contractual obligations can retard innovation, but also that the environmental and historical contexts in which institutions reside largely determine whether an institution's actors embrace or reject innovation and change. In higher education, progress toward organizational change has been muted partly because the traditions of faculty governance lead to deliberative, drawn-out change, driven by those who see little value in it.

LEVERS FOR CHANGE

We have argued that American higher education, although long considered the best in the world, is in need of creative and innovative ways to transform itself to meet the changed realities of the twenty-first century if it wishes to maintain its preeminence. Whereas reward structures and governance mechanisms once worked to help create a productive system, we suggest that they are now frequently retarding innovation in academe. Although consumers once wanted leafy campuses where their teenage children might spend four years studying for a degree, today the new majority of postsecondary learners—working, adult, part-time students—demand a different model. The conventional model—of a traditional curriculum taught by full-time tenured professors with a workload of a handful of classes a semester—certainly had its advantages, but it is impossible to scale this model to meet the growing demand for postsecondary education in an era of declining resources. A few entrepreneurial nonprofit traditional institutions, particularly privates, have begun to move away from this model. USC, for example, through a partnership with the for-profit company 2tor, Inc., has launched an online master of arts in teaching. The partner provides marketing, student recruitment, and technology support, while USC provides admissions, curriculum design, and instructional delivery. As part of the attempt to scale high-quality instruction, it has hired new clinical faculty who have the exclusive task of online instruction. The new barbarians at academe's gates are for-profit providers; whereas once they were but an insignificant number of trade schools in primarily urban locales, the demands of the knowledge economy have made these providers the fastest-growing sector in higher education.

Nevertheless, organizations will not automatically become innovative simply because the environment demands change. Our concern is that some may rise to the challenge, but many will remain wedded to past structures and fall into mediocrity, or even die out. The recent economic crisis and the resulting impact on state budgets have not yet brought about creative ideas that might lead to structural solutions. Instead, they have forced state policy makers and institutions to attempt quick fixes with little strategic foresight.

In order to stimulate the climate for innovation, we argue that federal and state governments must have a more active and purposeful approach in shaping the environment that colleges and universities face. Institutions themselves must recognize the changed realities and aggressively move to implement new approaches to instruction and other services. Several levers suggest themselves to us. Each can be spurred in part from action *outside* the institutions themselves—by more focused mission differentiation, smarter regulation, new funding mechanisms, systemic federal R&D, and so on—and in part from *inside* institutions themselves through creative use of online technologies, specialization of faculty and staff roles, more market-oriented labor contracts and working conditions, and so on. One is unlikely to happen without the other. Essentially, we argue that the key to the success of the postsecondary sector in the new millennia will be the resolution of several critical tensions.

Mindless Mimicry Versus Strategic Differentiation

We noted earlier that the history of the twentieth century was one in which postsecondary institutions tried to become more alike than different from one another. The result was not only that a teachers college became a university but also that the teachers college created the concomitant trappings of a research university—a campus, a research profile for the faculty, athletic facilities, and the like. The outcome is that four-year public institutions and two-year community colleges are more alike than different. However, to foster a creative environment, an institution's leaders need to determine the niche they want to fill. Once that is done, a variety of other changes may come into play. Tenure as a system, for example, may well suit some subset of institutions, but not all campuses. A traditional semester system may work for St. John's College, which caters to eighteen- to twenty-two-year-old students who wish to study the classics, but would certainly be inefficient for an organization that desires to speed up learning for a part-time adult clientele in need of immediate employable skills. New providers are particularly adept at market focus, whereas traditional colleges and universities have had a difficult time determining what their market niche should be. Productivity increases seem likely to come about across the sector if institutions become more focused and more differentiated from one another.

Although decisions about institutional strategy are under the purview of trustees, regents, donors, and administrators, federal, state, and accrediting agencies have considerable sway. Indeed, although it would be politically difficult, state legislatures could clearly define the missions of the institutions they fund. The California Master Plan for Higher Education of 1960 is often considered the benchmark. It clearly delineated UC as the primary academic research institution, responsible for undergraduate, graduate, and professional education, and with exclusive jurisdiction in public higher education for doctoral degrees. CSU's primary mission was undergraduate education and graduate education through the master's degree, including professional and teacher education. The California Community Colleges were to have as their primary mission providing academic and vocational instruction for older and younger students through the first two years of undergraduate course work. Over time, a combination of legislative, board, and institutional decisions have muddled this delineation, adding doctoral degrees to CSU's mission, remedial education to the community colleges, noncredit extension to UC, and so on. Extra campuses have been added that mimic existing ones, based only on the notion of geographic service. A disciplined state legislative approach could force public universities and colleges to become more focused and better delineated, eliminating duplication, and speeding up the time to a degree.

Guaranteed Funding Versus Incentive Funding

Although state budget cuts have challenged all entities receiving public dollars to find ways to save money, as we noted earlier, the response has generally been haphazard and reactive rather than strategic. Given that the long-term prospects for state support returning to prior levels are grim, the time has surely come to reexamine how higher education receives public funding, both at federal and state levels. Although there is no clear blueprint for guaranteeing that funding mechanisms ensure innovation—and any changes would likely be met with fierce political resistance from the state institutions themselves—it is plausible that current structures could be improved. For example, rather than ensuring funding simply on the basis of enrollments, some form of performance-based funding (for example, based on student graduation rates) for some fraction of revenues is possible.

Funding tied to real costs per student could be an incentive for institutions to find ways to drive down costs while maintaining quality. When a student has reached a particular credit limit, he or she could receive no more funding; for this formula to work, students would need to be able to take available courses and not take unnecessary courses because they are closed out of the courses they need. Courses also must be available year-round rather than when faculty wish to teach them. States could cap funding for certain levels of education (for example, first-year undergraduate student courses), thereby encouraging institutions to offer what they do best. States could also encourage large public research universities to become either private nonprofit or for-profit institutions.

Finally, similar to the Obama administration's changes in K–12, the funding of higher education could occur in part through competitive grants. This happens now on the research side, but not on the student side. If states removed automatic funding and instead made institutions competitive based partly on outcomes, they could strengthen incentives to innovate. Of course, probably sooner rather than later, states will need to face the reality that direct operation of public higher education institutions may no longer be viable. State legislators and the taxpayers will need to come to terms with whether they can maintain public commitment to educational opportunity without professors and custodians on the public payroll, and without dozens of state institutions offering every subject and every degree.

Responsible Regulation Versus Restrictive Oversight

Except for the starkest libertarians, most people will acknowledge that the government has a reasonable role to play in the oversight of various industries. The problem arises when that oversight is so restrictive that it stifles creativity and drives potential new entrants from a market or the regulations apply to some, but not all. Regulation is not inimical to innovation, and without it, consumers are left unprotected from those in the marketplace who seek to make a profit at the expense of the individual. However, much of the state, federal, and related oversight by regional and professional accrediting agencies now serves to stifle creativity in large part because those who make the rules and regulations are unable, or have no incentive, to keep pace with changes in technology, outsourcing, and globalization. The organizational literature is replete with examples of how policy incentives are generally more successful than sanctions if one wants to bring about long-term reform. Incentives that promote clear outcomes in student learning might appear to be a more fruitful avenue to explore, for example, than those that restrict new entrants to the market based on an unclear prediction about debt-load accumulation.

A fully fledged system of outcomes-based accountability in higher education is surely coming, but the pace of change has been slow. A system of largely autonomous institutions and a large public sector that receives funding on a per-student enrollment basis with little or no consequence for student outcomes is unlikely to ever have strong incentives to innovate. Although several states and accrediting agencies have moved toward measuring student retention, graduation rates, learning, or long-term labor success, progress has been painfully slow. Students still have virtually no comparable information on performance of colleges and universities, and policy makers have not based funding or regulation on systematic criteria that would spur innovation.

Business Models Versus Educational Models

The future is likely to lie in higher education organizations adopting a mixture of business and educational models rather than reflexively assuming that one set of institutions has nothing to learn from the other. For traditional, nonprofit, private institutions and public institutions, this means that many of the current ways of organizing are in need of reform—including everything from more flexible scheduling; streamlined program offerings; professional student advising, marketing, and recruiting; starker differentiation of roles among research and teaching faculty; and integration of IT in instruction. Though tenure may be confined to a handful of elite research universities, uniform salary schedules for professors are unlikely to survive, and light teaching loads will be a thing of the past. These kinds of innovations are, of course, controversial, but those entities that adopt them will likely grow and flourish, while those that resist will slowly wither and eventually die. Traditional providers will have to adopt some of the business models they fear and dislike. They may do so in the form of partnerships with new or existing companies that effectively outsource some of their functions, or which are able to make the needed investments in the development of technology.

Similarly, just as traditional public and private colleges and universities need to overcome their reluctance to reform and become more focused on costs, benefits, and outcomes, so too will the for-profit world need to reform its ways. Part of the challenge for for-profit providers has been that they are profit-seeking organizations in a traditionally nonprofit environment. The drive for federal and state oversight did not come out of thin air. Some providers were unscrupulous and some companies did bilk consumers—and these excesses were of consequence to the taxpayers. While we entirely concur that for a company to have long-term sustainability, consumer confidence is essential, we also know that in any environment there will be grifters and scam artists. The for-profit industry's response, however, has largely been one of extreme reluctance to open its books and an unwillingness to provide greater transparency. In the educational world, however, such transparency is critical; without it, for-profits will continue to struggle against the guilt by association that plagues their image today.

Disjointed, Lethargic Innovation Versus Purposeful R&D

Finally, for an industry to innovate, it must invest in new ideas, test and evaluate them, spread successful ones, and drop failed efforts. This requires an R&D process. In U.S. higher education, relatively few mechanisms exist for this process to take place. Most institutions have limited slack resources and are unable to make large-scale investments in potentially significant breakthroughs, particularly in the development of instructional technology, for example. Tuition or state-based subsidies, rigid labor rules, administrator perks, and aging infrastructures tie up resources, with few incentives for strategic investment capital. Accreditors and policy makers may spread innovation through rules and regulations, but game-changing innovation is unlikely to spread this way. The for-profit sector, by investing in innovation from marketing to recruitment to instruction, has developed an R&D process. But traditional providers have been slow to adopt many of its practices. Competitive forces will, over time, likely increase adoption, but slowly.

This point suggests to us a further redefinition of the role of government. As we noted earlier, through changes to financing and regulatory environments, both federal and state agencies might spur colleges and universities to develop and experiment with new techniques and products. But government could also be much more activist—in partnership with the private sector, think tanks, and academic researchers—in supporting large-scale efforts to develop innovations, particularly in instruction. An infrastructure could systematically test the efficacy of newly developed innovations and potentially spread them. Currently, we know very little about what works in college instruction and curriculum, and what we do know often comes from innovative online learning programs. Through the NSF, the

Department of Education, or some new entity, government could solicit competitive proposals that encourage traditional higher education institutions to develop and test operational innovations. It could give grants to test how an innovation already developed elsewhere could be transplanted to the university setting. Although not all institutions would play in such a competition, and many would oppose the effort entirely, such programs could effectively serve as federal incentives to innovate. States could do the same, but given the scale of investments needed, this seems like an appropriate role for the federal government.

CONCLUSION

We have not intended to draw a vulgar distinction between traditional colleges and universities that have not changed and the new entrants that have. As we noted at the outset of this chapter, the research enterprise within colleges and universities has gone through a sea change in the last generation, and these institutions remain the envy of the world. Different institutions and states also are undertaking experiments in teaching and learning that could have far-reaching impacts for students and taxpayers. Nevertheless, we remain troubled by an industry that all too frequently seeks answers to difficult problems by aping what it has done in the past rather than thinking about how it might do things differently in the future.

There is a clear imperative for greater innovation in U.S. higher education. Buffeted by demographic, economic, and technological forces that are unlikely to abate soon, the traditional way of doing things will lead to a deterioration in access and quality. Although the products, structures, and organization of the industry once served the nation well, that set of arrangements no longer appears sustainable. Without significantly greater innovation to drive productivity increases, many colleges and universities will struggle. Other labor-intensive industries provide some clues as to what is needed, as do the increasingly successful for-profit colleges and universities that were once confined to the fringes of the sector. We suspect that the increasing fiscal and competitive pressure on traditional colleges and universities will force many to change: movement toward the redefinition and even eradication of tenure in some classes of postsecondary institutions, higher class loads, use of contingent faculty, mission specialization, consolidation of programs, and outsourcing of some noncore functions (technology support, marketing, recruitment) are likely to accelerate. Some institutions that resist change may find themselves out of business altogether.

An institution's actors are capable of bringing about discrete changes within their institution; a more competitive environment is also likely to enhance the climate for innovation. Nevertheless, discrete internal changes and a competitive environment on their own will not bring about wholescale reform of the postsecondary industry. The solution to increasing innovation in higher education is not to abandon public funding or consumer protections. Rather, it is to redefine the state's role in a way that is much more purposeful: designing a regulatory framework for the twenty-first century that protects students but encourages new entrants into the market, compels mission focus, provides systematic incentives for existing institutions to reduce costs and devise high-quality-at-scale solutions, and reserves a federal role for R&D in instruction. Such changes are likely not only to enhance cost savings and increase economic competitiveness, but also to increase access to higher education and help the country become more equitable.

2

Old School

Four-Hundred Years of Resistance to Change

Jon Marcus

THAT NEW CAR SMELL. It's one of the first things you notice about Harrisburg University of Science and Technology—the smell of brand-new carpets in the halls and still-pristine furniture in the offices and classrooms overlooking Pennsylvania's capital city.

Harrisburg opened in 2005, the state's first new nonprofit university in a hundred years, operating from this single, sixteen-story, $73 million state-of-the-art academic center. Its approach to higher education is as new as its building.

There are no sports teams. The food court of an adjacent downtown shopping center serves as the de facto student union. There's no gym, though a health club in the mall offers student discounts. There are no dormitories; if they want, students can rent rooms in an apartment building shared with the local community college. A neighborhood restaurant is jokingly referred to as the faculty dining room.

What's more important are the other things this university doesn't have. There's no tenure. Faculty sign twelve-month contracts. There are no departments. Everyone has expertise in more than one subject. In addition to the full-time faculty, there are working professionals—called "corporate faculty"—drawn from the region's high-tech sector, something the state (by helping underwrite this school, among other things) is hoping to bolster as a means of replacing central Pennsylvania's vanished manufacturing industries.

Harrisburg University does allow at least one nod to tradition: it has an official seal. It's a stylized delta, the Greek scientific symbol representing change. This is a university focused on one thing: educating students. It was designed from scratch in a collaboration among experienced educators, government, and businesspeople frustrated by the barriers that thwart reform in American higher education—barriers like tenure and departments.

"If anybody believes that the curriculum at a mature institution is built for the students, think again. It's built for the faculty. The departmental structure, the college-within-the-university structure—these are silos within which people in traditional disciplines live," says Mel Schiavelli, Harrisburg's president and previously provost and interim president at the College of William & Mary and provost at the University of Delaware.[1] "I used to think you could knock those silos down," Schiavelli said. "Well, believe me, that is the most difficult thing in a university to have happen, partly because of the reward system for faculty. You're rewarded for contributions to your discipline, as opposed to contributions to your institution."

At Harrisburg, the idea that students and not faculty should be at the center of everything is as immediately obvious as it seems self-evident—when the security guard in the lobby helps one undergraduate fix his tie for a job interview, for example, or when a member of the board of trustees greets another student by name. Or when students seek help after hours in chemistry or algebra from faculty who teach microbiology or immunology, without worrying about the boundaries that traditionally separate departments. Or without worrying that the faculty won't be in their offices, because they almost always are, instead of working on research or publishing to bolster their campaigns for tenure.

Students learn such things as math and science not by copying long formulas off blackboards in large lecture halls, but by teaming up and applying these disciplines to problems that are socially current—studying the rates at which disease spreads, for instance, as a way of mastering statistics, or learning technical writing by designing a swine flu public-awareness campaign. They work at local companies with corporate faculty who are CEOs and managers in their chosen areas of study and who, unlike adjunct faculty at other universities, help design the curriculum to make it relevant to real-world career requirements. The average class size is twelve.

Professors can change the content of a course midsemester if it's not working out or if they need to add fast-moving new advances—a process that, at other universities, can take years. Core requirements such as ethics and critical thinking, taught at other universities as separate courses, are incorporated into every class here. Technology is pervasive, and faculty use it to its full effect.

This largely new model for delivering higher education was possible because this university itself is brand new. No one should be surprised, Schiavelli says, that what he calls mature institutions are unwilling or unable to change in such ways. "Think about it: How many human institutions that existed before the Reformation still exist today?" he says. Schiavelli pauses. "There's the Catholic Church—and how frequently do things change in the Catholic Church?—and the parliament of Iceland, maybe. And the rest of them are universities. When you start with a blank piece of paper, you don't have that."

WHAT HISTORY CAN TEACH US

Every few years in America, someone comes up with a new and better way to deliver higher education. It's not hard, given that the standard model is the one-way lecture, usually dispensed by a professor without pedagogical training or professional incentives to teach.

Recent examples of such new ideas include service learning, role playing, the case-study model, undergraduate research, small learning communities, capstone classes, writing in the disciplines, collaborative learning, and technology-based course transformation. Not all such approaches are new. Some are very old. Some schools have introduced small-scale seminars based on the Oxbridge tutorial, for example, to honors programs and for teaching traditionally underrepresented and underprepared students. New approaches in teaching have also encompassed *where* education happens—abroad, in a laboratory, in a classroom equipped for team projects, in a workplace. Innovation includes curricular decisions, too—the contentious debate between electives versus core requirements, for instance, or how or whether students are encouraged to work with each other.

Whatever form it takes, the innovation that does happen in American higher education tends to follow a familiar pattern: initial enthusiasm, proselytizing, promising assessments, growth from a small handful of institutions to larger handfuls, and then a plateau into a comfortable niche. Enough professors, departments, and, in a few cases, whole institutions adopt the practices to build small followings of enthusiasts. But the great mass of teaching continues more or less as before.

Most of the ideas about undergraduate teaching that have fallen in and out of favor in the nearly four hundred years of higher education in America turn out to have had several important and extraordinarily consistent things in common: They were imposed from outside universities at historic moments in which there were spurts of dramatic and significant social shifts propelled, in turn, by such epochal events as wars. They were as much in the universities' interests as the students'. And they occurred when reformers, frustrated by the slow pace of change at existing universities, opened new ones.

History shows that it is possible to develop and adopt new teaching methods under such circumstances. But it also makes apparent that, without self-interest or external pressures, existing universities have—not just recently, but for centuries—unswervingly exercised a stubborn resistance to systemic change that can hold off the smallest of reforms for years, stretching into decades. Not even major social movements have always resulted in changes to undergraduate teaching. The flood of returning veterans that inundated universities after World War II, for example, triggered only tweaks to the way that the schools provided higher education. Classes simply became much, much larger. The Soviet Union's successful launch of Sputnik on October 4, 1957, accelerated government involvement in subsidizing research and tuition, something many critics argue actually discouraged reform by ensuring a stable supply of revenue regardless of outcomes. After that, higher education settled in for several comfortable decades of general public and government financial support. Such interruptions as protest movements may have attracted a lot of attention, but they had little or no impact on classroom methodologies, other than allowing for more student freedom in choosing electives in the 1970s, before swinging back to the required core curriculum in the 1980s.

In this respect, universities "move with the predictability of a metronome," says Arthur Levine, president of the Woodrow Wilson National Fellowship Foundation and former president of Teachers College at Columbia University. "General education oscillates between moving toward free electives and moving toward required programs, just as the country also oscillates."[2]

Spiraling increases in costs, complaints from employers about work preparedness, the improvement of higher education in countries that are economic rivals, the challenge from the for-profit sector, and the general decline in economic competitiveness began to come together as early as the 1970s in a sort of slower moving, more spread-out, amalgamated crisis. Compounded by the acute financial pressures of the 1990s and 2000s, these problems are so dissolute that no single reform movement has risen to meet them, only a patchwork of proposals, many of which have not on their own picked up the momentum they need to overcome institutional interests invested in the status quo.

Why is it important for innovators to understand this history? Because it shows that change *can* happen in higher education, *when* it can happen, and how hard it can be.

When President George W. Bush's Secretary of Education Margaret Spellings convened a commission in 2005 to propose reforms, she discovered "just how adept organized higher education had become at 'ropa-dopa'—the art of stalling, dodging, and misdirecting until your opponent is too exhausted to be an effective threat," says Robert Zemsky, founding director of the University of Pennsylvania's Institute for Research on Higher Education, who was a member of the commission.[3]

"For nearly a century now, there has been no successful systemwide effort to change the environment in which undergraduate students learn," Zemsky writes in his book *Making Reform Work: The Case for Transforming American Higher Education.* "Nor have all that many institutions taken up the challenge of how faculty teach and hence how their students learn."[4] He writes: "Individual institutions can and do change, and very occasionally they transform themselves. But their successes tend to pale with time as the inertia in the system draws almost all institutions back to a mean that brooks only minor changes."[5] Instead, over the years, frustrated reformers have found it easier to give up and build new universities—for example, the University of Virginia, Rensselaer Polytechnic Institute, Johns Hopkins University, the aforementioned Harrisburg—than it is to transform old ones. And that isn't easy at all, which says a lot about how hard it is to change the way American universities deliver higher education.

The Deep Roots of American Higher Education

Most universities in America don't have the advantage of having just been built from scratch. They stand on foundations that do, in fact, predate the Reformation and even the Catholic Church and the tenth-century Icelandic parliament, if you consider the classical Greek and Latin with which most began and long persisted, and the enduring influences on them of the Renaissance and British universities founded in the twelfth and thirteenth centuries. Their resistance to change dates almost from their start.

Like their British forebears, colleges in pre-Revolutionary colonial America taught a simple curriculum of classical languages and literary or nonexperimental science, largely involving memorization and using the same tutorial system that had been in place since the twelfth and thirteenth centuries at Oxford and Cambridge. It would remain the norm at most for more than a century and, at the oldest, for nearly two. Only one of the early colleges was concerned with professional instruction—something that would take more than a hundred years for the rest to grudgingly embrace—and none with research or for that matter any particular form of active inquiry.[6] All operated under an administrative hierarchy similar to Cambridge's and Oxford's, though an American adaptation was to call the head of school the president.[7]

It was not surprising that, when the governors of the Massachusetts Bay Colony decided in 1636 to "advance Learning and perpetuate it to Posterity" by establishing America's first college, they adopted the curriculum of Emmanuel College, Cambridge.[8] After all, thirty-five of the one hundred-thirty university-educated Puritan men in New England by that time had attended Emmanuel, a Puritan stronghold.[9] Of the first nine graduates of Harvard, four became ministers. They got busy, spreading their approach to higher education like a virus or, more precisely, a gospel. Of the ten ministers who founded Yale, nine were Harvard grads. Six graduates of Harvard and three of Yale were among the twelve ministers who were charter trustees of the College of New Jersey, later renamed Princeton University.[10] Columbia University, originally called King's College, then adopted the curriculum of Princeton, which had, in turn, been modeled on those of Harvard and Yale.[11] Though not identical, most of these first colleges were, as a result, quite similar, and their graduates would largely determine the direction of other, newer schools for another hundred years. To this day, most American universities in their various classifications seem to prefer being more alike than different.

The single pre-Revolutionary college in the South and the second to be founded in America, the College of William & Mary, was as much inspired by the Renaissance as by the Reformation, including among its goals the idea of broadly educating southern gentlemen in the classics and the scriptures.[12] But it was also there and later in the other colonies that the influence of higher education institutions in another, hardly likely place began to take root: Scotland.

The first head of William & Mary, James Blair, was a product of the University of Edinburgh, while the first head of what became the University of

Pennsylvania, William Smith, had studied at the University of Aberdeen. They imported to American higher education the rudimentary Scottish system of dividing colleges into schools—at William & Mary, a school of Greek and Latin, a school of philosophy and mathematics, and a school of divinity and "Oriental tongues"; at the University of Pennsylvania (originally called the Publick Academy of Philadelphia), a school of Latin and Greek and a school of natural philosophy and science.[13] These earliest departments divided the academy by discipline.

Some of the most radical early education methods were imprinted on the University of Pennsylvania; many were decidedly domestic in origin and driven by its most enthusiastic advocate, Benjamin Franklin. The famously pragmatic Franklin, who had not himself gone to college, successfully pushed the novel idea of teaching practical skills above and beyond the usual theology and classical languages, beginning what would be a more than century-long (if not longer) dispute about the very purpose of higher education.[14] In 1765, Penn added a medical school, effectively becoming the nation's first real university by combining undergraduate and graduate education. It was the first to call its teachers *faculty*, a term that Harvard wouldn't use until 1825, and established another fateful precedent by giving them extraordinary powers over policy. The faculty would meet twice monthly with the provost and vice provost, the founding statutes decreed, to have "an immediate and general regard to the Manners and Education of all the Youth belonging to this College."[15] For all of the progressivism of the University of Pennsylvania, the authority it vested in the faculty would have significant repercussions for academic change, mainly by working against it as countless reforms disappeared into the seemingly bottomless process of faculty governance.

After the Revolution, America turned to France for all things fashionable, including the occasional new trend in higher education. For one thing, American colleges started teaching French, their first modern language, after France became an ally. Thomas Jefferson, U.S. minister to Paris, returned with other new ideas for higher education in America, foremost among them, that it be independent of organized religion. But Jefferson was among the earliest reformers to come up hard against the stubborn resistance of American colleges. Though governor of Virginia and chairman of the board of visitors of the College of William & Mary, his alma mater, he appealed in vain for changes in the traditional curriculum to add the same practical arts that Franklin pushed in Philadelphia—namely, agriculture, science, and modern languages. Finally, Jefferson gave up trying to reform existing colleges and famously began his own. "There are letters in the archives from him [Jefferson] to the masters begging them to change the curriculum to recognize the needs of the colonial society," says Schiavelli. "He tried for forty-five years and failed. So he went off and founded the University of Virginia on those principles."[16]

Jefferson's university finally opened in 1825, with its famous "academical village" shared by faculty, students, and classrooms. The most important part of the design is often overlooked: Where in other universities there would be a chapel, Jefferson put the library. Chapel attendance was not required.

There were other precedent-setting innovations. The university, at its inception, was divided into seven colleges, one each for ancient languages, modern languages, mathematics, natural philosophy, moral philosophy, chemistry, and medicine. The next year, an eighth college—law—was added.[17] Each conferred its own degrees, and while students were required to become a part of one college, they could take courses in another. It was the birth of the particularly contentious idea of the elective: letting students pick the lectures they attended. This model also finally met Jefferson's ideal that "all the useful sciences should be taught in their highest degree."[18]

If Jefferson believed that other schools would follow suit, he never lived to see it. Another twenty years passed, and the Industrial Revolution was under way, before Harvard or Yale started any sort of school for science. Harvard didn't drop mandatory chapel attendance until nearly the end of the nineteenth century. As for electives, Harvard added a total of one: a course in modern language that could be substituted for some of the requirements in Greek. That happened only at the urging of faculty who had attended German universities, where they became adherents of the idea of *Lernfreiheit,* the freedom to study anything they wanted—and a raucous student demonstration in support—in 1825. Most of those faculty and students, too, would be dead by the time Harvard acquiesced to make any electives available in the rest of the curriculum, which took another forty-seven years.[19]

Classical Versus Practical Knowledge

Notwithstanding *Lernfreiheit* and Jefferson, and in spite of the relentless flood of new knowledge, classical studies, taught in the original ancient languages, continued to dominate American higher education as the nineteenth century began. Universities were downright obstinate about it. For example, though Harvard was pressed to build an observatory for a program in astronomy as early as 1815—by, among others, John Quincy Adams—the university took twenty-four years to do it, and then only when a Boston clockmaker agreed to donate the equipment and work as "astronomical observer to the university" for free.[20]

In his broadly influential "Report on a Course of Liberal Education," Yale President Jeremiah Day explicitly railed against the introduction of experimental sciences and modern languages. A classical curriculum, he wrote, taught mental discipline: "Those branches of study should be prescribed, and those modes of instruction adopted, which are best calculated to teach the art of fixing the attention, directing the train of thought, analyzing a subject proposed for investigation; following, with accurate discrimination, the course of argument; balancing nicely the evidence presented to the judgment; awakening, elevating and controlling the imagination; arranging with skill the treasures which memory gathers; rousing and guiding the powers of genius."[21]

New universities were sprouting up all over the new nation at the time, and most subscribed to Day's philosophy, no matter how disconnected it seemed from everyday realities. "You had colleges in Tennessee adopting the Yale approach, teaching the classics in the original Greek and Latin," Levine says. "It was in pretty much every college during that period."[22]

Most of the many private colleges that started cropping up had religious affiliations and were driven by the Second Great Awakening of Christian evangelism. Where there were nine colleges before the Revolutionary War, another 182 were successfully founded between that war and the Civil War.[23] The widespread religious revival advocated reforms to prisons and the treatment of the mentally ill and led to the abolition movement, but where higher education was concerned, it embraced the status quo as Day promoted it, incorporating the Judeo-Christian tradition and the classics.[24] There things largely stood.

There were a few exceptions to Day's ideas. The wealthiest man in America and a convicted forger who taught themselves botany and geology in prison—Stephen van Rensselaer III and Amos Eaton, respectively—weren't particularly concerned about the opinions of the academic elite. They had met when Eaton delivered a series of lectures on the eminently practical topic of how the geology of New York State would affect the construction of the Erie Canal. In 1824, they opened the Rensselaer School, later renamed Rensselaer Polytechnic Academy, "for the purpose of instructing persons, who may choose to apply themselves in the application of science to the common purposes of life."[25]

Van Rensselaer and Eaton's new school was the first to apply field work to the study of botany and geology, and the first to use the laboratory method in a regular course in science, in this case, chemistry. It tapped into a rising swell of pent-up interest in higher education as a means to practical pursuits and attracted a flood of students, including many who had already graduated from Harvard, Yale, and Princeton.[26] But once again, those schools themselves did not respond to the demand for change.

Meanwhile, on what was then the frontier, the new midwestern states created universal education, different from the European model under which postsecondary study in the East had been largely reserved for the upper classes. Indiana, for example, in its 1816 constitution, promised education "ascending in regular gradations from township schools to a State University, wherein tuition shall be gratis and equally open to all."[27] So did Michigan, Wisconsin, and Ohio. These public frontier universities, not the elite privates, would finally lead the movement toward the simultane-ous instruction of basic and practical knowledge—practical knowledge, of course, being far more in demand on the frontier than Greek and Latin.

But that would take another fifty years, despite frustration that was building along with the demand that colleges teach the useful arts of ag-riculture, on which American society was then still based, and of indus-try, toward which it was inexorably heading. The center of this ground-swell continued to be the Midwest, where another botanist, John Baldwin Turner, led the fight for such industrial education against the staunch op-position of traditional colleges and advocates of their sectarian approach. In 1853, someone speculated to be a critic burned down his farm. But he gradually won support, including from Congressman Justin Smith Mor-rill of Vermont, who introduced a groundbreaking bill providing grants of land to each state proportionate to the number of its representatives in Congress—a formula that would benefit more densely populated eastern states like Morrill's—on which new public universities would be built.

President Abraham Lincoln signed the Morrill Act into law as the Civil War raged, on July 2, 1862.[28] It was to prove the single most dramatic turn-ing point in the history of American higher education, and, like many other such milestones, it was imposed from without. One hundred and thirteen years after Benjamin Franklin had pushed for combining practi-cal training with the traditional curriculum, the Morrill Act finally estab-lished new American universities, "without excluding other scientific and classical studies and including military tactics, to teach such branches of learning as are related to agriculture and the mechanic arts . . . in order to promote the liberal and practical education of the industrial classes in the several pursuits and professions in life."[29]

Sluggishly, existing colleges responded by beginning to add modern languages, the natural and social sciences, and professional studies includ-ing navigation and surveying, though the classical curriculum persisted.[30] Some were pushing to accelerate the pace of change, but not quickly enough for others.

The Movement Away from Classical Education

By the mid-nineteenth century, the most powerful conceivable force finally began working to transform conventional American higher education institutions: their own self-interest. As the Industrial Revolution picked up steam, students were increasingly reluctant to attend schools they thought could teach them nothing useful. Between 1850 and 1870, the proportion of the population that enrolled in college actually declined.[31] Angry alumni demanded change. The stalemate between classical and professional education began to break when Harvard and Yale both finally established scientific schools, though in each case, these were operated separately from the rest of the colleges.

Reform proceeded, if only in spits and starts. Henry Philip Tappan, president of the University of Michigan, followed the design of German universities in trying to integrate research with teaching. Francis Wayland, president of Brown University, added graduate study and emphasized such practical disciplines as modern languages and engineering in a system that gave students freedom to elect their own curriculum. Tappan was fired and Wayland quit, in both cases because of opposition and financial problems.

Not always smoothly, more educational reformers gradually began to rise to positions of influence at established universities and colleges. They included Charles W. Eliot, the youngest man to ascend to the presidency of Harvard; James B. Angell, who succeeded Tappan as the president of Michigan; Andrew Dickson White, who would become cofounder of Cornell; and White's Yale classmate, Daniel Coit Gilman, the second president of the new University of California. Each of these men had personal reasons to support new ways of doing business. Eliot had left Harvard at a low point in the college's history, when disparaging alumni were demanding change. One, the historian Henry Adams, summed up this criticism. "For generation after generation, Adamses and Brookses and Boylstons and Gorhams had gone to Harvard College, and although none of them, as far as is known, had ever done any good there, or thought himself the better for it, custom, social ties, convenience, and, above all, economy, kept each generation in the track," Adams wrote. In fact, he said, Harvard "taught little, and that little, ill."[32]

When he was denied a coveted professorship in chemistry at Harvard, Eliot took a position across the Charles River in Boston as a professor of analytical chemistry at the newly founded Massachusetts Institute of Technology (MIT), which would later move to Cambridge. Like Tappan's Michigan, MIT emulated German research universities, whose faculty had for more than half a century divided their time between research and teaching in seminars and laboratories, beginning in 1809 at the Friedrich Wilhelm University in Berlin, which conducted research in every field of instruction and broadly used the lecture, the elective, and the semester calendar.[33] Eliot had also witnessed this model up close on a two-year tour of Europe. Yet even he at first wasn't sold on the value of research. "I can't see that that will serve any useful purpose here," Eliot told a member of the Harvard faculty.[34]

White and Gilman also had traveled through Europe together, where White studied at the Friedrich Wilhelm University. After the Civil War, Gilman returned to Yale to serve as librarian and teach in the scientific school, but he left in a huff after being passed over for the presidency in spite of support from younger members of the faculty. He took the job of president of the new University of California. There, too, Gilman ran into problems, feuding with legislators who wanted the university to be primarily a school of agriculture, and his tenure in California was brief.

Angell chaired Brown University's department of modern languages under Wayland—who had, after all, elevated the status of his field—but left, as Wayland did, and went to Michigan when those reforms at Brown were unceremoniously reversed in the face of financial shortfalls and opposition from conservative faculty and members of the university corporation.

Confident of their cause and pressed by alumni angry that they hadn't learned much of value and prospective students who were convinced they wouldn't, these men advocated, to varying degrees, what became known as the "new education," which included undergraduate- and graduate-level research and teaching and immersion in technology and science. Eliot wrote:

> When institutions of learning cut themselves off from the sympathy and sup-
> port of large numbers of men whose lives are intellectual, by refusing to recog-
> nize as liberal arts and disciplinary studies languages, literatures, and sciences
> which seem to these men as important as any which the institutions cultivate,
> they inflict a gratuitous injury both on themselves and on the country.
>
> Their refusal to listen to parents and teachers who ask that the avenues
> of approach to them may be increased in number, the new roads rising to
> the same grade or level as the old, would be an indication that a gulf already
> yawned between them and large bodies of men who by force of charac-
> ter, intelligence, and practical training are very influential in the modern
> world.[35]

When Harvard restructured its board of overseers by allowing alumni to elect members, who had previously been appointed by the Massachu-setts governor and legislature, Eliot's activist reputation finally worked in his favor. The reform-minded alumni made him president—at thirty-five, the youngest ever. He finally added more electives, so that, by the end of his presidency (which was also the longest in the school's history), there was only one *required* course: English composition, though knowledge of a foreign language also was compulsory.[36] He expanded graduate and professional schools, along with scientific and technological research, and moved teaching from lectures and memorization to seminars in which the students were expected to participate.

Change still came slowly. It took Eliot four decades to accomplish what he did at Harvard, with fierce opposition within and outside the university. James McCosh, the president of Princeton, which stuck by the traditional curriculum, wailed:

> Tell it not in Berlin and Oxford that the once most illustrious university in
> America no longer requires its graduates to know the most perfect language,
> the grandest literature, the most elevated thinking of all antiquity. Tell it not

in Paris, tell it not in Cambridge in England, tell it not in Dublin, that Cambridge in America does not make mathematics obligatory to its students. Let not Edinburgh and Scotland and the Puritans in England know that a student may pass through the one Puritan college in America without having taken a single class of philosophy or a lesson in religion.[37]

While the going was slow on his own campus, Eliot was able to hasten innovation in another tried and true way. When entrepreneur and philanthropist Johns Hopkins bequeathed the then-staggering sum of $3.5 million to found a new university, Eliot, Angell, and White urged the trustees to hire Gilman as its president. Reforming higher education was after all easier on a blank piece of paper. Finally, Johns Hopkins University, started from scratch in 1876, could fully import the German university model, with research and teaching and undergraduate and graduate education in seminars and lectures to become America's first modern research university.

Eliot largely cemented his reforms at Harvard in 1890, when he made the faculty of arts and sciences responsible for undergraduate, nonprofessional education as opposed to the professional schools, in a system that was soon generally termed the comprehensive university.[38] Other colleges warily followed. At American colleges in 1890, 80 percent of the curriculum was required and 20 percent elective, on average. Ten years later, that ratio had nearly been reversed in more than a third of all schools.[39] Meanwhile, Clark University, the University of Chicago, Stanford University, and others followed Johns Hopkins in incorporating research into the curriculum. "There are institutions that are incredibly innovative," says Levine. "Gradually you see things beginning to move. We've gone from the classical college to the university to the megaversity."[40]

There, again, things largely stood. They still do.

Settling In

It took American universities 250 years to make the seemingly small hop from a classroom methodology based on recitation to one incorporating research, with lectures, seminars, and laboratory classes on a semester system. While the twentieth century would see a significant expansion of American higher education—and some universities did not even entirely welcome that—the research university, modeled largely on the 1809 German system with a calendar of summers off that originated in an agricultural economy, remained the most common method of delivery.

Some of the reforms in America at the end of the nineteenth century began to be reversed. After Eliot finally stepped down in 1919, Harvard's faculty restored requirements including that all students choose a major in a single discipline and take two or three classes outside it; by then, 55 percent were graduating having elected nothing but introductory courses.[41]

Decrying the "disunity, discord, and disorder" into which he argued higher education had descended, University of Chicago President Robert Maynard Hutchins launched a *revival* of the classical tradition there in 1930.[42] The Chicago Plan was built around the Great Books, taught in a series of cross-disciplinary lectures and small-group discussions that "purported to include all subject matter indispensable to every educated person."[43] There were no course credits, but there were examinations that a student had to pass before advancing to the upper divisions of the university. Hutchins also did away with football, fraternities, and other extracurricular activities he judged to be distractions. In their effort to be everything to everyone, said Hutchins, universities had become "service stations."[44]

Time magazine put Hutchins on its cover and said his plan would transform education.[45] A handful of other schools tried it. But enrollment at Chicago declined, and as soon as Hutchins left in 1951, the university dropped most of his ideas and even restored fraternities and football. The controversy he stirred up eventually fueled a backlash against American universities' stubborn and consistent focus on western civilization–based instruction.

Just after World War I, Nobel Peace Prize laureates Columbia University President Nicholas Murray Butler and former Secretary of State Elihu Root proposed the most widely adopted and enduring of the few twentieth-century innovations in higher education—study abroad. Their intention was idealistic—to encourage greater international understanding—yet their vision also was a completely fresh pedagogical model that immersed American students in modern languages and foreign cultures in the ultimate extension of Eaton's geological field studies.[46]

Those students' "ability to speak and understand a foreign language is likely to improve, especially if their stay abroad lasts for a semester or more and they live with a foreign family or are otherwise forced to use the native language frequently," former Harvard President Derek Bok writes admiringly in *Our Underachieving Colleges: A Candid Look at How Much Students Learn and Why They Should be Learning More.* "In all probability, a stay of substantial length in active contact with foreign nationals will also yield many of the fruits of a well-taught course on another culture."[47]

Many universities were skeptical of study abroad until the government eased visa rules and steamship lines introduced cheap student third-class passage. "If study abroad had been more expensive, it wouldn't have spread," Levine says.[48] In fact, universities discovered they could charge their students full tuition while paying just a fraction of that amount to foreign host institutions. Faculty who at first feared that the more students went abroad, the fewer would remain to take their courses, climbed aboard when they discovered they could travel, too. It was another reform that succeeded because of self-interest.

Again, external intervention next rocked American higher education: the Servicemen's Readjustment Act of 1944, more commonly known as the G.I. Bill. Like study abroad, the measure wasn't immediately concerned with education. It was meant to avoid a postwar recession caused by too many returning soldiers entering the job market and a repetition of the Bonus March on Washington that disaffected World War I veterans had staged in 1932. But it had an extraordinary impact on American universities, filling them with 2.2 million former servicemen, many of whom brought a seriousness of purpose to which preceding generations of students paled in comparison.[49] The ex-GIs were often lower- and middle-class students who would now expect their own children to follow them to college.

As more government money started streaming into higher education, more government scrutiny followed. Presidential and foundation commissions began considering how universities did their job—and could do it better. They would quickly find, like so many before and after them, that it was easy to propose pedagogical reforms, but nearly impossible to get them implemented.

The first commission, appointed by President Harry Truman, was chaired by Vannevar Bush, a former MIT vice president and dean of engineering who, during the war, had been director of the Office of Scientific Research and Development. Its report, *Science: The Endless Frontier*, proposed a massive federal investment in basic scientific research at universities, because they offered "an atmosphere which is relatively free from the adverse pressure of convention, prejudice, or commercial necessity."[50] Among other things, this led to the chartering of the National Science Foundation (NSF) and gave university science departments a new and important boost in influence.

Truman also convened a Commission on Higher Education for American Democracy, whose findings would expose a deep division between prestigious private universities and colleges and the fast-growing publics. Chaired by American Council on Education President George Zook, an activist reformer, it was implicitly critical of traditional higher education, calling for dramatically expanding access to college for students who might not have previously considered it, and for providing them with educations "that will prepare them more effectively than in the past for responsible roles in modern society."[51] That included global, rather than just western, cultural study and more practical education.

Zook's commission complained that universities spent too much time on "verbal skills and intellectual interests" at the cost of "many other aptitudes, such as social sensitivity and versatility, artistic ability, motor skills and dexterity, and mechanical aptitude and ingenuity."[52] Dominated by the presidents of public universities that emphasized professional education, plus a few experimental colleges, the commission wanted to expand the nation's higher education capacity to double the number of 18- to 21-year-olds enrolled, from the 16 percent then in line for bachelor's degrees to 32 percent by 1960.[53]

The other universities shot back in what became the most public airing of higher education's dirty laundry since Princeton's McCosh admonished Harvard's Eliot. Heads of the leading private universities got themselves appointed to a rival Commission on Financing Higher Education, sponsored by the Rockefeller Foundation and the Association of American Universities and chaired by Paul Buck, dean of arts and sciences at Harvard. Its report blamed any barriers to access not on the universities, but on students' motivation, secondary schooling, and family finances—a contention American universities still make—and argued against admitting many more. No more than 25 percent of the population would benefit from a college education, this elite commission insisted.[54] The Rockefeller report "affirmed the characteristics of higher education that the Zook commission attacked: its relative exclusivity, its emphasis on the development of individuals, and its focus on specialized knowledge," one historian observes. It "resisted the notion that major change was needed."[55]

Both sides, of course, were motivated by expediency. The Zook commission recommended that federal financial aid go only to public institutions, which would have benefited many of its own members and was "bound to frighten the establishment figures in the Rockefeller group, since it would shift the balance of academic power against" them.[56] Whichever side was right, the conversation moved away from what was best for students and become about what was best for universities, another historical hallmark of debate about reform.

Still, the debate marked important changes, all of them structural, and none pedagogical, despite the gap it exposed that still remained between adherents of traditional and practical educations. The first was the involvement of the federal government in considering higher education policy. Truman's pioneering commissions would be followed by many more, notwithstanding universities' ropa-dopa evasion of their eventual recommendations; now that they were awash in federal money, universities would have to tolerate the meddling of federal policy makers. Access to higher education did, in fact, expand. And the government began to provide financial aid at the federal level for students of given income levels at all universities and colleges, guaranteeing them a steady supply of customers and money, something critics say, even further diminishes their incentive to reform.

More money poured into the universities after another external crisis: the launch of Sputnik. "Much remains to be done to bring American education to levels consistent with the needs of our society," President Dwight D. Eisenhower said ominously at the signing ceremony of the National Defense Education Act in 1958.[57] The most significant effect of this on classroom learning was to expand foreign language instruction and accelerate the combination of research with teaching, something the universities did not resist, given the huge windfall they reaped in government research grants. More graduate fellowships were also funded, fueling graduate research and study.

Most of the Sputnik-era reforms in educational methodology, however, came at the primary and secondary levels. Still, combined with ever-growing enrollment, the national response to Sputnik had a broader impact on how universities delivered higher education. More faculty and more facilities meant schools could expand their course offerings and give students greater choices of majors and electives. While innovations also made their way into the classroom here and there, few of them stuck. "Ever since the demise of the classical curriculum," writes Bok, "faculties have clung to several different visions of education with no one model proving itself superior in a clearly demonstrable way."[58]

There were a few attempts. As universities grew bigger and opportunities more numerous, they made attempts to offer smaller classes, which assessments show improve success. Large universities launched honors programs, undergraduate internships, freshman seminars, and group tutorials. An "experimental college" movement dated back as far as 1927 when a Scotsman named Alexander Meiklejohn established a two-year school at the University of Wisconsin. Students and faculty lived and governed together in what

Meiklejohn, who had served as a dean at Brown and president of Amherst, called "an adventure in education." The school rejected both recitation and research. "Liberal education is not training in technical skill; nor is it instruction in knowledge," Meiklejohn wrote in a book about the project. Instead, he wrote, "The positive term which this book uses in the attempt to fix the aim of education is 'intelligence.'"[59]

Older forms of higher education, Meiklejohn wrote, "have lost, if not their vigor, at least their fitness for the new conditions in which men and their institutions have become so suddenly and rapidly involved . . . Never before in the history of the world was higher education so eagerly desired, so widely offered and taken, so lavishly endowed. And yet—or rather we should say, 'And hence'—it is at present largely futile, frustrated, dissatisfied."[60]

The principal and perfectly reasonable functional lesson of Meiklejohn's experiment was that educational planning and teaching should be entrusted not to large faculties, but to small groups of instructors working in close collaboration to coordinate their teaching. "It must be possible, it must be arranged, that all the members of the teaching force shall have genuine and intimate intellectual acquaintance with one another," he wrote.[61] The school also conducted classes one on one and gave students extraordinary freedom; some lived in trains like hobos for a while to see what it was like in a kind of early independent-study project. But the timing again was poor. Judged too radical, Meiklejohn's school lost public support and shut down in 1932.

In the 1960s, in the face of earth-shaking external factors including the civil rights and antiwar movements, the experimental college movement revived at Tufts University, the University of California at Davis, the University of Washington, Oberlin College, and other campuses. These programs confronted large social questions, of which there was no shortage at the time. Most did not give grades. They were part of a student-driven movement toward relevance in the classroom—something to connect the campus to the world—just as students in the nineteenth century had pressed for practical instruction. If there was a pattern to American higher education, that was it. It would come up again at the beginning of the twenty-first century and lead to new universities like Harrisburg.

Current Innovations

Some reforms have stuck—again, because of outside forces or self-interest, or in the form of altogether new universities built from scratch—and schools that practice them prove the remarkable consistency of the mainstream by remaining even a little bit outside of it. At Tufts, where the so-called Ex College (Experimental College) began in 1966 and continues today, students are voting members of the governing board, evaluate course proposals, and teach courses they design themselves. Classes are small and center around discussion, case studies, role playing, and simulations in such topics as adolescent fiction, the Vietnam War in film, legal and social aspects of domestic violence, and the politics of conservatism. By serving as a test ground for new courses, experimental colleges like Tufts's led to the addition of women's, African American, and peace-and-justice studies to the formal university curriculum.[62]

Another, newer innovation has been the extended freshman orientation, which helps acclimate arriving students to the university environment in small, seminar-style classes that afford them personal attention, and with tutoring and other support services that teach them study and research skills, at a time when they are otherwise thrown into huge, impersonal introductory lecture courses. Self-interest is the motivating factor here, too. Pressed by families and lawmakers to improve retention rates, universities have made this reform not only out of altruism, but because it costs less to keep a student than to have to go out and recruit another one. About 60 percent of American universities now offer some sort of extended orientation and support, showing the close connection between the spread of innovation and its impact on the bottom line.

Some colleges have taken the idea of smaller classes to its extreme—in the process returning to the earliest American models of higher education—by advocating variations of the Oxbridge tutorial system. Sewanee: The

University of the South in Sewanee, Tennessee, for instance, has created in itself not only an academic copy of Oxford, but a physical vestige of it. Ethereal spires rise from the dense woods of the Cumberland Plateau. The gothic-style buildings are arranged in quadrangles. The chapel includes a replica of Magdalen College's Great Tower. Faculty wear academic gowns. Even the governing structure is similar to Oxford's. The chancellor plays a symbolic function, while the vice chancellor is the institution's functional head. Sewanee emphasizes British literature and history, and sends more Rhodes Scholars to the real Oxford, per capita, than almost any other American liberal arts university.

"If you have a choice of being given a humanistic education or one that is based on a factory model, the humanistic education is very attractive," says John Mark Reynolds, director of the Torrey Honors Institute at Biola University in southern California, which also has a tutorial system.[63] Employers like the results, too, says Michael McLean, president of Thomas Aquinas College in California. "One of the virtues of this pedagogy is that students are practicing on a daily basis the arts of analysis, inquiry, careful reading, listening to one another, and engaging one another in serious conversations about serious issues," McLean says, sounding much like Jeremiah Day and Robert Maynard Hutchins.[64]

St. John's College in Annapolis and Santa Fe also uses a variation on the Oxbridge tutorial and is one of a few institutions to continue Hutchins's Great Books curriculum. Tutors work with students in small groups and one on one. Even the booths in the St. John's campus snack bar are equipped with chalk and blackboards for this purpose.

"The heart of the idea is that if you follow a student's passion and work with them very closely to find a fruitful way of combining their interests, you will create someone who is intellectually independent and will go off and solve the problems of the world," says Jerrilynn D. Dodds, dean of Sarah Lawrence College, which also offers only small seminar-style classes, student-faculty tutorials, and what it calls an "open curriculum" that frees students to design their own courses of study. "But if you create structures for education that are too guided, that are too deterministic—in order to become a lawyer, you will take this sequence of courses, and that does not include the arts—you will create people who think in proscribed ways and will not be ready with creative solutions when unexpected things happen."[65] Sarah Lawrence students don't have to declare a major or fulfill specific course requirements, though they do have to take courses in at least three of the four academic disciplines offered. The system has produced alumni the likes of Rahm Emanuel, Vera Wang, J. J. Abrams, and Alice Walker.

"The basic principle of the open curriculum is that faculty teach the courses that they want to teach, they teach in very small seminars to students, and the students are energized by the passion of the faculty," says Dodds. Before she came to Sarah Lawrence, Dodds was senior faculty adviser to the provost of the City College of New York for undergraduate education and spearheaded a freshman seminar program there modeled on the one at Sarah Lawrence. She quickly learned why, despite its evident effectiveness, the one-on-one and small-class-size style of education has remained confined to just a few isolated campuses: "It's expensive as hell."[66]

Barriers to Innovation

Cost, of course, is one significant and escalating reason that reform occurs slowly at American universities. ("Oh, have you noticed that?" quips Dodds.[67]) But there are many, many others, built into their structures in the last four hundred years, that favor intransigence—even stagnation— over innovation.

A key problem is the form of governance that the University of Pennsylvania pioneered, giving substantial authority to faculty, who worry about perceived threats—as anyone in their case would—to themselves or to their disciplines. "Humans are notoriously bad about change, especially when pay and reward systems all favor the status quo," says Eric Darr, who taught at UCLA and now is provost at Harrisburg University.[68]

As a result, writes Christopher J. Lucas, professor of higher education and policy studies at the University of Arkansas, "Much of the history of collegiate curricula in America over the past century and a half revolves around the struggle to legitimate new fields of scholarly inquiry and academic instruction, a struggle marked buy broad opposition to the incorporation of new professional specialties at the expense of older ones, and by a recurrent desire to preserve certain subjects or content bodies as timeless and immutable." [69] Lucas tracks the process by which innovation often dies with a precision that evokes Elisabeth Kübler-Ross: "Collegiate courses of instruction have always exhibited a certain inertia, evolving at first through a process of accommodation at the periphery and only later the core, and then almost always only as a result of strong pressure imposed from without." [70]

Departments also often stand in the way of teaching students whose interests cross disciplinary lines, the much ballyhooed interdisciplinary trend notwithstanding. That's why Harrisburg has done away with them. "The notion of not having departments may sound like a small thing," Darr says, "but it's actually a big deal in terms of getting different people with different talents to pull together for a common goal." [71]

Nor, in the complex and stressful progression to doctoral degrees and tenure, are scholars necessarily taught how to teach. Some universities now address this by offering support. The Eberly Center for Teaching Excellence at Carnegie Mellon University, for instance, distills research on how students learn and serves it up to faculty, along with advice about incorporating new technology and methods.

Accrediting boards and state departments of education can stifle innovation too, says Darr. They pronounce which standards must be met and proscribe such things as the permissible ratio of full-time to part-time faculty—a problem to a university like Harrisburg, which has full-time professionals from the fields students study serve as "corporate faculty." It gets around this by using a complicated formula that calculates the percentage of time students learn from part-time versus full-time faculty.

But there are deeper issues that prevent reform, says Arthur Levine, author of, among many other books on this topic, *Why Innovation Fails*. Universities, he says, have two missions: conservation and the advancement of knowledge: "And they have focused more on preservation than on advancement." [72] Just as the university representatives to the Rockefeller commission blamed motivation, family income, and poor secondary schooling for limiting student aspirations—not themselves—higher education still deflects responsibility and disapproval. It is "Teflon coated" and "remarkably immune to criticism," write Richard Hersh and John Morrow in *Declining by Degrees: Higher Education at Risk.* Even now, they write, universities and colleges prefer to think that when students don't learn, "it is because high schools have not prepared them properly."[73]

In a time of limited resources, as Dodds notes, universities also often say that they cannot afford reform. But some changes have been proven to reduce costs while improving outcomes. The University System of Maryland, for instance, ran a pilot program to revamp introductory lecture courses, which serve disproportionate numbers of undergraduates. The twenty-five largest courses at American universities, on average, enroll 35 percent of the students, but 40 percent of students at teaching universities and 15 percent at research universities fail them and have to take them again. The Maryland program, in collaboration with the National Center for Academic Transformation, reduced the failure rates in one redesigned, particularly tough, introductory math course from 67 percent to 50 percent and in another from 40 percent to nearly 30 percent, while cutting costs as much as 71 percent per student. It converted the course from exclusively lecture formats to a mix of lectures, online study aids and tests, team projects, and small classes led by undergraduate mentors.

Technology is part of the reform equation, but for all its promise, universities have largely used it only as a new way of delivering the same information in the same context, Zemsky says. "For the most part, faculty who made e-learning a part of their teaching did so by having the electronics simplify tasks, not by fundamentally changing how they taught the subject," he writes. "Lecture notes were readily translated into PowerPoint presentations. Course management tools like Blackboard and WebCT were used to distribute course materials, grades, and assignments, but the course materials, for the most part, were simply scanned bulk packs, and the assignments neither looked nor felt different."[74] Instead, writes Zemsky, most faculty today "teach largely as they were taught: that is, they stand in the front of a classroom providing lectures intended to supply the basic knowledge students need."[75]

CREATING AN INNOVATIVE UNIVERSITY—FROM SCRATCH

When central Pennsylvania business leaders first raised the idea that the region should have its own four-year university, Harrisburg was the largest state capital without one, only 23 percent of residents had bachelor's degrees, and the few high-tech industries that were finally beginning to replace the vanished manufacturing sector couldn't find qualified employees. They asked the presidents of the fourteen existing public universities in Pennsylvania what they thought of the idea of opening an urban campus to specialize in science, technology, engineering, and math with an innovative new curriculum. The presidents were unanimous: fourteen to none, against.

But the business group persisted, egged on by an entrepreneurial mayor and a vision born of the frustration with conventional universities they shared with Thomas Jefferson and Stephen van Rensselaer. "From the beginning we decided we didn't want this to be a traditional institution, because we in business who had been involved with other higher-education institutions felt that everything took too long," says David Schankweiler, publisher of a chain of local business journals, who chaired the effort. Still, the group invited existing universities to sit on the committee to develop the new school. "What a huge mistake that was," Schankweiler says. "I spent a lot of my time just handling their complaints, and it seemed like every corner we turned, they felt we were stepping on somebody's toes."[76]

The well-connected and determined group of backers got the state to give them $59 million in start-up capital for their university, and there was another $1.8 million from the federal government and $1.3 million from private and corporate donors. Just four years from the time it was publicly announced, Harrisburg University enrolled its first students—less time than some existing universities take to develop a new course.

Technology is woven into the curriculum at Harrisburg. The roomy classrooms (not having altogether abandoned the pedantic language of the academy, Harrisburg calls them "learning environments") connect to gleaming labs and conference rooms for team projects, and have iPad-sized remote controls from which instructors can project the lessons on computer screens and highlight them the way football commentators diagram plays on TV. Two cameras record each lecture and bank them for students to watch again if they need to. The average class size is twelve. The library (called the "learning commons") has only thirty-three hundred physical books, but thirty thousand e-books and journal databases. Everyone in it is typing on a laptop.

Harrisburg's fourteen charter faculty have no tenure, and many left tenured or tenure-track positions at other universities, including Fordham University, the University of Pennsylvania, Carnegie Mellon, and the University of Wisconsin. "My friends at William & Mary told me I was nuts not to offer tenure to our faculty," says Schiavelli. "No one would come here. It was unilateral disarmament." Schankweiler says, "When we advertised for our first faculty position we held our breath and wondered if anyone would come."[77] There were 150 applicants.

Microbiologist and immunologist Rene Massengale left Baylor University to come to work at Harrisburg because, she says, "it utilizes the talents of various faculty and focuses on interdisciplinary work. That is not typically what universities with tenure-track faculty do." In conventional universities, Massengale says, "one of the things I ran up against a lot was there was this idea that focusing on students wasn't necessarily tenure worthy, as opposed to getting published in the right journals."[78] On the whiteboard in her office are the formulas she's used to tutor students in everything from chemistry to algebra, evidence of the hugely different nature of a university that doesn't have departments. Massengale wrote a proposal four years ago at Baylor to create a degree in environmental health. It will take another three years to get up and running there, she says. At Harrisburg, says Christina Dryden, another member of the faculty, "We're still small enough and nimble enough to say, 'Well, that didn't work.' And instead of going to the curriculum committee and waiting two years, we can just change it."[79]

Harrisburg invited corporations to the table, "not to ask them what they thought and then have the full-time faculty go off and do what they wanted anyway, but to give them a vote on what the curriculum should be," Schiavelli says.[80] These corporations, after all, would be where students would eventually take their knowledge. Harrisburg offers a foundation in general education courses such as critical thinking and problem solving, effective communication, understanding global and societal issues, and quantitative reasoning, then undergraduate majors in biotechnology and bioscience, computer and information systems, geography and geospatial imaging, and integrative science.

Each major includes internships and classes with adjunct or "corporate" faculty. Each course incorporates such things as ethics and teamwork and collaboration. "If you think of it in the traditional way, you go out and take an ethics course," Darr says. "Or you do it our way, which is that you have some component of ethical thinking in all of your learning objectives."[81] These learning objectives are listed on the syllabus of every course. Most courses' topics are planned by connecting them to real-world social problems, providing the relevance American students have so long demanded. "I like to think of what we're doing," Schiavelli says, "as the new liberal arts."[82]

Now Harrisburg just has to bring this model to the rest of higher education.

Incubating Innovation

There are no technicians in white lab coats making notes on clipboards or students hooked up to monitors with wires at the National Center for Science and Civic Engagement. In fact, so far, its future home is just a huge unfinished room on the still-empty fourteenth floor of Harrisburg University. The center is an incubator for further reform, funded in part with a $2 million grant from NSF, which has been set up to help Harrisburg and other universities update undergraduate education, especially in the sciences, technology, engineering, and math, using an approach called SENCER (Science Education for New Civic Engagements and Responsibilities).

The idea is to make all-important science, technology, engineering, and math education in this century socially relevant in the same way that students in the last two centuries demanded other fields be relevant. It connects course content to civic questions about such things as public health, sustainability, and social justice—learning complex biochemistry and physiology, for example, by tracking asthma rates among minorities. And NSF assessments show that this approach improves science literacy, especially for women, nonmajors, and low-performing students.

"Too often science is taught as if it weren't about anything but itself," says Wm. David Burns, the executive director. "It's abstract, dry, and tough. This gives students a reason to study. You want a certain kind of nimbleness on the part of the instructor."[83] Most university instructors, he says, "have also got lots of obligations to not be nimble. They've got disciplinary obligations or the hegemony of a textbook. Generally speaking what we've tried to do is liberate the professionalism of the professoriate. And you have to start with an interest in the student." Burns stops for a moment and considers how something so seemingly obvious needs to be restored to universities. "It's painful, isn't it? It's awful. This is what's been lost." Burns has spent as much time figuring out ways of motivating faculty as he has designing a curriculum that works for students, he says.[84]

The faculty involved with SENCER—there have been three hundred so far, from seventy-five institutions, attending summer institutes, exchanging ideas, being mentored, and getting e-mail updates—"are all these St. John the Baptist types who thought they were out in the wilderness alone." Innovation happens, Burns says, when "you begin to create opportunities for people like this to associate with one another." Burns also writes letters to presidents praising faculty who are involved. "We take a lot of pains to make things have C.V. value," he says. He sees this as

> using a barrier to change as a means of encouraging it. It works against people when they want to change a department. It's a form of criticism. We try to at least make this not a risk for a person.
>
> There seems to be something of Eros in all this. There is something about working on things that are real and relevant and meaningful, and that get good responses from students who were otherwise pretty indifferent, that

seems to reconnect people to what motivated them to be interested in doing what they do in the first place. And the driving or sustaining force seems thus a bit more intrinsic or personal.

To call it love seems precious, but that's what it looks like to me . . . No doubt, however, there are other factors: the chance to be part of a community, to receive some recognition and support for innovation, to borrow some legitimacy from the NSF—all of these things no doubt play a part. But I think the fundamental thing is some kind of reconnection with desire—a reconnection that is welcome given the lusterless conditions of the modern professoriate.[85]

3

Creative Paths to Boosting Academic Productivity

William F. Massy

OVERWHELMING EVIDENCE SHOWS that, although America's universities are great in many ways, they are not as productive as they could be. The evidence lies in the things universities *don't* do: to paraphrase Sherlock Holmes, "the dog that isn't barking." This represents good news and bad news, because the ability to identify things not done points the way toward improvement.

There are two reasons why America's traditional universities need to pay more attention to productivity, and do it soon. The first relates to finance and competition. Public financing of higher education faces an indefinite drought, while concerns about tuition escalate and for-profit and other nontraditional providers mature and take ever-larger market shares. Efforts to expand participation rates will only increase the pressure, since it is apparent that growth at traditional unit costs is not affordable. Opinion leaders even now are eyeing the nontraditional and for-profit sectors as engines for leading the expansion, a decision that eventually could marginalize the traditional sector. The second reason is that ways to improve productivity—including paradigm-changing applications of information technology and new findings about teaching and learning from the cognitive and behavioral sciences—are becoming readily available. Adopting these methods would seem to be a moral as well as an economic impera-tive.[1] The barriers to doing so are cultural, not financial or technical. My goal in this chapter is help overcome these barriers.

Part of the problem stems from confusion about the meaning of *produc-tivity*. Old dictionary definitions define the word as a derivative of *produc-tive* ("having the power of producing; generative; creative."[2]) In interviews, faculty members seem to share this understanding of the term, as when one tells a colleague, "I've been very productive."[3] However, the economists' definition that *productivity* means "output quantity and quality per unit of input"—that is, producing the most or highest quality output possible given the resources on hand—is the appropriate one for our purposes here.

One should not think of productivity simply as cost cutting or applying business methods. Cost cutting that reduces quality is as likely to degrade productivity as to increase it, whereas boosting quality at the same cost increases productivity. Again, the goal in being productive is to get as good a result as possible given the available inputs, where good results encom-pass quality as well as quantity. No right-thinking person can be against this goal, but, of course, the devil is in the details. Crude attempts to apply business methods to academic productivity improvement miss important details and thus trigger immune reactions that lead to rejection. However, this kind of reaction is by no means inevitable.

In this chapter, I'll focus on teaching and learning productivity or, to state it more simply, *instructional productivity*—rather than productivity in re-search and administration—because the opportunities for improvement in the former are largely unexplored. But before describing the opportunities, I will describe briefly the barriers to instructional productivity improvement.

BARRIERS TO PRODUCTIVITY IMPROVEMENT

Some say nonprofit entities like traditional universities are inherently less able to pursue productivity improvement than their for-profit counter-parts. This is true to a considerable extent, but traditional universities can overcome the difficulties. To see how, we need to look at the fundamental economic model that drives nonprofits.[4]

The model holds that such entities seek to maximize value–where *value* means mission attainment—subject to constraints relating to market demand, production processes, and finance. In recent years, much attention has been focused on student enrollment management, particularly for undergraduates, and traditional universities now market themselves in much the same way as for-profits. Unfortunately, however, the same cannot be said for improving the instructional production process. One overriding reason for the lack of progress is that universities invest little systematic time and attention in this area. Time spent on task matters and the needed time has not been available where it matters most: within academic departments. Professors spend considerable time deciding *what* to teach, but relatively little effort on *how*. Individuals experiment from time to time, but departments rarely adopt even the most successful experiments, such as those that introduce new instructional software modules, as policy. Hence, teaching remains mostly a handicraft proposition. Three distinct problems, which I describe next, contribute to this result.

To anticipate potential objections, let me say at the outset that research is *not* a barrier to instructional productivity. Some side effects of research do present barriers, but there is no reason why robust efforts to improve instructional productivity cannot coexist alongside a vigorous research program.

Opaque Accounting Conventions

The first problem derives from a lack of transparency about what happens to the fruits of instructional productivity improvement. For the business firm, productivity gains fall to the bottom line as increased shareholder profits. For nonprofit universities, which cannot distribute the difference between revenue and cost to shareholders, better productivity augments the resources available for value creation in other areas. In other words, productivity improvement is another way of raising money—making additional resources available in a way that people within the university directly control rather than depending on markets or the actions of donors or governments. Viewed in this light, productivity improvement should be equally beneficial in the nonprofit and for-profit sectors.

Unfortunately, it's not that simple. Two centuries of accounting rules for public companies ensure the reliable quantification and disclosure of profits, which investors watch closely and compare across firms and industries. A company that fails to steadily improve productivity risks falling behind in earnings per share, with attendant adverse consequences for the stock price and its managers' careers. Universities rarely achieve such transparency. For example, how can one quantify the fruits of instructional productivity improvement when conventional accounting procedures don't even try to separate the cost of teaching from that of departmental research? Even when the requisite calculations are made, many institutions are reluctant to disclose the results for fear of stirring up conflict, either internally or on the part of stakeholders who may think they're paying for one thing but in fact are getting another. So because the benefits of improved productivity are seldom evident, it should not be surprising that such improvement tends not to be taken seriously.

Problematic Quality Measurement

The second problem stems from the difficulty of measuring the quality of higher education's instructional outputs. The lack of good measures has severely limited the degree to which market forces can discipline the provision of educational quality, especially for undergraduates. Indeed, it sometimes seems as if the marketplace values spending per se—such as on new faculty, facilities, and library materials—more seriously than it does teaching and learning themselves. The lack of measures also inhibits internal efforts to improve instructional productivity. People who work on quality in businesses, hospitals, and government say, "If you can't measure something, you can't improve it." The saying is based on the need for feedback about the consequences of one's actions, especially when the actions involve significant change from the status quo. Changing tried-and-true instructional methodologies without the ability to measure the effects on learning puts quality at risk, which accounts in part for the faculty's reluctance to attempt such changes.

There has been progress in recent years with, for example, the launch of the National Survey of Student Engagement (NSSE), which asks students about important characteristics of their college learning experience both in and out of the classroom, the Collegiate Learning Assessment (CLA), which measures improvement in students' core academic skills, and a variety of discipline-based measures. However, the state of the art remains imperfect, and few departments make a serious effort to adopt, adapt, or develop robust measures that are appropriate for their particular subjects and students. Others in this volume discuss the development of learning quality measures. Hence, it is enough here to say that universities and professors should pay careful attention to progress in this area, and they should quickly exploit whatever approaches promise a reasonable degree of success.

Pursuit of Prestige

The desire of many universities to pursue prestige presents the third barrier to productivity improvement. There is no doubt that the schemes for ranking universities that have proliferated in recent years have affected many institutions' sense of what's important. While the schemes differ from one to another, most commentators agree that prestige is the main driving force and that prestige is conferred much more by faculty research and admissions selectivity than by the quality of education per se. For example, research citations mostly drive the Shanghai Jiao Tong University international ranking system. America's *U.S. News and World Report* and the United Kingdom's *Times Higher Education* ranking systems use a combination of measures such as survey results, research prowess, student selectivity, and spending per student that they interpret as measures of prestige.

The impact of ranking systems on the higher education marketplace, coupled with the intrinsic desire of many professors trained in research universities to establish and maintain research reputations, directly impact the definition of value—the construct that nonprofit entities seek to maximize. Many boards, university administrators, and professors want to see their institutions rise in the rankings, and research gets a further boost from the faculty reward system and faculty participation in university governance. The result may well be that some institutions value research more heavily than many external stakeholders—such as state governments, students, and their parents—would like. How much teaching takes a backseat to research within institutions, and the resulting effect on instructional productivity, is masked by the shortfalls in learning quality measurement. And because the rewards accruing to prestige are never placed side by side with their costs, the pursuit of prestige can and does persist unchallenged.

Pursuing prestige accrues two kinds of cost. First, today's intense competition for research funding and top-notch research faculty make it very difficult and costly to move up in the rankings. For example, a team of RAND researchers found that, for institutions not already near the top of the prestige ladder, the substantial amounts of money spent pursuing prestige tend to cancel themselves out competitively in a kind of arms race and thus are largely wasted.[5] Such wastage certainly represents a drag on institutional productivity.

If the direct costs of pursuing prestige weren't bad enough, there is strong reason to believe that pressures to do research cause many professors to *satisfice* their teaching.[6] Satisficing in this context means that, although faculty want to do a good job for their students and usually will expend enough time and effort to achieve what they believe to be satisfactory performance, they are quick to turn their attention to research once they have attained the quality threshold. This diverts discretionary time from the continuous improvement of instructional productivity. The mantra of the quality movement, which also applies to productivity, is "Good enough isn't." The implication of satisficing is "Good enough is," which stops continuous improvement in its tracks.

OVERCOMING THE BARRIERS

The three barriers are formidable, but my experience in working with universities and their departments on quality improvement provides hope that they can be surmounted. The trick is to tap the intrinsic interest of faculty (at least for some professors some of the time) in doing a good job for their students—and in solving challenging intellectual problems—to a degree sufficient to overcome the urge to satisfice. Doing this requires: (1) a conceptual structure for productivity that professors can buy into; (2) a workload planning schema that allows time for productivity improvement work; and (3) a reward system that values such improvement, or at least does not undermine it.

Professors and whole departments differ substantially in their understanding of what it takes to produce high-quality undergraduate teaching and learning. Some succeed in doing so, for example, with coherent learning objectives, effective pedagogical activities that strongly engage students in the learning process, and well-aligned and timely learning assessments. However, graduate schools do not teach the art of doing these things, and they do not come naturally to people whose primary focus is on the canon of content in their disciplines. Another example, which I will discuss in the last section of this chapter, is the widespread failure to apply the lessons of cognitive and behavioral science to enhance teaching and learning.

I have called the time required to learn and do such things "academic quality work" to distinguish it from the act of teaching itself.[7] Such work falls under Boyer's "Scholarship of Teaching," but it is more sharply focused than most of his examples.[8] Universities that take the quality of undergraduate education seriously will provide faculty with the time and rewards needed to develop high levels of maturity in academic quality work, whereas a failure to do these things provides prima facie evidence that they carry a lower priority than one might expect. The same line of reasoning applies to the improvement of academic productivity, which, as we shall see presently, adds a cost dimension to considerations of quality. Indeed, quality and productivity are so closely intertwined that I'll refer henceforth simply to "academic productivity work."

My earlier mention of "the dog that isn't barking" referred to shortfalls in academic productivity work. The university can undertake such work at four different levels: for individual courses, at the level of whole departments or teaching programs, at the campus level, and above the campus level (which I'll call the "systems level"). I address the levels in the four remaining sections of this chapter. We shall see that each offers its own paths to productivity improvement. One can start at whichever level is easiest in the circumstances, because all the paths converge eventually.

COURSE-LEVEL PRODUCTIVITY IMPROVEMENT

We can liken the redesign of courses, and also course sequences and learning modules within courses, to business process reengineering, which is a key methodology for productivity improvement in business.[9] The idea was introduced in higher education about twenty years ago, when Rensselaer Polytechnic Institute (RPI) shifted its educational paradigm by introducing what it called "studio" courses in physics, chemistry, calculus, and, eventually (with variations), in engineering, computer science, and biology. The idea was to systematically incorporate the use of technology in a cooperative learning environment that consolidated lectures, virtual labs, and discussion sections, using simulation software to reduce or eliminate the conventional laboratory sections. I recall that at one point dozens of universities worldwide had adopted the studio model. The National Center for Academic Transformation (NCAT), founded in 1999 with a grant from the Pew Charitable Trusts, has carried the idea forward. The result has been to demonstrate remarkable instructional productivity improvements at almost a hundred U.S. colleges and universities.

RPI's Studio Courses

Rensselaer began by reexamining the conventional wisdom that the traditional lecture course with breakout sections or labs is the most cost-effective way to educate hundreds of students per semester.[10] It's significant that the innovation's initial impetus came from concerns about learning quality, specifically the observation that too high a proportion of students were failing the introductory math and science courses and thus dropping out of the university. Faculty interviews with students indicated that, despite the teachers' best efforts, the lectures failed dismally when it came to engaging learners in the subject matter, a finding that has been replicated countless times in many institutions.[11] Yet, teaching the introductory material through small seminars and tutorials was something the university could not afford, given its precarious financial situation. What to do?

The answer was unconventional to say the least. Instead of holding two one-hour lecture sections each week with thirty or so students, Rensselaer would teach the material in one two-hour studio session with forty-eight to sixty-four students. The difference would be technology: simulation software that the Annenberg Foundation developed ran on computers located in the studio, one for each pair of students. The hands-on attention of one professor, one graduate assistant, and one or two undergraduate assistants who guided the students through the assignments facilitated the learning. Instead of getting information from lectures, RPI expected students, with the instructors helping, to use print resources and computer technology to prepare more fully on their own, which led to a much more interactive class experience as the students used what they had learned for problem solving. The key to the process turned out not to be the simulation software itself, but rather that students had to report to their peers and the instructors during class about what they were doing, why, and how they were interpreting the results. This, in turn, helped the professor identify teachable moments for clarifying mini-lectures.

The effects were spectacular. Comparing the first five years of studio physics with the previous eight years showed that class attendance and pre-test versus post-test content knowledge gains were up sharply, while more topics were covered despite the reduction in student contact hours. Overall, the retention of students from freshman to sophomore year rose from 70 percent to 80 percent. When asked whether the course should be taught in the studio format versus some other way, 91 percent of the students voted for the studio, an opinion that also was reflected in better faculty teaching evaluations.

These results demonstrated a clear increase in teaching and learning quality. However, the gains extended beyond quality to the domain of cost. The method of analysis was a variant of "activity-based costing" (ABC). Developed in business as an alternative to conventional cost accounting, ABC analyzes the details of what actually occurs in production; at RPI, this is teaching particular courses. The core elements of the RPI model were: (1) the *activities* used to deliver instruction (class contact hours, out-of-class activities like preparation, office hours, teaching assistant [TA] supervision, and use of equipment and software) for a given number of enrollees; (2) the *resources* needed to animate the activities (faculty and TA hours as a function of the number and size of classes, number of work-stations, and size of facility); and (3) the *unit costs* of the activities (cost per faculty and TA hour, operation and depreciation of workstations and facilities). Once the model has been developed, a simple spreadsheet can multiply resource usage by unit cost and sum the result over the activities.[12] This contrasts with traditional cost accounting, which starts with a department's total cost (the *result* of the activity-based cost analysis) and then allocates it among the functions of instruction and research and perhaps, for the former, the various types and levels of courses.[13]

When RPI applied the course-based, activity-based costing model, it found that accommodating the required student throughput with the studio model required fewer faculty contact hours than the traditional lecture or lab format, that the amount of faculty preparation time decreased because much of the content was embodied in the software, and that TA supervision was dramatically reduced due to the elimination of recitation sections and labs. Adding up all the costs, including those due to the technology, showed the introduction of studio physics saved between $10,000 and $20,000 per semester for the introductory course—*at the same time it improved learning and student retention*. While these course-level savings may seem relatively modest, when taken to scale, they are significant.

NCAT's Course Redesign

"Doing more for less," in the sense of improving quality while expending fewer resources, has become the expected result of course redesign projects. NCAT, mentioned earlier, has developed a robust approach for working with faculty groups that have committed themselves to pursue productivity improvement at the course level. Professors work in teams to refine their course objectives and outcomes measures. Then they develop, deploy, and test one or more new instructional methods, compare them in terms of learning and cost outcomes, and make judgments about which are the most productive.

NCAT does *not* enter a redesign project with the idea that technology-based innovation is a necessary result, but things usually turn out that way. This certainly demonstrates the power of technology, but other innovative practices also are at work. Some of the most promising are increased interaction among students, online tutorials with student performance tracking, undergraduate learning assistants, and support services that ensure student engagement, many of which have become exemplars of good practice.

As in the case of the RPI studio courses, NCAT's course redesigns invariably deliver cost reductions as well as quality improvements. To quote NCAT director Carol Twigg, the first thirty courses redesigned under the original Pew grant "are reducing costs by an average of 37%, with specific savings ranging from 15% to 77%. Collectively the 30 courses on different campuses initially projected annual savings of about $3.6 million. Final results show [they] saved about $3.1 million. Some saved more than expected, others less."[14] She goes on to project that "if all institutions of higher education in the United States adopted NCAT's methodology to redesign their top 25 courses, the cost of instruction would be reduced annually by approximately 16%—while improving student learning and retention." Even accepting the fact that this is a very rough estimate, there is no doubt that universities can achieve substantial savings by applying course-level redesign.

Critics argue that departments cannot actually capture the savings because of tenure constraints and reluctance to take any action that might result in fewer faculty positions. These are formidable obstacles, but they aren't showstoppers. The necessary first step in productivity improvement is to *find ways to avoid cost*, even if one can't harvest the savings right away. For course redesign, avoiding cost can mean freeing faculty time for other important tasks. Sharing productivity gains with the people who create them (in this case, the faculty) is a good idea, even if it may turn out that some gains have to be sacrificed in the future as part of independently-triggered budget-reduction episodes. Universities are likely to require such reductions from time to time whether productivity has been improved or not, and they can achieve them with far less pain if they have achieved productivity gains beforehand. Furthermore, faculty will have enjoyed all the fruits of course redesign until the next budget-reduction episode.

DEPARTMENT-LEVEL PRODUCTIVITY IMPROVEMENT

Department-level productivity improvement initiatives take two forms: a decision to redesign individual courses as described earlier, and redesign of the department's *portfolio* of courses and teaching assignments, that is, its collection of instructional activities taken as a whole. Looking at the collection is harder than looking at individual courses, but the *departmental activity model* I describe in this section helps one visualize what's involved and, simultaneously, points the way toward improvement. In addition, such a model can help motivate the redesign of individual courses and also inform resource-allocation decisions by deans and provosts.

The following story illustrates what can happen to a department when a university imposes budget reductions without the holistic view an activity model provides. The English department in question had, over half a dozen years, lost a third of its regular faculty lines to budget cuts, despite enrollment increases. It responded by boosting teaching loads and the size of conventional classes, cutting seminars from the curriculum, and staffing more than half its general education and in-major class sections with low-cost adjuncts hired on the casual payroll. It assigned fewer papers (this was an English department!) and shifted most examinations from essays to multiple choice or short-answer questions that staff could grade more easily. Scholarship ground essentially to a halt, and some of the best professors decamped for other institutions. Like other departments facing similar problems, this one had lobbied the central administration for new faculty lines but had not been successful, so each year it simply hunkered down and made do with what it had.

The central administration benchmarked what they called departmental productivity against data for credit hours per faculty full-time equivalent (FTE), a system developed by the University of Delaware.[15] Not surprisingly, the department looked good on this measure. Some concern was expressed about equity—that "faculty were working too hard"—but the data were too ambiguous to alert administrators that there might be a quality problem.

The ambiguity is depicted in figure 3.1. Suppose a department rises above its benchmark: that is, it sits at the right of the figure. Does this imply high productivity? Not necessarily. It also could mean the quality of education has suffered, that heavy teaching loads are preventing faculty from meeting the university's objectives for research and scholarship, that faculty are working at an unsustainable and inequitable pace, or (as in the example) all of the above. The opposite is true for results below the benchmark, shown at the left of the figure.

FIGURE 3.1

Ambiguities in benchmarking student credit hours per faculty FTE

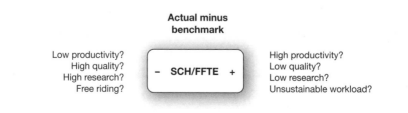

Actual minus
benchmark

Low productivity?   High productivity?
High quality?   − **SCH/FFTE** +   Low quality?
High research?   Low research?
Free riding?   Unsustainable workload?

What's needed is a more detailed way to analyze the data—for example, using the departmental activity model referred to earlier. Because the model depends only on information available in the university's central data systems, the central administration can initiate its development. Once constructed, the model can operate routinely to display results for all departments every semester. Though imperfect, it can focus attention on the available quantitative evidence about instructional productivity. I've been working on such a model, which consists of the four core elements I sketch briefly next.

Analysis of Instructional Activities

We begin the analysis by identifying the alternative approaches to instruction ("class types") that the department is using or might use. (We can also apply the model to cross-departmental teaching programs like general education.) For example, the alternatives might be:

1. Conventional courses with what are considered to be normal class sizes (see later).
2. Courses taught in conventional ways but that are large enough to inhibit interaction (such as large lectures).
3. Small multisection courses, such as seminars offered to all first-year students as part of general education and capstone courses for students majoring in the department.
4. Small single-section courses, which often proliferate in the catalog as faculty seek to teach their specialties.[16]
5. Studio courses as described earlier for RPI (also, perhaps, online and hybrid courses taught both face-to-face and on the Internet).

We include subtypes like breakout and lab sections where applicable. Class types also can be differentiated by level (for example, introductory to advanced, based on course number in the catalog) and what Robert Zemsky and I have termed *coherence* (based on the characteristics of students taking them).[17]

The next step is to extract data on each class type used during an agreed period of time. Data items should include, for example, the number of replications (sections taught including labs and breakout sections), average section size, class duration or credit hours, facilities and equipment needs, the fraction of classes taught by regular as opposed to adjunct faculty, and tenure-line faculty teaching loads.[18] Additional variables describing the fraction of students failing or repeating each class and the number of times the class has been closed to students desiring registration may be included as well.[19] Each university will define its own variables and, indeed, the list of class types itself, and these may vary to some extent across departments.

The analytical step is for institutional researchers to search out patterns in the data. Has the mix of class types shifted toward large classes or single-section small ones? Has the fraction of sections that adjunct faculty teach been moving up or down? How about teaching loads? Having consistent time series that cover all the departments in the institution can be a great help in understanding variations in productivity across units and over time. However, I have yet to describe the greatest benefits.

Activity, Resourcing, and Cost Models

Harvesting greater benefits requires development of activity, resourcing, and cost models. *Activity models* calculate the number of replications required for each class type and subtype, given the expected enrollment. For example, if two hundred students will take class type 1 and the normal class size is twenty-five, then eight (200/25 = 8) replications will be required. More complicated models include lab and breakout replications as well as appropriate activity representations for any online and hybrid courses.

The *resourcing models* relate teacher time, facilities, and other inputs to the number of replications and enrollments for each class type. Resource types typically include tenure-line and adjunct faculty, TAs, and facilities and equipment. Faculty time depends on the number of replications, class duration, and out-of-class workloads (which, as for grading, may depend on enrollment as well as sections taught). Applying the models gives the amount of each resource required to field a given configuration of class types. To anticipate what comes later, it is possible to conduct "what if" analyses by varying the distribution of enrollments and observing the effect on resource requirements. Among other things, we can use such analyses to explore the effects of substituting adjunct for tenure-line faculty and vice versa.

With the resourcing models in hand, it is fairly simple to calculate the cost of alternative class-type configurations. Institutional researchers estimate the *unit cost* of each type of resource: for example, the hourly cost for faculty, adjuncts, and various types of facilities.[20] Then one simply multiplies the unit costs by the resource requirements and sums to get the total cost of a given configuration. It also is easy to derive aggregate measures of productivity for comparison with, say, the Delaware benchmarks.

These models represent another application of activity-based costing. However, they differ from the approach many accounting firms apply in higher education. That approach does not model the department's instructional activities but instead uses only the percentages of time spent by faculty on teaching, research, service, and so on. This is problematic for at least two reasons. First, it treats instructional resource usage in terms of fixed ratios, i.e., the amount of each resource per FTE enrollment. Fixed ratios do not allow for substitution among inputs (for example, the use of regular faculty versus less expensive adjuncts) nor do they allow one to explore the effects of changing class types (as at RPI) or economies and diseconomies of scale. (Diseconomies occur, for example, when the need to cover a wide range of materials for a small number of students forces inefficiently small class sizes.) Second, the effort percentages usually are obtained from department chair judgments or faculty diary studies, both of which are notoriously inaccurate. In my view, the accounting firms' activity-based costing models should be enriched to include detailed instructional activity models of the kind I describe here.

Benchmarks, Norms, and Critical Values

I noted earlier that department-wide statistics like credit hours per faculty FTE can easily be computed from the activity models, which allows benchmarking against currently available data. However, breaking down the benchmarks by class type would make them even more valuable. Such a development does not seem far-fetched if a significant number of institutions were to engage in departmental activity modeling.[21]

The development of *internal norms* for the departmental activity variables is both natural and necessary even if external benchmarks are not available. The English department story implicitly assumes the existence of such norms, if only as the status quo before things got bad. The norms can always be changed, but people both inside and outside the department should be conscious of when the change occurs and why. Indeed, I would go further and ask departments and deans to agree on the following internal benchmarks for the key activity and resourcing variables:

- *A normal range* of values expected if things are operating as they should be, that is, to achieve a generally accepted level of educational quality. Using a range instead of a single value reflects the fact that the data are bound to shift by small amounts from year to year, even in the absence of structural change.
- *Critical values* for each variable, above and below the normal range, that would signal serious problems the department needs to address lest quality or productivity fall below acceptable levels.[22]

The normal ranges and critical values provide a basis for exception reporting; that is, the ability to compare each new tranche of data with previously agreed norms will help focus attention on anomalous situations or trends. The situation is made to order for the software industry's data dashboard technology, where one can look first at summary data that had been formatted to highlight anomalies and then drill down to get additional detail where needed.

Table 3.1 illustrates a crude dashboard, which more or less describes the situation in the English department. Entries outside the normal range are shown in bold-faced large type, with those that are outside their critical values also set off against a shaded background. A real dashboard would use icons and color to indicate the extent and direction of deviations, but even without these, it's hard to miss the dropping off of multisection seminars, the increase in large conventional courses, the skyrocketing use of adjuncts, and the increasingly heavy burden of faculty teaching loads. Drilling down is, of course, impossible on the printed page, but the ability to do so could show the kinds of courses and students being taught by adjuncts.

The English department's story might well have turned out better if the departmental activity model had been in place. It's hard to imagine that the changes highlighted in figure 3.1 would have gone unnoticed, especially if other departments were not seeing such changes to the same extent. This would have stimulated different budget-time conversations among the department chair, dean, and provost—conversations that might well have surfaced the quality-eroding shifts of examination style and numbers of written assignments. In other words, the greater level of detail that the departmental activity model offers (as opposed to aggregate statistics on credit hours per faculty) would have led to more evidence-based resource-allocation decisions.

TABLE 3.1

Illustrative developmental dashboard

Sections per year	2008	2009	2010	2011	2012	2013
Single-section seminars	45	45	44	43	44	43
Multi-section seminars	16	14	12	**9**	**7**	**6**
Conventional courses	61	59	57	56	53	50
Large courses	31	32	35	37	**42**	**45**
Adjunct	25%	27%	30%	35%	41%	**53%**
Faculty teaching load	5.1	5.2	5.3	5.4	5.6	**5.8**

Another reason for asking about normal ranges and critical values is to stimulate holistic thinking about the department's class-type portfolio (as represented by the list of class-type alternatives)—thinking that typically is not forthcoming when each faculty member plans his or her own courses. The department might decide, for example, that it's best to limit the number of classes of normal size and instead cluster them at the two ends of the size spectrum, that is, in multisection seminars and larger-than-normal classes. Such a barbell strategy exploits the fact that, for many subjects and instructional approaches, the loss of teaching effectiveness declines as class size increases, so that, for a particular student cohort, paying for a larger number of small classes with a smaller number of large ones produces better overall results than concentrating everything in the middle of the distribution. If properly configured, the departmental activity model invites the consideration of such strategies.

Use of the Model for Planning

Suppose a department wants to reduce its reliance on adjuncts but is not sure how best to compensate for this action while staying within its budget. As I described earlier, what-if analysis based on the model allows users to experiment with variations in adjunct usage, teaching loads, the mix of class types, and perhaps other variables.

While what-if analysis represents a big step forward, an even bigger step is possible with goal-seeking analysis.[23] The approach begins by using the normal ranges to calculate planning targets (the goals) and the relative importance of achieving them. Then we can employ a mathematical algorithm to find the plan that comes closest to the targets, while enforcing the applicable resourcing limits and keeping all results within their critical values.

Use of the goal-seeking model allows us to address a wider range of questions than we can handle using conventional what-if analysis. For example, it permits easy determination of whether departmental action can improve variables that threaten to fall outside the normal ranges or critical values, or whether the department requires additional faculty lines or enrollment adjustments. We can also use the model to make routine forecasts of how impending changes in enrollments and faculty lines are likely to affect departmental activity and whether the effect will be problematic.

CAMPUS-LEVEL PRODUCTIVITY IMPROVEMENT

What campus-level administrators can do to improve instructional productivity is mainly to stimulate and facilitate more effective work at the department and course levels. They also can improve the productivity of administration and support services—and of research and research administration, for that matter—but these are beyond the scope of this chapter. Instructional productivity improvement boils down to leadership, providing resources, and getting the incentives right. However, there are some specific actions that campus-level leaders may wish to consider.

The first such action involves developing models and data, such as the departmental activity described earlier. Administrators can work with faculty advisers to develop appropriate model specifications, extract the necessary data, and develop dashboard displays and other software, and then employ volunteer departments to work out the bugs and demonstrate efficacy before committing to a broader rollout. Embedding appropriate expertise in the institution's teaching and learning center is another good step, as is obtaining the support of the school deans. In addition to their other benefits, these actions send a needed signal that the university considers instructional productivity improvement a high priority.

Systematic follow-up also is very important. This can take the form of regular oversight of departmental productivity improvement activities or of more formal and episodic reviews of the kind I discuss in the next paragraph. Some may question the legitimacy of such oversight—by deans, or anyone else, for that matter—but there really is no alternative if the campus is serious about productivity improvement. This was brought home to me in the early days of academic audit, when we routinely interviewed departments about their attention to instructional quality (and now, by extension, productivity) and then discussed the results with the relevant deans. Often the deans were well aware of differences in their various departments' attention to quality and eager to discuss ways to improve the laggards. However, some deans exhibited no such knowledge or interest: they stated either that quality was someone else's concern (e.g., a senate or central administration committee) or that academic freedom precluded any intervention into departmental affairs. Not surprisingly, it was in the former situation where we found instructional quality to be best.

Oversight by deans is not particularly difficult, but it helps to know what one is looking for. A useful concept is what I've come to call the "principal of differentiation." For example, maintaining the same class-size norms across student levels and the same (or approximately the same) research workload assignments for all professors, regardless of their track records and prospects, shows a lack of differentiation, which provides prima facie evidence that productivity can be improved. Another telltale is whether the department regularly assigns at least some professors to participate in academic productivity improvement tasks.

Periodic formal reviews also may be needed. Of the various approaches, an internal academic audit seems to be the most effective.[24] Such audits focus on departmental processes including, importantly, their productivity improvement work, rather than on resource availability, research prowess, and curriculum, as is typical in traditional program review. Because such audits don't require deep disciplinary expertise, professors from within the university—but outside the department—can perform them inexpensively. Audits also can be formative and evidence-gathering exercises. This reduces faculty resistance, and because peers are used as reviewers, the audit process helps propagate good practice across the institution.

The final requirement for effective campus-level action is to link productivity with budgeting. A university should reward departments that truly are trying to improve productivity, whereas it should inform those not improving that they aren't getting all they might otherwise have gotten.[25] Even responsibility center management (RCM) systems can include such linkages, for example, through the use of special incentive funds and in the subvention-setting process. Linking effective productivity improvement work to a department's discretionary spending can provide a powerful incentive.

SYSTEM-LEVEL PRODUCTIVITY IMPROVEMENT

For the purposes of this section, *system* means "above the campus level," which aims at multicampus systems, higher education coordinating boards, and even institutional governing boards. The key proposition is that system-level judgments are less likely to be blinded or bound by the people, organizations, facilities, and culture of traditional campuses; in other words, system-level decision makers have more freedom to ask out-of-the-box questions and consider radically new structures and processes.

Some opportunities for system-level productivity improvement mirror those available to campus-level administrators. People at the systems level can encourage or even prod campuses to take productivity-improving actions. They can ask and re-ask tough questions and implement performance funding schemes. They can ascertain whether campuses have a system of internal academic audit and whether they are linking performance to budgets. Finally and importantly, system-level people can mount their own program of academic audit so they don't have to rely only on reports from the campuses. (Nations like the United Kingdom, Australia, Hong Kong, and New Zealand have turned academic audit into a fine art with a demonstrable track record of accomplishment.) In short, people concerned about academic productivity can take reasonable steps to determine whether the campuses for which they are responsible are engaging in the activities required for productivity improvement and, if so, whether these activities are making a difference.

Disruptive Innovation

Perhaps the most intriguing opportunities at the system level involve what's called *disruptive innovation*. As the name implies, disruptive innovation represents such a departure from the status quo that many, including those who do not normally oppose change, view it as alien or even damaging. Clayton Christensen of the Harvard Business School describes the emergence of personal computing and its effect on the Digital Equipment Corporation (DEC) as an example of disruptive innovation.[26] DEC had been doing very well with its line of minicomputers, and though it viewed the early Commodore PET, Apple, and IBM PCs with interest, neither it nor its customers saw a threat to the minicomputer business. This should not be written off as mere myopia. Because the early PCs and their software were extremely crude, their appeal was mainly at the very bottom of the computer market (i.e., with hobbyists). While inexpensive, the new microcomputers couldn't approach the jobs that DEC's customers wanted done. Yet, in the space of a few years, the PCs had almost put DEC out of business. What happened? Does this story have any relevance to today's traditional universities? Read on.

The key characteristic of a disruptive innovation is that, because it does things in an entirely new way, it starts crudely and low on the learning curve. It appeals mainly to those not well served by the traditional approach, often because the traditional approach isn't affordable. Yet, the experience of serving the underserved may allow the innovator to perfect the new ideas to the point where moving upmarket becomes feasible. Often this process occurs under the radar of the traditional supplier and its customers. For example, DEC's best customers reinforced the superiority of the minicomputer and kept demanding additional power and feature functions (at extra cost) right up to the point where they switched to banks of PCs. The company was caught flat-footed, because even though it possessed the technical expertise and had experimented with microcomputer development, its cost structures and corporate culture had prevented it from ascending the learning curve. Some commentators believe such a phenomenon may now be happening in higher education, as the best of the for-profit providers challenge traditional universities on their home turf.

For-profit university business models surmount or sidestep the three barriers to instructional productivity improvement that I identified in the opening section: opaque accounting conventions, problematic quality measurement, and pursuit of prestige. While such universities don't publish profitability by line of business and organizational unit, no one should doubt that such information is readily available and heavily used within the company. The for-profits also assess student learning to the maximum extent possible: to use the University of Phoenix's often-quoted phrase, "If it moves, we measure it." The resulting data feed directly into productivity improvement, and they also underpin the university's marketing to prospective students. Finally, prestige based on research and scholarship does not enter the for-profits' objective function because these enterprises don't include research as part of their mission.

Systems-level initiatives can address some of the same measurement and transparency issues in traditional institutions. For example, a state board or university system could require transparent accounting for instructional cost by discipline and organizational unit. (The ministry of education in Singapore already does this by requiring its universities to use activity-based costing, though their particular implementation fails to surmount the difficulties I described earlier.) State learning-assessment initiatives already have addressed the question of quality measurement, and though success has been elusive, I'm convinced that embedding assessment in a broader program of improvement work and academic audit can mitigate the problems.[27] Finally, the separation of research from teaching is an established fact in community colleges and some state college and university systems, and it is substantially so in the many private colleges that live or die in the marketplace for undergraduates.

Among other things, the departmental modeling initiative I've discussed in this chapter aims to halt the satisficing of teaching and its effect on continuous improvement, and to provide transparency about what alternative approaches to instruction actually cost. Finding better ways to get these innovations adopted at the campus level, where they are likely to be viewed as disruptive, should be a high priority for systems-level leaders.

Learning as "Job One"

To borrow from an old Ford slogan, the greatest challenge for those who would reform America's higher education system is to make learning "Job One" in the all-important instructional domain. Just such an experiment now is in process at the University of Minnesota's new Rochester campus (UMR). Descriptions of the experiment can be found elsewhere in this volume and in a recent book by Robert Zemsky.[28] Therefore, I'll limit myself to describing the goals of the experiment and the general strategy for implementation as I observed them while serving as the campus's lead strategy consultant prior to the admission of its first student cohort in the fall of 2009.

Stephen Lehmkuhle, the founding chancellor at UMR, insisted from the outset that undergraduate learning be Job One, and he had some very clear ideas about how to accomplish this. His ideas boiled down to the following:

1. Make the emergent lessons of cognitive and behavioral science central to UMR's teaching and learning.
2. Integrate information technology into the curriculum from the ground up.
3. Employ the precepts of education quality and productivity as key organizing principles for faculty activity.
4. Hire faculty who will enthusiastically pursue the new paradigm and reward them for so doing.

His first step was to appoint Claudia Neuhauser, Howard Hughes Medical Institute Professor and distinguished McKnight University Professor in the Department of Ecology, Evolution, and Behavior on the university's Twin Cities campus, as his vice chancellor for academic affairs. Working together, the two have developed a truly remarkable approach to teaching and learning.

Cognitive and behavioral science now offer much cogent advice about how students learn and, therefore, how professors should teach. Some is what most professors know anyway, but too often forget, such as the importance of motivation and engagement (and how teachers can further them), how the organization of knowledge (not simply its content) determines how students use it, and how goal-directed practice with timely and targeted feedback is critical to learning. Other insights are surprising: for example, that prior knowledge can hinder learning as well as help it, and that effective teaching involves recognizing and overcoming our expert blind spots. Zemsky provides a brief summary of these ideas and their potential. Readers who wish to explore them further can consult the Web site of Carnegie Mellon University's Eberly Center for Teaching Excellence,[29] and a slim but rewarding volume by Case Western Reserve University's James Zull.[30] The title of the Zull volume says it all: *The Art of Changing the Brain: Enriching the Practice of Teaching by Exploring the Biology of Learning.* I believe that absolutely every university teacher eventually will need to be familiar with these concepts. Teaching without such understanding will be recognized as akin to practicing engineering without a good knowledge of mathematics—one can build bridges using rules of thumb, for example, but they will require an extravagant use of material and, even so, won't always stand.

Technology is the second key building block in the Lehmkuhle-Neuhauser schema. The application begins with the use of learning objects to provide students with a first exposure to most subject-matter modules. A learning object consists of three elements, all embedded in Web-based or local software: (1) content knowledge or links to where to find the knowledge; (2) an interface to facilitate the student's access to and interpretation of the content; and (3) a learning assessment method based on a combination of behavior-tracking data from the interface and purpose-designed exercises and tests. By way of an example, consider a program that teaches Newton's laws of motion through a series of computer-mediated tutorials that include text, dynamic diagrams or cartoons, audio, and video, followed by test problems that continuously assess the students' knowledge gain and cause the program to backtrack when further instruction is necessary.

Learning objects supported by peer interaction and on-call faculty (discussed later) allow students to proceed at their own pace even as they participate in a vibrant on-campus learning community. Deep interpretive conversations with faculty remain very important, but they are deferred until a student has mastered a given module's content. That's only half the story, however. The other half is that the software collects, as a by-product of student assessment, data on the performance of each learning object—data that faculty can use continuously to improve the learning process. Accumulating such data will enable evidence-based decisions about what works and what doesn't, which over time will produce further advances in the emergent science of learning.

The third requirement for ensuring that learning is and will remain Job One is to maintain an organized set of processes for productivity improvement. This means implementing ideas such as those I discussed earlier. Traditional universities often fail to apply these ideas, but UMR made them a central element of its development plan.[31]

The final building block, a faculty structure purposely designed for the new learning schema, was facilitated by the fact that UMR was a start-up campus. Lehmkuhle and Neuhauser are fond of saying, "The bad news at the beginning was that we had no faculty; the good news was that we had no faculty." This enabled them to hire based on some distinctly nontraditional faculty job descriptions:

- *Design faculty*: one person for each major discipline taught at UMR, whose job it would be to develop curricula, apply the cognitive science principles, acquire or develop learning objects, oversee the teaching process as it evolved, and do research on learning in his or her area. These people would be tenured or on the tenure line.
- *Student-based faculty:* permanent team members with full fringe benefits who would staff the smart classrooms and learning laboratories, be available for on-call student consultation, perform other hands-on teaching duties, and identify students with learning difficulties and offer timely interventions. Their numbers would fluctuate

with enrollments so as to maintain a target student-faculty ratio. Most would have PhDs, but they would not be on the tenure line.

- *Postdocs:* recent doctorate recipients with a strong interest in cognitive science and learning processes, who would spend a few years perfecting their skills as teachers in the new environment, doing research, and preparing to innovate at other institutions. Their duties at UMR would be essentially as utility infielders: helping the design faculty and the student-based faculty wherever needed as well as pursuing their own projects.

UMR had just finished its first year of operations at the time of this writing, and the jury is still out as to whether the experiment will be successful and sustainable. Initial reports have been good, however, as evidenced by a feature article in the fall of 2009 in the *Chronicle of Higher Education*.[32] But whatever the final result, this scheme represents an important breakthrough, and the fact that a traditional research university could launch such a path-breaking and disruptive innovation is highly encouraging.

I shall close with a comment, or perhaps a challenge, aimed at the kind of university where I spent my own career. Stanford and similar prestigious universities create great value both in the reputational value of their degrees and the quality of their research and scholarship. They have little to fear from disruptive innovators, at least anytime soon. Yet they should pay attention to the ideas I discussed in this chapter, if not for their own immediate purposes, then as a contribution to the academic community generally. Carnegie Mellon University, the Massachusetts Institute of Technology, the University of Minnesota, and perhaps other schools as well are already introducing important innovations. Imagine the impact if additional research-intensive and well-financed institutions were to embrace and further develop something like the UMR schema.[33] Not only do such institutions have the human and financial resources to be truly and disruptively innovative, successful applications in these venues would go a long way to legitimatize the new paradigm—to make learning truly Job One.

4

Rethinking the Professoriate

Ronald G. Ehrenberg

FOR THE LAST THIRTY-FIVE YEARS, I have been a tenured faculty member at a selective private research university, whose faculty members are predominantly full-time tenured and tenure-track. I am a longtime, active member of the American Association of University Professors (AAUP) and have chaired two of its committees. I have published papers on the importance of the tenure system and conducted empirical research that showed that persistence and graduation rates at four-year American higher education institutions are positively associated with the share of an institution's faculty members who are full-time tenured and tenure-track. While I wish that the type of faculty position that I have had is the one that the majority of future generations of faculty will have, the handwriting is on the wall. Major changes will continue to occur in the way that U.S. academic institutions educate their students, leading to continued erosion of the tenure system. The goal of this chapter is to foster an acceptance of the reality of these trends while exploring new strategies for developing the faculty that American colleges and universities will need in order to respond to the challenges they face.

The stereotypical model of undergraduate instruction in American higher education is outdated. The image of a full-time faculty member with a doctoral degree, who has tenure or who is on a tenure-track and will eventually be evaluated for tenure, lecturing to or leading discussions with undergraduate students could not be further from the truth at most colleges and universities in the United States. The most recent data on faculty appointments reveal that slightly more than 50 percent of faculty members at colleges and universities are full-time professors. Of those full-time professors, only about two-thirds of them are tenured or on the tenure-track.

As I detail later, this trend away from tenured and tenure-track faculty represents a fundamental departure from past patterns of instructional staffing and from the conventional view of undergraduate education, and its roots go much deeper than the recent financial difficulties. Even before the great recession that we have recently experienced, the failure of private higher education institutions to moderate tuition increases and to expand their enrollments to meet social needs have driven these changes. The arms race of spending in which institutions try to maximize their prestige and the failure of states to maintain adequate funding for their public higher education systems have also driven these changes. The decline in state finance has led to percentage tuition increases at four-year public institutions that mirror the percentage tuition increases at four-year private institutions, but the tuition increases at the publics have only partially offset the decline in state support and have left public higher education in many states unable to meet demands for undergraduate slots.[1] These changes have also been driven by technology, including the growth of the Internet, and the nature of the modern job market, which has led to working adults' increased demand for higher education that is delivered at convenient times and places for them.

The American higher education system faces tremendous pressure to enhance access and graduation rates. In a period of increasing financial difficulties, how will the nation's higher education institutions achieve these goals and how will they recruit faculty and staff their classes in the future? The answers to these questions, which are the focus of my chapter, will likely vary across different types of higher education institutions and will reflect the nature of the classes that they offer and the types of students that they educate.

First I describe the changes in the staffing patterns that have occurred in American higher education over the last thirty-five to forty years, a period marked by a decline in full-time tenured and tenure-track faculty, and discuss the reasons for these changes and their implications for the professoriate and for undergraduate students. Next I focus on how and why our nation's research universities have increased their use of full-time nontenure-track faculty. I follow this with a discussion of efforts to use technology to restructure how we educate undergraduate students and the implications of these efforts for the composition of academia's instructional staff. I then turn to a discussion of what private nonprofit and public institutions can learn from the rapidly expanding for-profit higher education system about delivering instruction and staffing courses and then how improvements in system effectiveness will influence who will educate American college students. Although economists are not well known for the accuracy of their long-run forecasts, I conclude by venturing some thoughts about what the future will bring for American higher education and the professoriate.

HISTORICAL CHANGES IN STAFFING PATTERNS

A wide range of metrics vividly illustrates the extent to which colleges and universities have progressively turned away from the traditional model of full-time, tenured, or tenure-track faculty as the instructors of choice. While close to 80 percent of the instructional faculty at American colleges and universities were full-time in 1970, by 2007, this percentage had fallen to only slightly more than 50 percent. Moreover, these numbers overstate the true percentages of faculty that are full-time because they ignore graduate students in instructional roles who have titles such as teaching assistants or teaching fellows (see table 4.1).

To say a faculty member is full-time does not necessarily mean that the faculty member is tenured or on a tenure-track. As table 4.2 indicates, the percentage of full-time faculty nationwide that were not on tenure-track appointments more than doubled between 1975 and 2007 increasing from 18.6 percent to 37.5 percent. These faculty are often on one- or multiyear-term appointments, with titles such as instructor, lecturer, or senior lecturer. Empirical studies suggest that they are paid much less than their

TABLE 4.1

Percentages of instructional faculty that are full-time in degree-granting institutions in the United States

Year	Percentage full-time
1970	77.9
1975	70.1
1980	65.6
1985	64.2
1989	63.6
1995	59.1
1999	57.5
2007	51.3

Source: U.S Department of Education, *Digest of Education Statistics: 2009* (Washington, DC, 2010), table 249, http://nces.ed.gov/programs/digest/d089. Instructional faculty include faculty with professorial ranks including instructors, lecturers, and adjunct or interim professors. The category *excludes* graduate students with titles such as graduate assistants or teaching fellows.

TABLE 4.2

Percentage of full-time faculty (FTF) with tenure or on tenure-track nationwide at Title IV degree-granting institutions

Year	Percent FTF with tenure	Percent FTF on tenure track	Percent FTF not on tenure track
1975	52.3	29.1	18.6
1989	52.0	21.3	26.6
2003	44.9	20.4	34.8
2007	42.6	19.1	37.5

Source: U.S. Department of Education, IPEDs Fall Staff Surveys.

tenure-track and tenured colleagues.[2] It should be clear from tables 4.1 and 4.2 that in recent years, less than one-third of the faculty in American higher education are tenured or on tenure tracks.

Predictably, these trends have not been constant across the wide range of institutions within the American higher education system. Postsecondary institutions range from public and private research and doctoral universities that offer bachelor's, master's, doctoral, and professional degrees; public and private comprehensive universities that offer primarily bachelor's and master's degrees; liberal arts colleges (largely private) that offer mainly bachelor's degrees; and two-year colleges that offer associate's degrees and certificate programs and also perform a variety of other functions that are important to the local communities in which they are located. Within private higher education, there is a growing for-profit sector that focuses largely on adult learners. As table 4.3 indicates, institutions from each of these sectors employ different mixes of full-time and part-time faculty, and the percentage of faculty with PhDs varies widely across the groups. The public research and doctoral universities come closest to the stereotypical model, where only about 20 percent to 30 percent of their faculty are part-timers and upward of 70 percent of their professors have PhDs. Not surprisingly, the two-year schools lag behind on both of these indicators. But

TABLE 4.3

Percentages of part-time instructional faculty and percentages of instructional faculty with doctoral degrees, by institutional type, Fall 2003

Year/Institution type	Percentage of part-time faculty	Percentage of full-time faculty with doctoral degrees	Percentage of part-time faculty with doctoral degrees
Total	43.7	59.6	17.6
Public research	19.7	73.7	35.6
Private research	26.8	69.4	28.7
Public doctoral	28.8	71.9	24.1
Private doctoral	41.5	75.4	35.0
Public comprehensive	36.0	72.1	22.7
Private comprehensive	56.4	65.0	22.6
Private-liberal arts	36.4	69.1	22.2
Public two-year	66.7	17.9	8.7

Source: U.S. Department of Education, *Digest of Education Statistics: 2008* (Washington, DC, 2009), table 252, http://nces.ed.gov/programs/digest/d08. Instructional faculty include faculty with professorial ranks, including instructors and lecturers, and adjunct and interim professors. The category *excludes* graduate students with titles such as graduate assistants or teaching fellows.

even across other bachelor's degree-granting institutions, like public and private comprehensives, the percentage of part-timers has climbed toward 40 percent and above.

The usage of part-time faculty and faculty without doctoral degrees also varies across fields. As table 4.4 indicates, the percentages of faculty that are part-time are highest in professional fields such as business, education, and the fine arts, where institutions make heavy use of practicing professionals who bring unique skills to students, and in the humanities, where adjunct faculty and full-time nontenure-track faculty shoulder much of the introductory course load.[3] Moreover, the fine arts and health (including nursing) fields employ the smallest percentages of faculty who hold doctoral degrees.

Why have institutions changed their patterns of staffing so dramatically? There are convincing economic arguments for why tenured and tenure-track

TABLE 4.4

Percentages of part-time instructional faculty and percentages of instructional faculty with doctoral degrees, by subject area, Fall 2003

Subject area	Percentage of part-time faculty	Percentage of part-time faculty with doctoral degrees	Percentage of part-time faculty with doctoral degrees
Agricultural and Home Economics	30.2	63.0	15.5
Business	51.0	61.9	11.5
Education	55.5	57.7	19.4
Engineering	29.5	77.1	31.2
Fine Arts	52.5	34.6	7.1
Health	38.1	28.9	11.1
Humanities	50.0	63.2	13.4
Natural Sciences	33.4	80.6	29.7
Social Sciences	37.4	86.0	37.7
Other	48.7	44.6	11.7

Source: U.S. Department of Education, *Digest of Education Statistics: 2008* (Washington DC, 2009), table 254 (http://nces.ed.gov/programs/digest/d08). Instructional faculty include faculty with professorial ranks, including instructors and lecturers, and adjunct and interim professors. The category *excludes* graduate students with titles such as graduate assistants or teaching fellows.

positions are declining. The substitution of part-time and full-time nontenure-track faculty for tenured and tenure-track faculty is due to a host of factors: the growing financial pressures public and private higher education institutions face, the lower costs associated with hiring nontenure-track faculty members, the increased flexibility that hiring such faculty members gives academic institutions in uncertain economic times, and the end of mandatory retirement for tenured faculty that took place in 1994.[4] Finally, changes in the profession itself have driven the trend, such as the increased emphasis on research at major research universities that has led tenure-track professors to increased specialization in research and the universities to depend more on nontenure-track faculty to provide undergraduate instruction.[5]

As economists are fond of pointing out, there is no such thing as a free lunch. A growing body of research suggests that reliance on lower-cost, full-time, nontenure-track faculty and/or part-time faculty may adversely affect student outcomes. For example, my own research with Liang Zhang, which used institutional-level panel data, found that, holding other factors constant, when a four-year academic institution increases its use of either full-time nontenure-track faculty or part-time faculty, its undergraduate students' first-year persistence rates and graduation rates go down.[6] Daniel Jacoby similarly found that those public community colleges that relied more heavily on part-time faculty had lower graduation rates, while M. Kevin Eagan and Audrey J. Jaeger found that increased community college student exposure to part-time faculty appears to reduce the likelihood that community college students transfer to a four-year college or university or that they complete their associate's degree.[7] Finally, Eric P. Bettinger and Bridget Terry Long found that students attending Ohio public four-year colleges and universities that take "adjunct heavy" first-year class schedules are less likely to persist after their first year, a result also found by Jaeger and Eagan. (However, in later research, Bettinger and Long found that in some fields having an adjunct in an introductory class increases the likelihood of a student taking additional classes in the fields.[8])

Why do researchers often find that nontenure-track faculty members are associated with poorer undergraduate student outcomes? After all, many nontenure-track faculty members are dedicated teachers and, without any research expectations placed on them, can devote themselves fully to undergraduate education. This argument ignores the haphazard and ad hoc nature of nontenure-track faculty appointments, which often require instructors to take on higher teaching loads and multiple affiliations in order to make a living. Full-time nontenure-track faculty teaching loads are typically higher than tenure-track faculty teaching loads, which may leave the former less, rather than more, time for individual students. Part-time faculty members, especially those in urban areas, must often find employment at multiple institutions to make ends meet and have little time (and often no place) to meet students outside of class.[9] The forces that pull nontenure-track faculty in many directions across multiple institutions also suggest that full-time tenured and tenure-track faculty members, who may be more connected to their institutions and more up to date on their department's curriculum, may also be better prepared to advise students.

Given that faculty who do not have doctoral degrees do a large share of the teaching in American higher education, it is natural to ask whether the education level of a faculty member per se is a predictor of how much students learn.[10] The evidence on this point is ambiguous and surely depends on the academic aptitude of the students, the level of the class, and the field of study. Moreover, it is likely that the share of undergraduate instruction done by faculty with doctoral degrees will be declining in the future because the increasing scarcity of faculty positions that are full-time tenure or tenure-track positions will likely dampen the already decreasing interest of American students in pursuing doctoral study. It is reasonable to expect that four-year institutions that emphasize primarily undergraduate and master's-level education, except perhaps the most selective and wealthiest liberal arts colleges, will increasingly have to more heavily depend on faculty without doctoral degrees to staff undergraduate classes.

In doing so, they will be reverting to a pattern that existed prior to the late 1960s when PhD production in the United States greatly expanded.

FIGURE 4.1

Share of full-time faculty with doctorates in mathematics departments

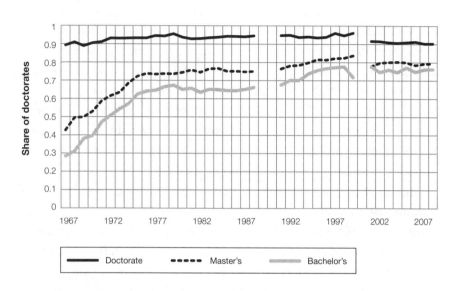

Source: Annual survey data, American Mathematical Society, *Notices of the AMS*. The data are available at www.ams.org/employment/surveyreports.html.

The American Mathematical Society collects the best historical data on the composition of faculty in annual surveys. Figure 4.1, which is constructed from these annual surveys, shows the share of full-time faculty members with doctorates in mathematics departments at bachelor's, master's, and doctoral universities during the 1967 to 2007 period. While over 90 percent of the doctoral universities' full-time faculty had doctoral degrees throughout the period, the master's-level percentage rose from about 40 percent in 1967 to about 80 percent in the mid-1980s, while the bachelor's-level percentage rose from about 30 percent in 1967 to over 70 percent in the mid-1980s.

One may speculate about whether the amount students learned in undergraduate mathematics classes increased during the period and whether a return to the degree patterns of faculty in the earlier era would have an adverse impact on student outcomes. Of great concern to me is that a decline in the share of faculty with doctoral degrees at the master's and lesser selective baccalaureate institutions will likely lead to a decline in undergraduate student involvement in research at them, which in turn would be associated with a further decline in the number of undergraduate students going on to PhD studies.[11] While almost half of new American doctorates who were graduates of American baccalaureate institutions in 2006 were people who earned their bachelor's degrees at research universities, a substantial fraction, probably close to one-quarter, received their undergraduate degrees from master's or less selective bachelor's institutions.[12]

This is not the place for me to discuss in detail the arguments in favor of a tenure system for faculty.[13] But it is important to briefly outline the arguments to give the reader a sense of why many in higher education are so supportive of the tenure system. In addition to the traditional justification of academic freedom, which suggests that faculty members require job security in order to engage in scholarship that may prove controversial, there are arguments about incentives for information sharing, cooperation, and continued productivity. Some argue that because a tenure system provides senior faculty with some job security, they have incentive to fully share their expertise with junior colleagues without fear of losing their jobs. In this way, tenure facilitates the intergenerational transmission of knowledge. Other arguments posit that a tenure system can be thought of as an implicit long-term incentive contract or a winner-take-all tournament that provides incentives for both tenure-track and tenured faculty to work harder than they would otherwise; that tenure is a desirable job characteristic and, in the absence of a tenure system, colleges and universities would have to pay higher salaries to attract top faculty; and that a tenure system helps to align the interests of faculty with the interests of their institution.[14] While each of these arguments has merit, the key point to stress from all of my earlier data is that only a minority of faculty members at American higher education institutions, and a shrinking minority at that, either have tenure or are on tenure tracks.

INCREASED USE OF FULL-TIME NONTENURE-TRACK FACULTY

Professional schools at U.S. major research universities, including law, business, medicine, and architecture schools, have long had nontenure-track positions with titles such as professor (or assistant professor) of practice or clinical professor. They use these positions to bring to their campuses practicing professionals who can provide instruction in areas in which the tenure and tenure-track faculty do not have expertise. With the increased pressure for faculty at major research universities to specialize in research, increasingly these institutions have made more use of full-time nontenure-track faculty in undergraduate instruction and have tried to improve the status of such faculty. Duke University has long been at the forefront of these efforts, and President John Sexton of New York University has articulated the goal of creating a professional class of teaching faculty at his institution.[15]

Efforts to rethink the roles of professors that are underway at Duke, NYU, and other leading research universities may provide a model for other schools that still hire nontenure-track teaching faculty in a fragmented, ad hoc manner. Luckily, there is evidence that such jobs can attract talented PhDs. The relatively poor academic labor market conditions that currently exist for new PhDs, coupled with the large and growing differentials in faculty salaries between major private research universities and master's universities, have made full-time nontenure-track teaching positions at these private research universities an increasingly attractive alternative for new PhDs, even though these positions pay lower salaries than their full-time tenure-track colleagues receive.[16] While teaching loads of these faculty are often higher than their tenure-track colleagues', because the teaching loads of the former have declined over time, teaching loads for the nontenure-track faculty teaching at these institutions are often lower, or at least no higher, than they would have if they were employed at other institutions in tenure-track positions.

Table 4.5 presents data from 2008–2009 on average faculty salaries for professors, assistant professors, and lecturers, by institutional type and form of control from the annual AAUP salary survey.[17] While the average

TABLE 4.5

Average faculty salary by rank and institution type (2008–2009)

Institution/Rank	Professor	Assistant professor	Lecturer	Lecturer salary at private doctoral/ Assistant professor salary in the category	Lecturer salary at public doctoral/ Assistant professor salary in the category
Private doctoral	151,403	82,295	62,799	0.763	0.630
Public doctoral	115,509	68,048	51,827	0.923	0.761
Private master's	99,555	61,986	54,408	1.013	0.836
Public master's	88,357	59,416	49,159	1.057	0.872
Private bachelor's	98,808	58,882	58,014	1.067	0.880
Public bachelor's	84,488	56,997	49,708	1.102	0.910
Two-year colleges	74,933	53,427	50,415	1.175	0.971

Source: American Association of University Professors, *2008-2009 Report on the Academic Status of the Profession*, table 4, www.aaup.org.

salary of lecturers at private doctoral universities is about $20,000 a year less than their assistant professor counterparts at these institutions, the average salary of lecturers at private doctoral universities is only slightly lower than that for assistant professors at public doctoral universities and is higher than those of assistant professors at public and private master's and bachelor's institutions, as well as at two-year colleges. Admittedly, the lecturers' average salaries include those of senior lecturers who may have many more years of teaching experience than the most experienced assistant professors, and there are salary gains associated with promotion for assistant professors. However, these data suggest that the financial costs to accepting a lecturer position at a private research university may not be that high relative to accepting an assistant professor position at other types of institutions, at least in the short run.[18]

Moreover, these nontenure jobs need not come at the expense of a modicum of job security for those professors who take such a position. Conversations I have had with colleagues at several of these private research universities, who either are in such positions or are chairs of departments that hire such faculty, suggest that contracts are now often "rolling multi-year contracts." For example, an instructor will teach under a three-year contract that is annually extended for a year if performance is satisfactory, so that the faculty member has greater job security than if decisions on renewal are made only when a term contract is about to expire. Of course, these contracts are all contingent on the availability of funding, so they provide less job security than a tenured faculty member would have. On the other hand, the nontenure-track faculty member does not have the stress of worrying if his or her research will be sufficient to achieve a tenured position and gets to teach at a major university with high-quality colleagues and bright students.

To give the reader a sense of the importance of these faculty members in major research universities, in March 2010 a graduate assistant of mine looked at the Web pages of the faculty in the top twenty departments, as measured in the 1995 National Research Council rankings, in four fields—chemistry, economics, English, and electrical engineering—and calculated the number of the full-time faculty who were either tenured or in tenure-track positions, as well as the number not in tenure-track positions, in each department.[19] She based this calculation on the titles of faculty members, counting instructors, lecturers, and professors of practice as nontenure-track faculty. I then summed up these numbers over all the departments in each field and computed the shares of the full-time faculty in these departments that were not on tenure tracks.

These shares appear in table 4.6. They vary from a low of 0.115 in electrical engineering to a high of 0.225 in English; both of these numbers are considerably smaller than the share of full-time faculty that are nontenure-track nationwide (see table 4.2). In two of the fields, English and economics, the share is higher at private institutions than it is at the publics, but in the other two fields, the pattern is reversed (perhaps reflecting the more serious financial problems of the public doctoral universities). These shares mask the wide variation in the use of full-time nontenure-track faculty that currently occurs across departments in the same field. For example,

TABLE 4.6

Share of full-time faculty in the top 20 departments in the 1995 National Research Council study that are not on tenure tracks

Department	All (number of departments)	Private (number of departments)	Public (number of departments)
English	0.225 (19)	0.260 (11)	0.182 (8)
Economics	0.159 (20)	0.169 (13)	0.143 (7)
Chemistry	0.146 (20)	0.103 (10)	0.170 (10)
Electrical engineering	0.115 (20)	0.108 (8)	0.125 (12)

Source: Author's calculations from faculty data on departmental Web pages in March 2010.

Note: One top-20 department in English was excluded because it was impossible to determine which faculty members were full-time from its Web page. Some electrical engineering departments are electrical engineering and computer science and, in those cases, when it was possible to identify and exclude the computer science faculty, they were excluded.

four top-twenty economics departments employed no full-time nontenure-track faculty members, while four others had shares of full-time faculty that were nontenure-track in the 0.28 to 0.33 range.

Given the dismal job market conditions that now exist, for students nearing completion of PhD programs, these nontenure-track positions at major research universities are likely to be attractive. However, students considering PhD study are likely to view them as less attractive, and their continued growth, in the long run, may well lead to a decline in the numbers of top American college graduates going on for PhD study.

My research with Liang Zhang showed that the expansion of full-time nontenure-track positions at major doctoral universities was less problematic than at other institutions, such as the public master's-level institutions, in the sense that the adverse effects of increasing the share of full-time nontenure-track faculty on undergraduate students' persistence and graduation rates were smaller at the doctoral universities.[20] This is not surprising because the higher compensation levels and lower teaching loads at the doctoral institutions allow them to recruit very talented faculty for these positions. Further expansion of full-time nontenure-track faculty at other institutions is likely to be much more problematic for undergraduate students. If we are to avoid such a troubling future, colleges and universities must look for new strategies to mitigate the damage by thinking more systematically about the way they hire and allocate faculty, rather than simply plugging holes with part-time instructors. These institutions have the most to learn from the initiatives underway at Duke, for instance. The expansion of nontenure-track faculty need not be as disastrous as it could be, provided colleges and universities are open to new solutions.

TECHNOLOGY: CHANGING TEACHING METHODS AND STAFFING PATTERNS

During the debate over health care reform from 2009 to 2010, proponents of the Obama administration's proposals argued that the status quo was not an option. The same can be said for how we teach students and staff our classes in higher education. The financial pressures academic institutions are facing, coupled with the demands on them to increase access and persistence, is forcing institutions to think much more about how they educate their students. Moreover, institutions are learning that the prevailing "lecture/discussion" format that many instructors use does not necessarily promote optimal educational outcomes. In the future, institutions will increasingly use technology to help improve learning outcomes and to simultaneously reduce the costs of instruction. In doing so, they will have substantial impacts on how institutions of higher education are staffed.

A growing number of evaluation studies suggest that online education can be as effective as regular classroom contacts, especially for more mature students. These same studies suggest that a blend of online and face-to-face instruction is typically more effective than online instruction alone (a point that I will come back to shortly).[21] While the marginal costs of delivering online education may be low, the start-up costs and the infrastructure needed to support such activities are high. Greg von Lehman, provost of the University of Maryland University College, which offers more than a hundred bachelor's and master's degree programs and certificate programs fully online, has stressed the need for "robust IT systems and staff to maintain them, a flexible and reliable learning management system, online student services that cover the range of student needs, online library resources, course development . . . and the staff necessary to train and manage faculty, while maintaining quality control."[22]

Fully online classes, either at academic institutions that exclusively offer online classes or at campuses that offer online as well as regular classes, represent only one way to use technology to improve the effectiveness of the U.S. higher education system. Two examples illustrate this point.

The National Center for Academic Transformation (NCAT), an independent nonprofit organization, has been at the forefront of using information technology to improve learning outcomes for students and reduce costs for institutions. NCAT lists over a hundred large-enrollment introductory courses that have been redesigned with its help in quantitative (mathematics, statistics, computing, and science), social science, humanities, and professional studies fields at a wide range of academic institutions (community colleges, comprehensives, doctoral universities). The NCAT Web site also provides links to descriptions of each of the redesigns.[23]

While the NCAT efforts have led to a variety of different models, the projects tend to focus on enhancing active learning (often replacing lectures with interactive computer-based learning resources such as tutorials, exercises, and low-stakes quizzes that provide frequent feedback, as well as individual and small group activities), mastering learning objectives, and offering on-demand help (often in computer labs or online—staffed by faculty, graduate assistants, peer tutors, or course assistants). Evaluations of these efforts' success provide evidence of each redesign's effectiveness in improving learning outcomes and/or reducing costs. Some of the cost reduction comes from a reduced reliance on costly full-time faculty and graduate assistants and an increased use of less costly peer tutors and course assistants to staff classes. The course assistants troubleshoot technical questions, monitor student performance, and alert the instructor to difficulties with teaching materials, among other tasks. Put simply, they allow expensive faculty to focus on educational matters, not organizational and technology matters. This distribution of responsibilities effectively increases ratios of students to full-time faculty. This permits either increased student enrollment for a given number of faculty members or a smaller faculty size for a given number of students. Both of these outcomes represent potential cost savings to institutions and might also enable them to more effectively leverage their best teachers.[24]

A second example comes from the Open Learning Initiative (OLI) at Carnegie Mellon University.[25] OLI has designed more than a dozen classes in introductory subjects in primarily mathematics and science fields that make use of advances in cognitive knowledge about how learning occurs and employ technology to create intelligent tutoring systems, virtual laboratory simulations, and frequent opportunities for assessment. OLI has made these classes freely available on its Web page. Serious evaluations of an introductory statistics class taught at Carnegie Mellon in 2005 and 2006 found no significant differences in learning outcomes between the traditional instruction methods or the OLI online approach. Moreover, the evaluations also showed that when a hybrid model that combined online learning with classroom instruction was used, students learned as much or more than they did in classes using traditional instructional methods in half the time.[26] With funding from several foundations, OLI is now building a version of its initiative specifically for use by community colleges and will test if the education gains (and cost savings) it found for Carnegie Mellon students from OLI will also hold in the community college context.[27]

The activities of both OLI and NCAT suggest that, at least initially, technology can improve educational outcomes and reduce the time (per student) that faculty spend in introductory-level classes at institutions ranging from community colleges to doctoral institutions. In the short run, these initiatives appear much less likely to influence methods of instruction in specialized upper-level elective classes. To the extent that such redesigns expand the number of students that full-time faculty can educate, they may reduce the pressure that public and private, nonprofit, higher education institutions have felt to expand their use of part-time adjuncts. However, as we shall see, some for-profits have adopted a completely different staffing model that increases reliance on part-time faculty.

Furthermore, the activities of OLI and NCAT suggest that the comparison is not between lecture classes taught by adjuncts and those taught by tenured professors, but between the various ways of organizing and staffing a course and traditional lectures taught by any type of faculty member. Academic institutions focus in the future should be on how classes are structured and taught, as well as on who is teaching them.

LESSONS FROM THE FOR-PROFIT HIGHER EDUCATION SECTOR

In contrast to traditional public and private nonprofit institutions of higher education, which have largely avoided any fundamental restructuring of the traditional tenure-track models of staffing, most institutions within the growing set of for-profit providers have developed new ways of recruiting, training, and assessing faculty members. Though for-profit institutions are a heterogeneous group, three examples from this growing sector clearly emphasize both the shift away from full-time tenure-track faculty and the use of technology to improve educational effectiveness.[28] I discuss in turn the University of Phoenix, Capella University, and StraighterLine/ SMARTHINKING.

University of Phoenix

The University of Phoenix (UOP) is now the second-largest accredited university system in the United States.[29] As of February 2010, it had enrolled over four hundred fifty thousand students at its various physical locations and in online classes, employed approximately thirty thousand faculty members, and it offered twenty-two associate's degree programs, forty-four bachelor's degree programs, forty-five master's degree programs, and eleven doctoral-level programs.[30] Its focus is on adult learners. It is an open admissions institution at the undergraduate level. Most of its programs prepare students for careers in professional fields such as business, criminal justice, health care, information technology, education, nursing, counseling, and organizational leadership, although at the undergraduate level, it now offers bachelor's degrees in a few liberal arts subjects.

The way that UOP staffs its courses is almost entirely different from the way that traditional universities do things. None of its faculty are tenured, and their retention and promotion are linked to student outcomes. Only about fifteen hundred of its faculty members are full-time core faculty; these core faculty members' duties include instruction, curriculum oversight and development, and academic and faculty administration. The vast majority of its faculty members are associate faculty—practicing professionals with whom UOP contracts to teach individual courses. Approximately two-thirds of these associate faculty members have a master's degree, and nearly one-third have a doctoral degree. They are required to have a minimum of five years of professional experience and must be currently employed in the field they teach and to go through an extensive orientation and training program.[31] Classes, with an average of fifteen, usually working students, meet primarily in the evening, which allows full-time professionals to take on these associate faculty positions. Content experts develop the curriculum, which is therefore fairly standardized, although faculty members are allowed to make modifications as long as they cover all the essential learning outcomes.

The typical associate faculty member teaches six courses a year (an undergraduate UOP campus-based course requires twenty classroom hours of instruction plus an additional twenty hours of participation in a supervised learning team), and the faculty are paid the average offered adjuncts in similar geographic regions for comparable hours of teaching, which ranges up to $1,900 per undergraduate class.[32] David Breneman interviewed over twenty longtime UOP associate faculty members and concluded that they did not teach for the money, but rather for the professional contact and stimulation they received from teaching adult students in their field and for the prestige they felt as faculty members.

Because the associate faculty are by far the majority (almost 95 percent in 2009), they do not feel like second-class citizens, as many adjuncts at more traditional academic institutions do.[33] One would expect that this would lead to relatively low turnover in the ranks of these faculty members, and this is the case. Of all the faculty members who taught six or more classes in 2007, nearly 92 percent taught in 2008, and over 81 percent taught in 2009.[34]

Phoenix evaluates faculty members in two ways, via self-reported feedback from students and from an assessment of how well their students have mastered the subject matter. The university is extremely data-driven and presents numerous comparisons of its students' learning outcomes relative to those of comparison groups in its annual reports.[35] Critics of for-profit higher education, and some supporters, believe that analyses of the educational effectiveness of the sector will be credible only if independent researchers are granted access to the data needed to do independent evaluations of performance.[36]

In addition to structuring its faculty in ways that are different from most traditional institutions, the University of Phoenix also makes extensive use of technology to facilitate student learning in a number of ways.[37] For example, it provides all course materials and textbooks electronically via the Internet and has a university library (also online) with over sixty-five thousand publications and one hundred fourteen databases in 2009. "Virtual Organizations" is a Web-based tool that offers a problem-based learning environment for students in a variety of contexts (business, health care, schools, and government). It also provides writing and math support services online. Students can get almost instantaneous feedback on papers through an electronic writing tutor, work with math tutors online in real time, and do self-assessments of learning outcomes in a number of areas online.

Capella University

Another example comes from Capella University, which is physically located in Minneapolis.[38] Capella awards master's and doctoral degrees to adult learners in primarily professional fields, although it also has some bachelor's degree programs. In the fall of 2009, it enrolled over 33,000 students of whom about 90 percent were part-time and over 80 percent were graduate students. In the previous year, it awarded over four hundred-fifty bachelor's, two thousand master's, and eight hundred doctoral degrees. While Capella is categorized as an online institution, its programs actually are hybrid programs, because most programs require face-to-face meetings, typically for a week at a time, that occur in airport hub cities.

Given its emphasis on graduate education, over 80 percent of its faculty members have doctoral degrees. More than 25 percent of its faculty members are full-time employees. Capella requires that its newly hired faculty have a minimum of three years of teaching experience. As at the University of Phoenix, Capella has no tenure system in place. However, unlike Phoenix, because Capella has such a high proportion of doctoral faculty, it is very cognizant of the need to pay competitive salaries to attract and retain quality faculty. As a result, Capella relies on comparative faculty salary data in setting salaries, much the way many private nonprofit and public colleges do. Salary decisions are merit-based and predicated on performance evaluations by chairs of departments and reviewed by the associate deans of the various schools. Most of its faculty members are long term, turnover is relatively low—with a turnover rate of 8.7 percent during calendar year 2009—and the faculty are surveyed to give Capella a sense of their job satisfaction. Capella feels that its compensation policies are validated by its faculty members' levels of job satisfaction and engagement, their low levels of turnover, and the rate at which it attracts candidates for open positions.

Both Capella and Phoenix heavily base their educational strategies on instructional models that focus on learning outcomes and prescribed rubrics.[39] Capella faculty members are evaluated by their students' success in achieving these outcomes, and they have considerable flexibility in the materials they choose for their classes. However, because all materials are posted online, they must get prior approval from Capella for use of all materials to ensure that the institution abides by all intellectual property rules.

While neither Phoenix nor Capella has a tenure system, their staffing patterns (full-time versus part-time) and compensation practices differ greatly. So, even within the for-profit sector, there is no single model of staffing and compensation. They also differ in the share of faculty that has doctoral degrees because Capella is primarily a graduate institution. This heterogeneity in staffing patterns, compensation, and degrees held by faculty illustrates the diverse array of faculty models within the for-profit sector. This heterogeneity also mirrors the status quo in the rest of higher education, where the distribution of traditional tenured or tenure-track faculty versus nontenure-track faculty differs greatly across institutions. These two facts together suggest that competition from the for-profit sector will differentially have an impact on staffing patterns at different types of academic institutions.

In particular, we might expect that the institutions that compete most directly with the for-profits for undergraduate students, such as community colleges and comprehensives, will most likely to try to emulate the for-profits' model of offering classes at times and places that are convenient for students. Such competition will increase pressure on them to expand their use of part-time faculty. Indeed, many community colleges now trumpet that they are using their facilities twenty-four hours, seven days a week, both because of physical capacity constraints and to meet employed students' needs.[40]

Another important feature of both Phoenix and Capella, as well as of OLI and NCAT, is their concern with proving that they produce comparable or greater student learning at the same or lower cost than more traditional forms of instruction. Indeed, professors at both Phoenix and Capella are evaluated and rewarded based largely on their students' performance. This is in great contrast to public and private, nonprofit, higher education institutions, which currently base evaluations of faculty members' teaching performance on student evaluations, peer evaluations of lectures, or faculty colleagues' and administrators' perusal of class reading lists and (at tenure time) faculty members' teaching portfolios.[41]

StraighterLine

The for-profit sector also includes firms that are not stand-alone, degree-granting institutions, but that provide college-level course work in a piecemeal fashion. One such firm, StraighterLine, offers yet another prototype of how institutions might structure course offerings and student learning. StraighterLine offers low-cost, online remedial and introductory-level college classes, based on McGraw-Hill materials, in a number of subjects at relatively low costs.[42] These classes are self-guided, and students can utilize a tutor from SMARTHINKING and receive instant feedback online. The tutors go through an extensive training process before being employed. Students also submit assignments and papers to the tutors for feedback and grading. Founded in 2008, StraighterLine had served nearly a thousand students by early 2010.[43]

About 90 percent of SMARTHINKING's tutors have master's or doctoral degrees.[44] SmartThinking does far more extensive training and evaluation of its tutors than most colleges. The tutors come from all over the world. They are organized in a call-center model rather than in an instructor-led model, which SMARTHINKING's developers believe leads to much better service levels for students. Tutors' pay is comparable to that of an adjunct professor for comparable hours, but once they are trained, there is no prep time for classes or follow-up after class. Most of the tutors work for SMARTHINKING as a second job. Its high share of tutors with advanced degrees is due, in part, to the state of the PhD labor market and the excess supply of PhDs.

StraighterLine classes allow students who are unsure about whether they want to or are qualified to attend college to test the water in a low-cost, convenient way. Moreover, three colleges have agreed to accept these classes for credit if a student subsequently enrolls at them, although there has been some faculty backlash to the administrations agreeing to do so.[45]

StraighterLine's approach obviously reduces the need for faculty members. Currently, it cannot provide automatic college credit for its classes because institutions can be accredited only if they offer degrees.[46] To the extent that either StraighterLine rapidly expands and more colleges arrange to accept its classes for credit, or the system of accreditation changes to allow providers such as StraighterLine to provide classes for credit, its approach could potentially have a large impact on the need for faculty in the future.[47]

CHANGING WHERE STUDENTS ARE EDUCATED AND IMPROVING SYSTEM EFFECTIVENESS

While the professoriate has changed, so too have student enrollment patterns and the demands placed on institutions of higher education. Changes in the types of institutions that increasingly attract college-going students as well as the efforts to improve the effectiveness of the U.S. higher education system will have an impact on the types of faculty members who deliver undergraduate instruction. For example, expanding two-year colleges as ports of entry to higher education and improving articulation agreements between two-year and four-year colleges will shift more remedial and introductory-level instruction to the two-year colleges. These institutions employ relatively few full-time faculty members and relatively few faculty members with doctoral degrees (see table 4.3), so a shift toward two-year colleges will reduce the demand for faculty with doctoral degrees. So too will the expanding numbers of students enrolling in Advanced Placement (AP) classes, international baccalaureate programs, and dual-degree programs while in high school.[48] These trends will shift more teaching of introductory college classes to high schools and two-year colleges, neither of which employs many faculty members with doctoral degrees.

On the other hand, the evidence is mixed on the effectiveness of AP classes relative to traditional college-level introductory classes in preparing students for advanced classes in a field and for college success more generally.[49] Moreover, some colleges—mostly high-tuition, selective, private institutions—are beginning to restrict or eliminate the granting of college credit for AP classes, instead using the classes only for placement purposes. These protectionist efforts, which are at least partially an effort to protect an institution's tuition revenue flow, may lead to increased demand for faculty with doctoral degrees to teach upper-division elective classes. This is particularly likely to happen at the more selective institutions that enroll students who have typically taken AP classes while enrolled in high school.[50]

LOOKING TO THE FUTURE

Given the pressure on both private and public colleges and universities to expand enrollments and graduation rates and to meet the changing needs of an altered student population, we have to give serious thought to how we can improve the educational efficiency of individual academic institutions and the U.S. higher education system, especially through reevaluating faculty roles and incentives. I have discussed several examples of how technology can both reduce costs and improve learning outcomes. I have also discussed how some of the important organizations in the for-profit higher education sector have embraced efforts to do so and, in turn, have positioned themselves as leaders in changing how college students are educated and how faculty are evaluated.

So what will the future bring? Economists are not much better than meteorologists in making long-run forecasts, but I will venture some here. The leading private liberal arts colleges and the wealthy private and flagship public research universities are in a world of their own. There we are most likely to see the full-time tenured and tenure-track faculty maintained.[51] These institutions will increasingly employ technology in introductory-level classes in an effort to expand active learning and to reduce costs, with the cost saving going toward enhancing the quality of upper-division classes and furthering the research enterprise. An expansion of full-time nontenure-track faculty will likely occur at the research universities to further free up the time of the tenure-track faculty for research. The pay levels at these institutions and their relatively low teaching loads may be sufficient to keep the nontenure-track positions attractive to new PhDs. Some new PhDs, such as those attracted to places like Capella University, may actually find these jobs preferable to the "up and out" tenure-track positions with high-research expectations. New PhDs concerned with finding a balance between work life and family issues may also find these positions attractive.

The public regional doctoral universities, the public and private comprehensives, the other private liberal arts colleges, and the two-year colleges are likely to be under increased financial stress, while facing growing pressure to expand enrollments and to improve efficiency. A deskilling of their professoriate is likely to occur in the sense that a greater share of their faculty will not have doctoral degrees and a greater share will not be full-time or on tenure-track lines. But the move away from tenure-track PhDs does not have to be as problematic as the research on student outcomes that I cited earlier may suggest. If public and private nonprofit institutions put much more effort into selecting, training, evaluating, and supporting their nontenure-track faculty, and these faculty adopt teaching methods based on advances in our knowledge of how learning occurs, this deskilling will be accompanied by a reskilling of the faculty and may actually increase the amount that students learn.

The use of technology to reduce costs and improve learning will likely occur more rapidly in introductory-level courses at these institutions than it will at the wealthy research universities and selective liberal arts colleges. People in nonfaculty positions will undertake a greater share of instruction at these institutions. One can easily envision the widespread growth of the types of tutors that SMARTHINKING employs or the types of people employed in some of the innovative positions that institutions participating with NCAT have developed in redesigning classes.

Pressures for accountability surely will increase, and colleges are increasingly being asked to demonstrate student learning outcomes as part of the accreditation process. This will likely put more focus in academia on the quality of undergraduate instruction and the need to ensure that the best instructors are rewarded and promoted. If so, we might expect to see an increased focus, especially in remedial and introductory classes, on evaluating faculty at least partially by their students' outcomes, as the for-profits do. The institutions that compete the most directly with the for-profits are where the pressure for this would be the greatest.

Old-timers and many in the professoriate will bemoan the decline of the golden age of American higher education, with its heavy reliance on tenured and tenure-track faculty, just as many people bemoan American corporations' substitution of automated answering services for human operators. But economic forces will continue to accelerate the trends that we have already begun to observe. There is no such thing as a free lunch, and higher education is not immune to fundamental economic forces and trends.

Of course, there are some complicating factors and other concerns that I need to stress. First, the growing use of adjuncts and their perennially low salary levels may lead to increased unionization for them, which could in turn lead to a decline in the economic benefit of hiring adjuncts. While there is a case for the use of practicing professionals as part-time professors in fields such as business, education, engineering, and nursing, substituting long-term, full-time faculty for part-timers in arts and science classes would likely lead to improved student outcomes. This would be a desirable side effect of increased unionization of adjuncts, if it were to occur. Increased adjunct unionization might also lead to increased use of online classes to economize on faculty time. Whether collective bargaining agreements for adjuncts could prevent this type of outsourcing is unclear. Pressure may also grow for increased unionization of full-time nontenure-track faculty at institutions in which job stability and compensation are not sufficiently attractive.

Second, the declining use of tenured and tenure-track faculty nationwide as well as the decline in the number of faculty with doctoral degrees at all but a subset of institutions will likely increasingly discourage American college students from going on for PhD degrees. This would reduce the supply of PhDs available to take full-time and part-time nontenure-track positions. A reduced supply of PhDs may also have serious implications for the academic research enterprise and our nation's rate of productivity growth. More generally, the United States needs to worry about how to finance doctoral education in order to ensure an adequate supply of the best and brightest students going on for PhD study and research careers.

Finally, rethinking the way faculty are recruited and allocated at colleges and universities is not the only issue in the quest to improve undergraduate learning, retention, and completion. In particular, policy makers must not lose sight of the importance of noninstructional inputs in student success. The best for-profits realize this and devote considerable resources to counseling and supporting students. Research that Douglas Webber and I conducted showed that the amount colleges and universities spend on student services, broadly defined, influences the persistence and graduation rates of students at four-year colleges and universities, and that these expenditures have a greater impact on students at institutions with large fractions of disadvantaged students in terms of entry test scores and family income levels.[52] The nation will increasingly try to enroll these students in higher education; they will be the focus of efforts to improve persistence and graduation rates. If we care about student success, we need to focus on more than how we staff our classes and the characteristics of the faculty of the future.

5

The Promise, Performance, and Policies of Community Colleges

Paul Osterman

AMERICA HAS MADE CONSIDERABLE strides in opening higher education to its citizens. In 1980, 49.3 percent of brand-new high school graduates attended a postsecondary institution the following October. By 2007, that figure stood at 67.2 percent.[1] Among those high school graduates whose families were in the bottom twentieth percentile of the income distribution, 32.2 percent were in postsecondary education in 1980, whereas in 2007, that figure, while still lagging the rate for wealthier students, stood at 55 percent.[2]

Community colleges have played a central part in this story. In the fall of 2008, they enrolled 7.1 million students in credit courses compared to 9.3 million undergraduate students who attended four-year institutions. Put differently, community colleges account for 43 percent of postsecondary enrollment. And, as we shall see, millions more attend noncredit-bearing courses in community colleges. The success of the so-called community college access agenda is clear when we consider that between 1963 and 2006, community college enrollment grew by 741 percent compared to 197 percent for public four-year colleges and universities and 170 percent for private.[3]

Community colleges do many things well. Students who receive an associate's degree or a certificate earn a high rate of return.[4] From the business side, a recent focus group of employers in three cities concluded that, "Among respondents community colleges and vocational colleges were associated primarily with high quality training . . . [they] were generally considered by respondents to be the most credible teaching/training entities . . . Graduates of community colleges were considered to be more ambitious, motivated, disciplined, physically accessible, and literate."[5]

Community colleges are a central component of America's human capital development system. They dwarf in scale any other institution in terms of providing vocational training, and they are also a resource for firms in training their incumbent work force and for obtaining new skills in emerging technologies. Education is not simply an economic tool. Higher education helps grow young people into citizens and enriches the cultural life of communities in numerous ways. These noneconomic purposes must be respected, and as we shall see, tensions can arise between the different missions of higher education in general and community colleges in particular.

But while there is much to praise, there is also much about which to worry. Those who obtain a certificate or degree enjoy high rates of return, but the fraction of students who successfully obtain these credentials is shockingly low. The majority of students who enter community college do not succeed, and this failure comes at great cost to them and to society.

This chapter aims to help us think about how to improve community colleges. In much of the chapter, I examine these institutions and ask what steps we might take to obtain better outcomes. However, I also ask broader questions: How do community colleges fit into what might be termed our human resource development system? Therefore, what alternatives to community colleges might be viable? One of the great strengths of the U.S. human capital system, compared to other nations, is that we offer multiple pathways to success. While community colleges must, simply by virtue of their scale, be the anchor of any strategy, everyone will benefit if we also strengthen alternative pathways.

Thinking about how to improve community colleges and help them fulfill their promise is very challenging and not simply due to the standard problem of inadequate resources, although that is a serious issue. The difficulty lies in the very fact that community colleges have multiple missions, each of which is legitimate and important but each of which implies a somewhat different approach to teaching and to the very organization of the enterprise. Unless we think sharply about just what each of these missions is and what each requires for success, then reform policy will be a muddle. We need to make hard choices in order to focus on the most essential goals. In addition, community colleges are underfunded, and they need additional resources to improve outcomes. Finally, I argue that the problem is not one of knowledge about what succeeds. We may not understand best practice, but we do understand good practice. Our challenge lies in execution and the resources to support that execution, not in research and development.

In the next section, I provide some basic facts regarding the reach and performance of community colleges and the challenges we face. I then turn to strategies for improvement, both within the context of community colleges and in terms of alternative pathways.

THE LANDSCAPE AND THE FACTS

There are over 1,177 community colleges that enroll over 7 million students in credit-bearing courses.[6] We are not sure how many students are enrolled in noncredit community college courses—on topics ranging from the directly vocational to the recreational—because not all states keep data on these enrollments, but experts agree that the numbers are very close to those in credit courses. Hence, roughly 12 million Americans are enrolled in community colleges. Among students who are enrolled for credit, most are in degree programs, but a substantial minority seeks certificates.

Another way to grasp the magnitude and importance of the community college system is to consider the activities that they undertake. A typical community college prepares students for transfer to a four-year institution, offers terminal associate's degrees in a wide range of vocational fields, offers less-than-two-year certificates in other fields, provides customized training for incumbent workers for local firms, offers one-off courses (both in skills and for recreation) for area residents, provides Adult Basic Education (ABE) and English as a Second Language (ESL) courses under contract with their state department of education, and provides training as part of a contract with a federal job training program. The range of activities is impressive but also represents a very significant management challenge and may well have an impact on performance. Table 5.1 begins to describe the landscape of sub-baccalaureate education.

These data direct our attention to several important patterns. First, public community college students do not resemble the traditional image of a college student. Nearly 40 percent are over age twenty-four, and 60 percent attend part-time. Indeed, the rhetoric regarding the diminishing importance of the traditional college student is really about community college students. By contrast, among undergraduates in four-year institutions, 79.5 percent attend full-time and about 70 percent are under age twenty-four.[7]

TABLE 5.1

Postsecondary enrollment patterns, Fall 2007

	Total enrollment	Percent enrollment age 24 or younger and full-time	Percent enrollment age 25 or older and full-time	Percent enrollment age 24 or younger and part-time	Percent enrollment age 25 or older and part-time
Public two-year	6,374,554	29.8%	8.7%	29.4%	31.3%
Public less-than-two-year	54,598	20.7%	30.8%	21.7%	23.3%
For-profit two-year	321,221	49.1%	38.6%	4.4%	6.6%
For-profit less-than-two-year	232,934	45.6%	38.7%	6.5%	7.5%

Source: U.S. Department of Education, National Center for Educational Statistics, *Enrollment In Postsecondary Institutions, Fall 2007, First Look*, NCES 2009-155, tables 1 and 2. Row percentages do not add to 100% because of rounding and because a small number of students have missing age data. Data on student age were not collected for the 2008 report that is cited earlier and hence this table refers to 2007.

At the same time, we should acknowledge that about one-third of community college students are young and attend full-time. Later, I will argue that in the rush to serve older—perhaps more vocationally oriented—students, we should not overlook these younger, more traditional students.

The second striking pattern in the data concerns private for-profit schools. In terms of enrollment, they are dwarfed by community colleges, even if we add together two-year and less-than-two-year institutions. This conclusion might be slightly softened if we consider two-year degrees awarded by four-year institutions, since many private, for-profit, four-year institutions offer this option. However, the same is also true for public four-year institutions.[8] Overall, it is apparent that the private, for-profit sector is quite small relative to the public sector.

The difference in enrollment patterns between public and private institutions is striking: a far larger fraction of private, for-profit students attend full-time, and they are also much more likely to be older than are the students in public institutions. I will explore the implications of these differences later. In addition, while less-than-two-year institutions are essentially irrelevant in the public realm, they represent a significant fraction of for-profit two-year schools or less enrollment.

While community colleges enroll 43 percent of all postsecondary credit students, if one looks only at June high school graduates who are attending college the following October, then community colleges enroll about 24 percent.[9] This points to the first key fact about the community college population—it is more weighted toward working adults than is enrollment in four-year institutions.

Table 5.2 provides additional demographic data on community college students compared to those who attend public four-year colleges and universities. Recall that we have already seen that community college students are older and more likely to attend part-time. The additional differences are also notable. Community college students are more likely to be minority, are more likely to be self-supporting, and are more likely to be first-generation college students.[10] There are, however, two ways to read these data. In one reading, community colleges are a pathway for upward mobility. In another, they are a

TABLE 5.2

Demographic composition of postsecondary enrollment, 2003–2004 academic year

	Community college	Public four-year institution	Private nonprofit, four-year institution
% Black	15.3%	10.4%	13.0%
% Hispanic	14.4%	8.9%	12.0%
% Asian	5.3%	5.9%	4.2%
% Parents' education high school or less	40.8%	26.7%	27.6%
Dependent students	38.8%	65.7%	62.3%
Single parent students	17.2%	6.3%	5.0%

Source: U.S. Department of Education, National Center For Education Statistics, *Community Colleges: Special Supplement To The Condition of Education* (Washington, DC: U.S. Department of Education, 2008), 40. The data refer to the 2003–2004 academic year.

channel that less-advantaged students are shunted toward while others enjoy the advantages associated with a four-year school. This tension in fact goes to the heart of the question of how to improve community colleges.

Expectations of Students

Understanding the goals of community college students is important because helping them achieve these goals is the ultimate objective of the system. And as we will see later, sorting through these goals will shape this chapter's recommendations for how to narrow and focus the mission of the institutions.

One source of data on student goals is the National Postsecondary Student Aid Survey conducted in 2000. In their analysis of these data, researchers at the Community College Research Center distinguished three groups of community college students: those in occupational programs who accounted for 50.7 percent of students, those in academic programs who accounted for 25.3 percent, and the remaining 23.8 percent who at time of survey were undeclared.[11] Of those on an occupational track, one-third were seeking a certificate, and two-thirds an associate's degree.

These distinctions are useful but are also hard to interpret in terms of student goals. For example, the academic track is defined as people who majored in humanities, mathematics, science, or social science, while the occupational track consisted of a list of majors in fields such as engineering, information technology, and various health-related areas. The problem is that it is totally plausible that many of these occupational students hope to eventually obtain a BA or BS degree. Enrollment in an occupational major does not necessarily imply a truncation of expectations. In fact, the demographic profile of students in the AA degree occupational track (the two-thirds of occupational students) is similar to that of students in the academic track, and the fraction who report wanting to transfer to another institution is not very different and shows a pattern of falling with age (or, to put it differently, rising for younger students).

That many community college students have aspirations beyond community colleges is demonstrated in another survey focusing on graduating high school seniors in 2003–2004.[12] Twenty-eight percent of those who directly entered community colleges reported wanting to eventually obtain a BA or BS degree, and an additional 39 percent reported that they had applied to a four-year school but for various reasons were instead attending a community college. One reading of these data is that 67 percent of high school seniors who directly enter community colleges have further aspirations.

None of this is to deny that a substantial fraction of community college students have more narrowly defined occupational goals. This is clearly true for students in certificate programs and certainly also true for many students, particularly the older ones, in AA degree programs. But at the same time, it is wrong to think of community colleges as simply two-year vocational training institutions.

COMMUNITY COLLEGES AND THE LABOR MARKET

Community colleges are tightly linked to the job market in their communities. Most states do not collect systematic data on noncredit enrollment; hence, there is some disagreement about just how many students take noncredit courses. However, all observers agree that the numbers are very close to the 7 million in credit courses.[13] These students take courses in a range of topics from ESL and ABE to health and information technology certifications to recreational courses. The majority are clearly vocational. There is remarkable variation across states in whether noncredit teaching receives any state funding and whether any formal record of student attainment is kept in these courses. In addition, there is some concern that students who enroll in noncredit courses find themselves unable to transfer any credit into a credit program, should they subsequently be interested in doing so. Another indication of the core economic role of community colleges has been the surge of attendance during the recent economic downturn as adults return to school seeking new skills in the hopes of improving their labor market prospects.

The strength of these linkages and the tilt of community colleges toward vocational training have been a source of controversy, as some have argued that these trends have led the schools to diminish their traditional goal of assisting students who seek to transfer to four-year schools.[14] Others argue that the opposite is true, and that, if anything, community colleges "warm up" rather than "cool out" potential transfers.[15] Regardless of where one stands on the debate regarding what *should* be, the facts about what *is* are clear: community colleges have a strong vocational training component. Indeed, given the magnitude of the community college system, it is no exaggeration to say that community colleges are America's primary vocational training system and are an approach toward providing vocational skills that is distinct from many other developed nations.[16]

The connection of community colleges to the local economy is more than passively enrolling students with a vocational interest. Community colleges have been aggressive and entrepreneurial in working with firms to provide customized professional development for incumbent workers and to train students for openings projected by the local employer community. The local community colleges in the San Diego region exemplify this role, as they work closely with biotechnology firms to develop training programs for the technicians those firms need. The curriculum was created in cooperation with the companies, and the firms provided some of the instructors and the equipment. [17] Community colleges in North Carolina launched a similar effort in the same industry.[18]

As another example, the Milwaukee Area Technical College, with funds from the American Recovery and Reinvestment Act, is beginning a nondegree training program to prepare employees for careers in health information technology.[19] Such cases can be multiplied endlessly across the country.[20] In addition, community colleges are often contractors and sometimes the administrative agency, under the Workforce Investment Act.

The community college connection to the job market is so wide and deep that many institutions have created a separate administrative division that offers the noncredit courses to adults seeking to improve their skills. In addition, these units engage in a wide range of entrepreneurial activities with firms such as the customized programs I've described.

What can we say about future demand for the skills community colleges produce? This is a key question at the heart of any argument regarding the future of these institutions. There are two, not necessarily consistent stories that one can tell in response to this question. It is important to be clear about just what lessons to draw.

The first story is that the demand for what has been termed "middle skill" jobs of the kind produced by community colleges will be strong and is likely to grow.[21] There is a good deal of truth to this expectation, and it does provide an important counterweight to an assumption that one might infer from the standard economics literature that the only postsecondary attainment of importance is a four-year degree. As an example, the bread and butter of many community college programs is health careers, a field for which there will be increasing demand for professionals. Information technology is another example of a growing field served by community colleges. Indeed, the U.S. Bureau of Labor Statistics (BLS) projects that for 2008 to 2018, occupations requiring an associate's degree will experience the most rapid percentage growth rate.[22]

The second story is less optimistic. At the anecdotal level, hospitals are increasingly seeking to hire BS rather than associate's degree nurses, and in another signal of possible trouble to come, a prominent community college president recently worried in print that employers were increasingly expecting more education than a community college credential.[23] Turning again to the BLS projections through 2018, when we look at new openings rather than percentage growth, job openings are projected to be 2.3 million jobs for associate's degree holders and 2.9 million for employees with other forms of postsecondary vocational training. If we take these BLS numbers literally, there will be fewer job openings for associate's degree graduates than the community colleges will produce. Recall that there are nearly 7 million community college students currently enrolled, of whom about two-thirds are in associate's degree programs. Even more distressing, that figure is just the current enrollment, whereas the projected openings are for the entire period until 2018.

We should not, of course, take the occupational projections that underlie the educational demand projections as gospel truth, but their track record is reasonably good.[24] However, it is also possible, and indeed likely, that the BLS underestimates the demand for education for jobs that in the past did not require extensive schooling. For example, observers note that whereas in the past automobile assembly workers did not require much in the way of school, auto firms now want even assembly-line employees to have a community college degree because of the skills involved in quality programs. There is a conservative, backward-looking bias in the projections that may miss some of this kind of development. However, even if the BLS underestimates the future demand for community college–level skills by fully a half, there is still good reason for concern, given the magnitude of enrollment.

These projections provide an important note of caution in what may well be a somewhat overheated optimism about future demand for community college–level skills. The implication of this line of thought, which I develop later in the chapter, is that we should continue to take the transfer mission of community colleges very seriously and that we should think of community colleges as more than two-year vocational training institutions.

OUTCOMES

For students who obtain a credential—either a certificate or an associate's degree—community colleges perform well and are an excellent investment. The first widely noted research on rates of return to community college credentials reported positive results, and more recent research has updated these findings and managed to control for a large range of personal and family variables.[25] The rates of return range from 13 percent for men who obtain an associate's degree to a remarkable 38.9 percent for women. In general, the results are more robust for women across all specifications, but for both genders, the overall message is clearly positive for those who manage to obtain a credential.

Thus far, the news has been good. However, when we ask what proportion of students who enroll in community college obtain a degree or certificate, or even accomplish a full year of attendance, the picture darkens considerably. This failure rate is without question the greatest challenge confronting community colleges.

The federal government collects data on graduation rates via its Integrated Postsecondary Data System (IPEDS), and according to the most recent figures, only 22 percent of public community college students who entered in 2005 had obtained a degree or certificate within 150 percent of the expected time, or by 2008.[26] However, the problem with these data is that they only refer to full-time students, whereas, as we saw, a strong majority attend part-time. Another federal source, the Postsecondary Students Longitudinal Survey, includes both full- and part-time students. In these data, among students who enrolled for the fall of 2003, 5.5 percent had obtained a certificate, 10 percent an associate's degree, 39.8 percent were still enrolled, and 44.6 percent were no longer enrolled by June 2006. In other words, the three-year success rate, as measured by a credential, was an even lower 15.5 percent, presumably reflecting worse outcomes for part-time students.[27]

These outcomes are more than a little discouraging. However, many observers would point out that they are also somewhat unfair. Given the substantial fraction of part-time students in community college, focusing on a three-year completion rate may be too stringent. The U.S. Department of Education does not collect outcomes for a longer enrollment period; however, a recent effort, executed by Jobs for the Future—part of the Lumina Foundation for Education's Achieving the Dream initiative—did collect detailed outcome data from six states for a six-year period since enrollment. These data are shown in table 5.3.

These data paint a brighter picture than do the three-year federal figures, but the assessment is still grim. Even assuming that the story for transfer students has a uniformly happy ending, at best only four of ten students reach their goals within six years of enrolling, and in most of the states, the results are even worse. When the data are broken out by full- and part-time status, the results get grimmer still, as table 5.4 shows. It is hard to know what is worse: that in three of the states, only around 20 percent of part-time students achieve success after six years or that among students who are devoted full-time to community colleges, the highest success rate is only 45 percent.

TABLE 5.3

Outcomes after six years, 1999 entering class

	Award, less than AA degree (certificate)	AA degree	Transfer (no award)	Total award or transfer
Connecticut	1%	9%	14%	23%
Florida	6%	22%	7%	36%
North Carolina (five-year result)	10%	16%	14%	40%
Ohio	2%	23%	6%	30%
Texas	5%	12%	25%	42%
Virginia	3%	19%	13%	35%

Source: Jobs for the Future, *Test Drive: Six States Pilot Ways to Better Measure and Compare Community College Performance* (Boston, MA: JFF, July 2008).

TABLE 5.4

Success rates after six years by full- and part-time status, 1999 entering class

	Award and transfer for full-time students	Award and transfer for part-time students
Connecticut	31%	16%
Florida	43%	26%
North Carolina	45%	31%
Ohio	37%	19%
Texas	45%	39%
Virginia	42%	22%

Source: Jobs for the Future, *Test Drive: Six States Pilot Ways to Better Measure and Compare Community College Performance* (Boston, MA: JFF, July 2008).

Sources of Failure

Why are failure rates in community colleges so high? As is true for school reform at the K–12 level, characteristics of the students have a significant impact on outcomes. Community college populations are both diverse and challenging: many enter with reading and math skills well below grade level; many are part-time and are distracted by work and family demands; and many more are unsure of what they want to accomplish and lack a clear plan.

All of this said, there are sufficient examples of postsecondary institutions that do succeed with this population, and a "blame the student" response is unacceptable. Instead, it is more fruitful to ask what characteristics of the community college experience lead to such high failure rates.

When students enter community college, nearly 60 percent are channeled into remedial programs, typically called "developmental education."[28] In many community colleges, the developmental education courses and faculty are housed in a separate administrative unit from the credit faculty. The typical outcome is that students spend several semesters in developmental education—sometimes not realizing that they are not obtaining college credit—then use up all their financial aid and drop out due to exhaustion and frustration. According to one study, only 25 percent of students who took three developmental courses completed all three five years later, only 4 percent graduated, and 78 percent left school without a credential.[29] Another study found that less than 40 percent of students referred to developmental education completed their sequence of assigned courses.[30] There are similarly poor results for students who enroll in ESL and ABE programs.[31] To make matters worse, across community colleges, the criteria and cutoffs for placing students in developmental education are a "bewildering plethora."[32]

In addition, the vast majority of students recount an experience in community colleges in which there is virtually no counseling or support, in which the pathways to the desired degree or credential are very unclear, in which there are few signposts of progress or intermediate achievements, and in which most flounder and give up. The typical student is simply admitted and then implicitly told to sink or swim, and far too many sink. Given the complications and pressures in the lives of the typical students who are part-time, holding a job, and coming from an economically stressed background, the failure to sustain commitment to what on average is a five- or six-year slog to a degree or certificate is not surprising.

EXISTENCE PROOFS: IT'S POSSIBLE TO DO BETTER

A core argument of this chapter is that the challenge of improving community colleges lies not in discovering what works, but rather in finding ways to afford and diffuse good practice. In making this statement, I use the term "good practice" rather than "best practice." It is certainly the case that we do not know everything and that we can extend our understanding of just what practices are optimal. It makes sense to continue engaging in research and demonstration. In my view, we have in hand good evidence of practices that lead to outcomes that are far superior to what we now achieve, and the continued search for the optimum should not delay the very substantial improvements that are now possible. This argument gains additional force because of the long time lag inherent in community college research. Given a three- or, more realistically, six-year span from implementation to outcome, and then adding the time required to analyze and present results, the delay between the execution of an innovation and useful findings is prohibitively long.

The evidence that we understand good practice comes from a variety of distinctive programs in different parts of the country. These programs are not small boutique experiments within a larger community college structure, but rather substantial stand-alone efforts that offer educational success to a population that is the same as that which normally attends community college programs.

Project QUEST, Inc., and its replications welcome students in an intensive and accelerated remediation component organized by the program, offer a wide range of supportive services and counseling, and then enroll the students in community colleges in a wide range of degree and certificate programs. [33] While in the community college, QUEST counselors provide continuing support and assistance. Year Up, which began in Boston and has been replicated in several cities, enrolls recent high school graduates in a six-month classroom training and remediation experience that is then followed by an additional six-month internship with an employer. The students attend full-time, receive considerable support throughout the experience, and any additional required remedial work is integrated into the regular classroom instruction. The Tennessee Technology Centers require full-time enrollment in certificate programs in a limited range of fields, and classes are scheduled to permit as much flexibility as possible in student schedules.

Project QUEST has been the subject of several extensive evaluations, while data on Year Up and the Technology Centers largely come from the programs' own administrative records. Taken as a whole, the outcome data are far more impressive than is normal for standard community college programs.[34]

Although the programs differ in their design, what they have in common points to the strategy for moving forward.[35] First, remediation either is integrated into the credit curriculum or else is intensified and collapsed into a brief period. In addition, organized peer groups—or so-called "learning communities"—are utilized to provide additional support and motivation. The key point is that developmental education is not allowed to soak up a great deal of time or resources. Second, the programs are focused with a clear but narrow path provided for success. Students are not permitted to flounder as they try to piece together a set of courses that add up to their goals.[36] In some cases, this is achieved through a rich set of counseling supports and, in other cases, simply by limiting the range of choices. Third, the students are encouraged to attend full-time or as close to full-time as is practical, enhancing the strategy of focus and speed. Fourth, counseling and support services play a core role in maintaining enrollment and progress. Finally, courses are scheduled in a way that makes attendance easy, and much of the material is presented in stackable modules so that progress is visible and cumulative.

Exactly how these principles are implemented varies with the nature of the program and of the students. Those students for which full-time attendance is feasible—most typically younger students—can benefit most if the elements can be combined in their "purest" form. The example of the City University of New York's plans for a new community college built from scratch so that the elements are virtually all incorporated in the new design illustrates this point.[37] On the other hand, many working adults simply cannot be full-time students, and for these students, additional flexibility is necessary, but the core elements of the good practice principles are still relevant.

MOVING FORWARD

How should we think about moving the community college system down the road in the direction of good practice? Turning around this massive but diverse enterprise will be far from easy, and in some respects, it is even more challenging than the case of K–12 school reform. Multiple missions, multiple constituencies, and very differentiated governance and finance systems across locales make it difficult to devise a coherent and plausible reform strategy.

The importance of community colleges has not escaped the attention of the policy community, and several national foundations are devoting substantial resources to the effort. In addition, the Obama administration—via the American Graduation Initiative—has sought to make community college reform a centerpiece of its domestic policy agenda, although the effort was substantially trimmed in the tightening fiscal climate.

As we think about reform, we must keep in mind two principles: first, it is important to build a system that offers multiple options, and second, the system should not track students—particularly low-income or minority students—into a narrow vocational path. These principles make the reform project so hard. The vocational functions of community colleges are significant both to young students and, increasingly, to older ones who rightly view community colleges as central to their efforts to navigate and succeed in a volatile labor market. Indeed, this is one of the core missions of community colleges, and it fulfills a vital function in developing human capital and bolstering the national labor market system. However, as we have seen, a substantial number of students, particularly students who enter community colleges directly from high school, aspire to a bachelor's degree. The colleges should encourage and nurture these aspirations and not shunt the students into a purely vocational path. There is, in fact, reason to fear that the current system does track low-income students who are qualified for and aspire to four-year degrees into community colleges.[38] The challenge then becomes how to create a system that can provide both high-quality vocational training and also serve as an effective pathway to higher levels of education.

As I discuss how to move ahead, I will devote little attention, with the exception of distance learning, to efforts to understand best practice. To date, a substantial amount of policy energy has gone into experiments and demonstration programs to test different versions of best practice.[39] These are worthwhile efforts; however, as I argued earlier, while we may not have an understanding of perfect practice, we do know enough about good practice to move forward with more aggressive reforms.

ALTERNATIVE PATHS

One approach for achieving better outcomes is to strengthen alternative pathways, particularly for young people and adults who are primarily interested in vocational training. Two strengths of the American system have always been flexibility and choice, and any steps we can take to support these values are all to the good. Competing pathways also offer some degree of competition to community colleges, as well as providing laboratories to study alternative practices that can act as release valves for the enrollment pressures that community colleges now face.

The categories of alternative pathways that seem worth considering are private, for-profit, proprietary schools; apprenticeships; ; and a select group of employment and training programs. In thinking about alternative pathways, we should avoid any stratification or, more specifically, avoid the reality or impression that one pathway is reserved for a relatively more disadvantaged group of students. Long experience with social programs demonstrates that when such stratification emerges, the "poor person's pathway" loses support and funding over time. The key here is to ensure that choices about pathways are in the hands of students and that these choices are not constrained by family income.

Proprietary Schools

Proprietary schools have grown rapidly since their students became eligible to receive federal Pell Grants. In 2007 to 2008, students at proprietary schools received 19 percent of all federal financial aid funding. [40] Four-year institutions account for 57 percent of proprietary schools, two-year schools account for 24 percent, and less-than-two-year programs account for 19 percent.[41] As we have seen, proprietary school students are older and more likely to be minority and female than are students in public institutions. In addition, a significantly larger fraction of proprietary students attend full-time than do students at public institutions.

According to reported federal data, graduation rates for two-year proprietary schools are better than those in public institutions. The most recent IPEDS data are that 22 percent of public and 59.7 percent of proprietary school students receive their credentials within three years of entry.[42] These figures are biased against public institutions because they only include full-time students, and some observers have expressed concern that the figures are subject to some manipulation, for example, by changing the status of students in trouble to part-time so that they are not included in the IPEDS data. Nonetheless, other observers agree that at least some proprietary schools perform better than does the average public institution, likely because of the more tightly focused program and the more extensive support the proprietary schools provide.[43] However, the comparison to public community colleges may also be unfair, given that a higher percentage of for-profit students are older and attend full-time. Although some researchers argue that the profile of students in the two types institutions is similar, these patterns cast significant doubts on that argument, while also reinforcing the point that full-time attendance is desirable and should be encouraged.[44]

Given their growth rate and their apparent success with many students, proprietary schools seem to represent an important alternative to public community colleges. However, three considerations counsel against becoming too optimistic. First, the growth rate in percentage terms notwithstanding, proprietary schools remain small compared to the community college universe and are thus unlikely to exert a great deal of impact on the distribution of outcomes. Second, proprietary schools are much more costly than community colleges, a fact that both limits their range and also helps explain their success. And third, there are serious reasons to worry about how well a significant minority of proprietary schools treat their students.

As we saw in table 5.1, two-year and less-than-two-year for-profit schools add up to less than 10 percent of public community college enrollment.

This is not trivial, but it is hard to say that these schools represent a significant alternative.[45] Another way of seeing this is to note that proprietary schools get almost no enrollment from graduating seniors: 18.8 percent of graduating seniors went to public community colleges and only 1.4 percent to private ones.[46]

The second problem with relying to any great degree on proprietary schools is their cost. Whereas public postsecondary schools receive only 30 percent of their revenue from tuition, proprietary schools rely on tuition for 88 percent of their revenue. The average two-year tuition for a proprietary school is six times that of an average public institution (roughly $12,000 versus roughly $2,000).[47] From the student perspective, Pell Grants cannot offset this cost disadvantage.

The final, and perhaps most serious, worry is performance. Many observers believe that the best-performing proprietary schools have much to teach the public system and that these schools do in fact serve their students well. However, the darker side of this picture is that there appear to be significant problems among a nontrivial set of proprietary institutions. The history of these schools has been marked by periodic scandals and newspaper reports of fraud or near-fraud.[48]

The debt load of students in proprietary schools is considerably higher than that of students who attend public institutions. According to the College Board, in 2007, 43 percent of students in for-profit associate's degree programs carried a debt load of $20,000 or more, compared to 13 percent of students in public AA degree programs. The median debt load in the proprietary institutions was $18, 783 compared to $7,125 in publics.[49]

Not surprisingly, this debt load has consequences. The Government Accounting Office (GAO) recently compared student loan default rates at proprietary and public community colleges and projected that the four-year default rate at proprietary schools is 27.2 percent versus 16.6 percent at public community colleges. Among less-than-two-year schools, the proprietary default rate was 26.6 percent.[50] In the same report, the GAO documented evidence of outright fraud—for instance, providing students with answers on placement tests or helping them obtain high school degrees from diploma mills—although the GAO also notes that it is not claiming that this fraud is typical.[51]

Apprenticeships

The term *apprenticeship* refers both to a pedagogy—a combination of practical instruction and classroom learning—and to a particular formalization of that style of teaching. As a pedagogy, it holds great promise in many settings. As a specific institution, its possibilities are considerably more limited but still worth exploring.

There are more than four hundred fifty thousand people currently in registered apprenticeship programs and about the same number in nonregistered ones.[52] A program is registered if it is formally certified by the U.S. Department of Labor or a state agency and meets certain standards regarding instruction and practice. It is not clear what "nonregistered" means, and it may be hard to distinguish these from relatively well-structured, firm-based training to which the employer simply appends a label. The evidence on rates of return is that completing a registered apprenticeship program pays off very substantially.[53]

More than half of registered apprenticeships are in construction (56 percent) with another nearly 11 percent in the military. These patterns do narrow somewhat the scope of apprenticeships as an alternative pathway, as does the fact that virtually all registered programs are linked to a labor movement that is not growing. Nonetheless, it is certainly reasonable to encourage deeper penetration of the apprenticeship model in current apprenticeship occupations. It is also worth noting that nonconstruction apprenticeships use community colleges as the most common source for their formal instruction.[54]

Alternative Training Providers

There are a wide range of employment and training programs that, taken together, constitute an alternative job training system. Some of these programs are funded by the WIA and many others—such as the intermediaries supported by a consortium of foundations called the National Fund for Workforce Solutions—are funded privately by foundations. Some programs rely on a mixture of public and private funding, while others draw their resources from state training funds that are often based on the Unemployment Insurance Tax.

Although there is a widespread perception that the training programs that fall into this grouping are ineffective, the data point to a quite different conclusion. Evaluations of intermediary models are quite positive, intensive training programs show excellent results, and even WIA performs better than the popular perception.[55] After many years of experimentation and the involvement of national technical support organizations, a promising best-practice model has emerged. The model involves a dual customer focus, with the programs responding to the needs of both trainees and the firm, and a higher level of support to trainees than is typical in job training programs. The problem is more one of reach and resources. While the best of these efforts do represent viable alternative pathways, they remain very small relative to the universe of need. WIA trains just over three hundred thousand people annually in occupational skills, and its funding has fallen by over 40 percent in real terms in the past two decades.[56] Several of the good practice models that have demonstrated success are considerably more costly on a per-student basis, or even a "per graduated student," basis than the cost of community colleges.[57]

Another promising source of training is public vocational institutions that enroll students for less than two years. In the fall of 2007, these institutions enrolled a total of 54,598 students, so the scale is small.[58] However, at least some of these appear to be very successful and offer a model for community colleges. As an example, the Tennessee Technical Colleges report a graduation rate of 75 percent, which they achieve via a tightly focused curriculum, a requirement that students attend full-time, and teaching that is organized in blocks or modules and scheduled at times that are convenient for students.[59]

IMPROVING COMMUNITY COLLEGES

Expanding and strengthening alternative pathways is important but, given the realities of scale, we need to direct most attention squarely on the community college system. The key to improving community colleges is to think sharply and ruthlessly about the missions of the institution and to focus on what it takes to achieve each mission and on how to prevent overlapping missions from interfering with each other and providing excuses for failure.[60] This is even more vital as some community colleges continue to expand their responsibilities.

Community colleges have three distinguishable missions:

- Serving young high school graduates, some of whom want to enter a vocational track, many of whom want to transfer to a four-year school, but virtually all of whom want and would benefit from a "traditional" college experience. As we saw earlier, these students overwhelmingly aspire to a four-year degree. In the rush to think of community colleges as an extension of America's vocational training system, these students and their aspirations can be too easily overlooked. Furthermore, as we saw earlier, occupational projections suggest that the demand for associate's degree graduates may be insufficient to provide opportunities for future supply, and this adds additional weight to the transfer mission of community colleges.

- The second core mission of community colleges is serving older students and adults who are returning to school largely for vocational reasons. For these students, a narrower and more focused vocational program is appropriate, and part-time attendance is frequently unavoidable.

- The third mission is encompassed in the activities of the continuing education activities of community colleges. The most important of these activities is working with employers to design customized training programs and offering noncredit courses to local residents.

What is gained by sharply identifying these missions and distinguishing between them? The point is that community colleges should organize themselves to optimally achieve each mission rather than offer an undifferentiated menu that tries to serve all purposes. What we know about good practice suggests that for the younger students, school should be full-time and intense. The curriculum, support system, and financial aid should be structured to move students rapidly toward attainment of their degree or their transfer. For these students, smaller learning communities are a promising approach, and to the maximum extent possible, faculty should be full-time and as committed to the success of their students as are faculty at the best four-year schools. By contrast, adults who are returning to school to obtain new skills typically cannot attend full-time. The good practice keys to success here involve flexible scheduling and a modularized curriculum. In addition, the realities of scheduling make some elements, such as learning communities, more difficult to implement but make other components, such as day care, more essential.

In a simple world, we would stop with the first two missions described. Today, community colleges do neither of these well, and making substantial improvements is such a challenge that, at first glance, it makes little sense to ask anything else of the institution. However, this is not realistic. Community colleges cannot turn away from their local community of employers, because this mission speaks to an important need, because there are powerful internal and external constituencies that would resist such a move, and because employer support is essential for political and budgetary reasons. The challenge, then, is how to prevent this set of activities from diverting attention and resources from the core missions of the institutions. This consideration implies that the more entrepreneurial activities of community colleges—ranging from noncredit courses to customized training to ABE to serving as a WIA contractor—should be housed and administered in structures that are distinct from the degree-granting efforts.[61] This unit should be self-supporting and internally "taxed" to support the more core missions of the institution (although there also should be more effort in terms of local and state policy to facilitate transfer of credit for students who want to move into a credit degree program).[62]

Resources

Although arguing for throwing resources at problems is easy, any serious attempt to improve the performance of community colleges must start with an understanding that more resources are needed. Some key facts regarding finances are presented in table 5.5.

As is apparent, community colleges spend far less per full-time equivalent (FTE) student than do four-year schools, even when expenditures are limited to direct instructional expenses. In addition, consistent with their commitment to access, community colleges have not sought to make up the funding shortfalls via increases in tuition that exceed those of four-year institutions. Adding to the difficulty is that state support for community colleges has declined in recent years, and expectations are that, even in the face of growing enrollments, the declines will continue.[63] There are

TABLE 5.5

Community college finances

Sources of revenues for community colleges	38% from state, 20% local, 15% federal, 17% tuition
Average expenditure per FTE student	Community colleges = $10,500 Public four-year colleges = $31,900
Average instructional expenditure per FTE student	Community colleges = $4,100 Public four-year colleges = $8,000
Tuition and fees	Public community colleges = $2,017 In-state public four-year colleges = $5,685 Private two-year community colleges = $12,620
Increase in tuition and fees, 1976–2006 (after inflation)	Public community colleges = +105% Public in-state four-year colleges = +165%

Source: National Center for Education Statistics, *Community Colleges: Special Supplement To The Condition of Education*, NECS, 2008-033.

certainly tweaks that can be made in community college operations that will improve outcomes, but very substantial progress will unlikely be made without additional funding.[64]

The realities of budgets underlie two personnel issues that have a significant impact on the performance of community colleges: the widespread use of part-time adjunct faculty and the very high student–to-counselor ratio. Across the country, two-thirds of community college faculty are part-time.[65] In addition, the resources that community colleges devote to faculty development are minimal even for full-time faculty and almost nonexistent for part-time.[66] Second, although we have seen that good practice entails counseling and support, the availability of these resources is scarce. Ironically, at Macomb Community College, where President Obama announced the American Graduation Initiative, there are fifty-eight counselors for thirty-three thousand credit students and fifteen thousand non-credit students.[67]

Loosening the Constraints

I have argued that we know enough about "good practice" or "effective practice," and hence an excessive focus on demonstration programs and boutique experiments may not be wise. The exception to this point is the possible role of information technology and distance learning in loosening the fiscal constraints that confront reform. A full 45 percent of public community colleges offer at least one certificate or degree course that could be completed entirely via distance education, and nearly all institutions offer at least some distance options.[68] The annual rate of increase in online instruction in recent years has been 12.9 percent, substantially above the overall increase in higher education enrollment.[69] Whether these efforts lead to improved results is an open question, but pilot programs suggest that distance learning can be effective even in groups that have not had a great deal of exposure to computers and information technology.[70] Whether this represents a strategy that can be successful at scale is very much worth exploring.

Incentives

It is simply unrealistic to expect substantial improvement without the resources to underwrite it. What we know about good practice, for example,
the importance of support services, makes this clear. However, it is also
irresponsible to call for additional resources without being adamant that
they must be conditioned on performance. Just how to do this is not entirely clear, and the problem is made more difficult by another current reality. In the past two years, as the recession has deepened, community colleges across the nation have been inundated with adults who are returning
to school in search of new skills. This huge demand poses two challenges.
First, resources are stretched even thinner and hence reform is even more
difficult. Second, the pressure on community colleges to do better is softened by the overwhelming success of their "access agenda." As things stand,
there is no penalty in terms of enrollment or finances for the current level
of success or lack thereof.[71]

The record of efforts to impose accountability is very mixed. In the past
three decades, twenty-six states have adopted incentive funding schemes,
but fourteen of those states subsequently discontinued the effort. Even in
those states that continued, the amounts of money involved relative to
the overall budget were very small and often unstable.[72] The fraction of
budgets used as incentives varied, and both internal and external political
pressures led to frequent changes in the indicators used for determining
the incentives. Researchers found that community college opposition, unstable higher education budgets, and highly variable political support all
undermined the effort.

The story of incentive funding is not entirely negative, and the best case
appears to be in Tennessee. The percentage of each institution's budget
available for performance funding steadily increased to 5.5 percent, and
the indicators remained reasonably stable. However, a moment's consideration suggests that the impact of this program is largely symbolic. It is a
rare, if nonexistent, institution that receives none of its potential performance funding, and hence the actual budgetary swing is relatively small.

Also notable is that the IPEDs graduation rate for two-year schools in Tennessee is 11 percent.[73] The state has recently taken important steps to strengthen its performance funding system, but, for now, our overall judgment has to be cautious. What the foregoing suggests is that a state strategy has to involve a more aggressive and consistent use of incentive funding, with governors and legislators exhibiting strong leadership and strategy development.

Currently, the greatest source of pressure and incentives for improvement is coming from the foundation community, notably the Bill & Melinda Gates Foundation and the Lumina Foundation. Lumina, in its Achieving the Dream initiative, has focused on data in an effort to develop a "culture of evidence" that forces leadership and faculty to understand the outcomes of their institutions and the sources of failure.[74] The Gates Foundation has a three-pronged strategy that aims to improve institutional practices, help students make smarter choices, and encourage public debate and political support for improving community colleges. This sophisticated approach holds very considerable promise, but at the end of the day, a strong governmental role must replace foundation resources and stimulation of new thinking.

Just as it has pushed K–12 educators to improve through initiatives like Race to the Top and i3, the federal government needs to become more actively involved in incenting, encouraging, and in some cases requiring community colleges to improve. As the GAO has pointed out, there is a need for stronger oversight regarding proprietary schools, but this need can also be generalized to the community college system overall. The current failure rate is simply unacceptable, and, via oversight, links to financial aid or to accreditation or both need to be addressed. Since the federal government provides substantial resources to community colleges through Pell Grants, there are many opportunities to leverage this investment to incite better performance.

Improving community colleges will require that other constituents, notably the business community and public interest groups, push for community college reform with the same intensity that they have pushed for reform at the K–12 level. There is simply no national movement or pressure currently comparable to that for public schools.

CONCLUSION

Community colleges are a source of great educational and economic promise. Nearly half of America's postsecondary students attend these institutions, and the returns for those who obtain a credential are impressive. At the same time, community colleges are falling well short of their promise. The fraction of students who actually manage to obtain a credential is far too low; indeed, it is well below the success rates of high schools in graduating their students or four-year postgraduate schools in graduating theirs. Improving this record is an urgent priority.

This chapter argues that the search for best practices should not obscure the fact that we know enough about good practice to move forward. The key lies in thinking sharply about the mission of community colleges and the strategies for improvement. Not only do community colleges try to do too many things, but they also suffer because the current discussion has tended to treat them as purely vocational training institutions. This goal is important for many students, especially working adults and younger students who are seeking certificates. But many students see community colleges as a step toward a four-year degree, and we should also support this objective. It is important to avoid creating a class- or income-stratified higher education system because we should respect student aspirations and be concerned that the demand for community college skills may fall below the number of students the institutions may produce. Indeed, this latter point is often underappreciated in contemporary discussions but is potentially very significant.

One strategy for improving outcomes is to build up alternatives to community colleges; however, the scale of these alternatives will never match that of community colleges, and an improvement strategy aimed directly at these institutions is imperative. Any such strategy faces very difficult realities: the underresourcing of the institutions, the large fraction of faculty who are part-time, the paucity of support and counseling for students, and the political inertia created by the multiple missions and their constituents. Forward progress requires additional resources that are aggressively linked to performance.

6

For-Profit Sector Innovations in Business Models and Organizational Cultures

Guilbert C. Hentschke

IN RESPONSE TO INCREASED demand over the last quarter-century, for-profit institutions of American higher education have grown much more rapidly, on average, than their traditional public and nonprofit counterparts—due in large part to their ability and willingness to provide innovative programs and services to the growth segments of the higher education marketplace. This chapter examines the largest and fastest growing of those for-profit institutions—primarily those publicly traded—in order to identify the most fundamental innovations, underlying business models, corporate cultures, and resulting market impact of these educational organizations.

In recent years, criticisms of the motives, educational quality, recruiting practices, and even legitimacy of for-profit colleges and universities have been highly publicized, in contrast to largely unexamined issues of their internal governance, corporate strategies, and pedagogical practices. I examine all of these organizational attributes here with the aim of understanding how these institutions are different—and why. Specifically, I suggest that governance differences associated with for-profit status provide incentives and opportunities for institutional leaders to pursue organizational growth and, of necessity, innovation. This fundamental differentiator from traditional public and private, nonprofit colleges and universities, in turn, provides administrators at for-profit colleges with the opportunity to create organizational practices and operations that differ from those in traditional colleges and universities, and these new practices also better enable them to pursue growth through innovation.

Viewed from this perspective, the emerging innovations that we see in for-profit educational services and programs are logical extensions of the growth strategies that these institutions pursue as a function of their profit motive. Retaining the positive attributes associated with this sector, such as growth orientation and demand sensitivity, while mitigating problems associated with the sector, such as quality control and consumer protection, will require a more institution-sensitive regulatory environment than is currently in place.

I begin by reviewing the incentives that underlie for-profit institutions of higher education, and how these incentives shape institutional governance and practice. The chapter then outlines how these governance differences affect various organizational practices, from program structure and curricula to faculty recruitment and training. Many of these practices are fundamentally different from what goes on in traditional colleges and universities. I then move on to discuss some innovative attempts to expand market share and serve traditionally underrepresented students that some for-profit institutions have undertaken. The chapter concludes with a few implications for traditional colleges and universities and for federal, state, and nongovernmental organization regulators.

GROWTH, GOVERNANCE, AND INNOVATION— A THREE-LEGGED STOOL

Within the short span of about forty years, for-profit colleges and universities have emerged as a significant presence in American higher education even as enrollments at *all* institutions, both domestically and around the globe, have exploded. From 2000 to 2007, the number of tertiary students in the United States and Western Europe more than doubled, from 16 million to 38 million students. At the same time, however, the share of tertiary students from these developed countries relative to the rest of the world shrank from 48 percent to 23 percent, as global tertiary enrollments over that period grew by nearly a factor of five, from 35 million to 165 million. During this surge, for-profits have been growing *proportionately* as well as absolutely, expanding much faster than traditional colleges and universities, especially in the United States. Between 1967 and 2007, the number of degrees that American colleges and universities awarded mushroomed by a factor of almost three, from 6.9 million to 18.2 million degrees granted. Against the overall growth during this period, the market share of for-profit institutions increased from 0.3 percent to 6.5 percent of the degrees granted. If we fast-forward to the present and include awarded certificates as well as awarded degrees, for-profit colleges and universities now account for about 10 percent of the U.S. higher education student market, which represents an incredible expansion in recent decades.

These for-profits are growing through the creation of new institutions, but existing for-profits are also expanding at a much faster rate than traditional institutions. Institutions created since 2000 accounted for 24 percent of the growth in degrees awarded among for-profits, but only 2 percent of the growth among traditional institutions. Among higher education institutions existing before 2000, enrollments at for-profits increased 107 percent between 2000 and 2007, compared to only 15 percent at private nonprofits and 17 percent at traditional publics.

For-profit colleges and universities have grown as a group because they have greater incentives and capacity to grow than their public and nonprofit counterparts. By the very nature of their governance arrangements and business models, for-profit colleges and universities seek profitability, and profitability results from the interaction of growth in volume and in unit margins, or in other words, the gap between revenues and expenditures. The incentives that shape the behavior of for-profit postsecondary institutions are therefore quite different from those of traditional colleges and universities, which are more concerned with increasing prestige than with growth and cost effectiveness. For-profit colleges and universities that provide value for money can (and do) expect to grow.

The causes of low growth rates at traditional institutions vary across different types of institutions. Traditional colleges define *success* differently from for-profits and do not often include growth in enrollment as an indicator of success. Traditional institutions seek the highest-quality students, subject to capacity constraints. Some of these institutions are more competitive and better positioned to attract abler students than others, but all seek to attract the most able students and to enroll as many as they can up to a physical capacity constraint. These institutions define success as getting the highest-quality students possible to enroll in the school, what analysts characterize as the pursuit of prestige.[1] Institutions with greater prestige are prestigious in part because of their higher rates of rejection.[2] In light of these incentives, increasing the size of the student body doesn't make sense for elite institutions. To do so would mean, among other things, admitting students who are further down the quality scale and greater proportions of nontraditional students. Increasing the size of entering classes by admitting larger proportions of those who apply leads to *decreases* in student quality, as defined here. Further, it could lead to more work on the part of current employees but may only indirectly lead to increases in their salaries, if at all.

Unlike elite privates, public colleges and universities, which enroll the bulk of all higher education students, are fiscally constrained. Recently, for example, California had to reduce admissions to its state higher education systems by a hundred thousand students. Because of these financial constraints, significant growth is not a viable short-run option for institutions in the public sector. *Elite* private nonprofit institutions, on the other hand, have little incentive to grow, preferring to pursue prestige by limiting access to high-quality admissions. *Non-elite* private nonprofit institutions would like to grow enrollments but are limited by lack of sufficient demand at their high price points. Published fees across all private nonprofits average $25,243, compared to $13,246 across all for-profits.[3] Despite different growth incentives and circumstances, the net impact is the same: for-profits are serving increasingly higher numbers *and proportions* of postsecondary students because they have incentive to grow and the flexibility to do so.

In contrast to traditional institutions, which are constrained by state funding and the pursuit of prestige, for-profit institutions start with a pre-defined description of what constitutes a qualified applicant and enroll as many of them as they can attract. Most for-profits (and the federal government) define a qualified applicant as a student who has earned a high school diploma or a GED. For-profits enroll students who are less likely to have a high school diploma (79 percent have a diploma) than those at public (88 percent) and nonprofit (91 percent) institutions.[4] For-profits seek to enroll as many of these students as they can, and, like most other profit-seeking businesses, they seek to grow their capacity through new sections, campuses, programs, and delivery modes to accommodate larger numbers of students, rather than turn away eligible students.[5] After enrolling, some of these students do drop out of their programs, as they do in traditional institutions. However, this is not because the students were not admissible, as defined by government eligibility criteria. Rather, it is usually due to student characteristics and circumstances that reduce their likelihood of completion at *all* institutions of higher education, for-profit or otherwise.

The different motives that characterize for-profits, including their pro-growth, revenue maximizing, and (now diminishing) anti-selectivity mindsets, have sometimes been conflated with a presumption that for-profits are inclined to pursue growth at the expense of quality. The roots of this negative presumption started to grow during the 1970s and 1980s when for-profits operated with less aggressive oversight, in particular, of recruiting, instructional, and placement practices. They grew especially in urban areas where low-income students would qualify for federal Pell Grants and guaranteed student loans. When scandals arose over fraudulent recruiting practices; high loan default rates; and low completion, placement, and wage outcomes, Congress mandated stricter eligibility requirements for institutions participating in Title IV federal student loan assistance programs, primarily applied to vocational and technical schools. The 1992 regulations increased the minimum length of eligible programs, decreased institutional reliance on Title IV funding sources, tightened recruiting and admissions procedures, and removed incentive compensation for recruiters, and established more stringent accreditation standards.[6] Over the next ten or so years—in large part as a result of the tighter regulations that followed—a large number of for-profits left the field. Between 1991 and 2005, the number of eligible proprietary schools shrank from 3,770 in 1991 to 1,906 in 2005, a drop of over 1,800 institutions, or nearly one-half.[7] The vast majority of proprietary institutions that left the field during this time were those with very high dropout rates, which are reflected in student loan default rates. Of these, "more than 1,100 schools had lost student loan program eligibility" between 1991 and 2001.[8]

More recently, several institutions were accused of illegal employment and recruiting practices, in several instances, paying recruiters on the basis of the number of students they successfully enrolled (ruled illegal after 1992). One institution ultimately was required to pay over $80 million in penalties as a result of the lawsuit.[9] The earlier *legislative* reaction to for-profit excesses was aimed at the entire sector, whereas the more recent *judicial* response targeted a small percentage of the sector. Nonetheless, the negative publicity generated during both periods has tarnished the brand of the entire sector, fostering a spate of independent print and electronic media exposés, as well as legislative hearings on for-profit higher education practices that have also been covered by the media.[10]

The most sweeping and widely quoted recent criticism came from hedge fund short seller Steven Eisman, who shorted the housing/financial industry and made a fortune doing so. "Until recently, I thought that there would never again be an opportunity to be involved with an industry as socially destructive and morally bankrupt as the subprime mortgage industry," said Eisman, of the hedge fund FrontPoint Financial Services Fund. "I was wrong. The For-Profit Education Industry has proven equal to the task." "We just loaded up one generation of Americans with mortgage debt they can't afford to pay back," Eisman noted. "Are we going to load up a new generation with student-loan debt they can never afford to pay back?" [11] His critique is based on debatable presumptions that, while for-profits enroll fewer than 10 percent of American college students, they accounted for 23 percent of Pell Grants and federal student loans in 2008, and for 44 percent of defaults among borrowers who entered repayment in 2007.[12] He and other critics of for-profit higher education use these data to support their claims that for-profits are talking unfair advantage of students. Proponents of for-profits, on the other hand, use these same data to support their (factually accurate) claim that they are serving disproportionately high numbers of low-income students with higher likelihoods of dropping out, often those who are most in need of higher education. High loan defaults, they argue, are a function of the students served, not of the sector location of the institutions providing their education.

Despite the negative publicity that has surrounded for-profit higher education, the implication that *all* for-profits always seek to maximize profits at the expense of quality is problematic, and does not reflect the incentives and behavior of these and most other businesses. There are firms in every industry that seek largely short-term gains and will behave accordingly, often promising one thing now and delivering another later. Likewise, every industry has firms with unhappy investors and/or employees who have sued their firm for numerous forms of alleged misconduct. Issues of consumer protection may be to some degree different with education services. Prospective students may find it particularly difficult to "buy higher education" because they don't purchase educational programs frequently; it is unusually difficult for most to thoroughly comparison-shop prior to purchase. For example, just the financial analysis of weighing the short-term program costs against long-term estimates of future revenues from better paying jobs can be daunting for any prospective student.

In most fields, however, firms that continually provide poor-quality services and cannot earn profits tend not to last long, not unlike some of the for-profit colleges and universities that left the higher education field during the 1990s. Most businesses, however, seek to succeed and grow in value over time and to satisfy customers by meeting or exceeding their expectations. In addition, apart from the incentives to serve customers that spring from for-profit incentives, changes in the overall regulatory environment can also greatly influence a firm's performance, as reflected in the recent history of the for-profit colleges and universities that were forced out of business.

Even as traditional institutions of higher education continued to grow over the past two decades, for-profits successfully increased their market share dramatically. Clearly, as a loose confederation of several thousand businesses, they are doing something different in comparison to traditional institutions. The most visible differences—in growth rates, in the markets they serve, and the programs they offer—are important educationally, but are also symptomatic of more fundamental differences in governance, which I examine later in this chapter. These differences enable for-profits to structure and operate in ways that differ from traditional colleges and universities.

For-Profits Are Different

I make the generalization that for-profits are different with some caution, due to the wide variety of for-profit colleges and universities in existence. For example, these institutions vary greatly in size: the spectrum ranges from single proprietorships with one or two vocationally oriented certificate programs to massive, publicly traded, multinational comprehensive universities offering all levels of degrees in dozens of vocational and academic fields to hundreds of thousands of students. Near the small end of the spectrum, the American College of Hair Styling serves hundreds of students on its two campuses in Iowa, traces its proprietary roots back to 1899, and offers programs five days per week in barbering, hairstyling, and cosmetology that can be completed in thirty to seventy-five weeks, for which it charges between \$12,960 and \$13,360.[13] Laureate Education, Inc., near the other end of the size spectrum, enrolls about half a million students, operates thirty-five accredited institutions with seventy campuses in twenty countries, generates about \$2 billion a year in revenue, and is growing by about 30 percent each year. American College of Hairstyling and

Laureate, both for-profits, differ not only in size but also in growth rates and on many other dimensions. The very large (usually publicly traded) for-profits as a group are growing on average about twice as fast as the smaller (usually privately held) for-profits.

Despite this great variation, most for-profits generally address nontraditional student markets and offer highly structured and focused programs of study with relatively few electives; these programs are explicitly designed to lead to initial employment and career advancement. They tend to be geared for completion as early as feasible, provide identical programs in multiple locations proximate to high-demand markets, and are offered at price points roughly between public universities on the low end and private nonprofit universities on the high end. I explore each of these generalizations in turn.

NONTRADITIONAL STUDENTS. Unlike traditional institutions that seek to fill their seats with the most able students they can find, for-profits disproportionately serve the nontraditional students traditional institutions are less likely to seek. These students have demographic and social characteristics that, in a statistical sense, make their chances of successful school completion less certain. The criteria underlying the nontraditional student label are based on a collection of student characteristics that depart from the stereotypical characteristics of the archetypal undergraduate: eighteen to twenty-two years of age, Caucasian, from at least a middle-income family, single, successfully completing high school with above-average grades, and with relatively little need for separate financial assistance.[14] Departures from this traditional stereotype are often considered risk factors, in that most data suggest that they reduce the likelihood of successful admission, retention, and completion of programs in higher education—and consequently raise the probability that the student will default on any loans made while in school.

Seven student characteristics, in addition to age and race, have been identified as risk factors, in that students who share those characteristics have a lower probability of receiving a degree: (1) not graduating from high school; (2) delaying enrollment in postsecondary education; (3) being financially independent; (4) having dependents; (5) being a single parent; (6) attending part-time; and (7) working full-time while enrolled.[15] These risk factors are additive, and many nontraditional students have a mix of them.

Each risk factor and student is unique, and students at for-profits are more likely to have these characteristics than students at traditional schools. For example, students at for-profit colleges are generally older than the typical undergraduate. They are about 1.3 times as likely to be minority students. They tend to be financially independent in that they do not have parental support (about 1.5 times as likely among for-profit students). Students at for-profits are also twice as likely to have dependents for whom they must provide support, and are about three times as likely to be single parents themselves.[16]

The U.S. Department of Education defines a high-risk student as someone who has at least three of these factors. Such high-risk students constitute about 36 percent of the enrollments of traditional institutions; they constitute about 54 percent of enrollments of for-profit institutions.[17] For-profits are often criticized for seeking out high-risk students, implying that these students are somehow less astute or more gullible consumers of education services. Ironically, these are the same students who are both underserved by traditional institutions currently and the *only* students who must be served if the United States is to significantly increase its proportion of individuals with a college education.

CAREER ENTRY, CAREER ADVANCEMENT FOCUS. The mix of career-related curricula and broad liberal education curricula in for-profits differs from the mixture at traditional colleges and universities in two ways. First, for-profits tend to place greater emphasis on specific career-focused programs than do traditional colleges. Collectively, the twenty-eight hundred for-profits provide programs in over two hundred diverse career fields, including art, business, information technology, allied health, and culinary arts. These programs offer a range of awards, from certificates (less than two years) through PhDs and other professional degrees such as JDs. The majority of for-profits are still less-than-two-year institutions (52 percent), but the trend is for greater proportions of schools and programs to migrate up the degree hierarchy. Three-quarters of the for-profits that the National Center for Education Statistics classifies as "two-year or longer" now offer full degrees, and 8 percent of the for-profits offer graduate degrees.[18]

Second, as for-profits move their programs up the degree hierarchy, they often increase the (small) proportion of content devoted to general or liberal arts education. The change in the professional–liberal arts ratio as one moves up the degree hierarchy is roughly the opposite of that found among traditionals, where lower degrees have higher proportions of general education and graduate degrees focus on narrow specialties. The difference between the two sectors, and the logic behind it, is reflected in Corinthian Colleges' program-building strategy in health sciences.[19] Corinthian Colleges medical assistant program focuses on preparing nontraditional students for entry-level careers in health sciences. In this context, the traditional liberal education framed around disciplines that guide students toward a career funneling into graduate professional schools is not viable for a number of reasons. Corinthian's one-year certificate program is designed to provide students with the skills and content knowledge that they need to start a job exactly one year after beginning the program.

A lot of the program-design work is, thus, devoted to ascertaining, designing, and executing everything—including cognitive, attitudinal, and behavioral outcomes—that must go into the program, including content sequencing and appropriate instructional modalities. The designs are then reformatted into a comprehensive recipe, not a menu of what teachers are to teach. The obligation of the teacher is to have the students succeed, not only in the courses and the program, but also later in the workplace. The explicit attention that Corinthian pays to preparing students for success in a particular job is common across the for-profit sector, and the data suggest that this focus on employability pays dividends. According to some estimates, across *all* for-profits and certificate or degree levels, 76 percent of the students who successfully completed a program in 2005 were employed directly following graduation.[20]

HIGHLY STRUCTURED PROGRAMS.   Unlike traditional institutions with majors, minors, concentrations, and electives—all of which can be switched while pursuing one degree—for-profit institutions tend to offer highly structured, sequential, and focused programs with little choice for students within programs. Both types of institutions build programs around sets of courses, but for-profits emphasize the integrity of overall program content (and often its relationship to specific occupations), which is distinct from the collections of individual, stand-alone courses that predominate at traditional colleges and universities. Career orientation comes first, and general education gets folded in later, in part because employers are themselves asking for a broader curriculum at the associate's and higher degree levels.

Highly structured programs permit a greater degree of quality control over programs, because all graduates of a given program have taken the same course work and all instructors who teach the same courses are expected to have taught the same content. Student choice is largely concentrated in the decision about program choice; after they choose the program, students have very little opportunity to make further choices.

SPEEDY ENROLLMENT AND DEGREE COMPLETION.   In order to speed completion and entry into the job market, for-profits offer more full-time programs than their traditional counterparts. Eighty percent of the students at for-profits attend full-time, compared with 57 percent of students at public institutions and 75 percent of students at private, nonprofit institutions.[21] For-profits also reduce the wait time before starting a program. About 60 percent of enrollments at for-profits are on a rolling basis, enabling students to start a program at frequent intervals during the year.[22] Course work can be offered at convenient times and places, but all else equal, full-time enrollment speeds completion and the resulting improvement in employability. Statistically, shorter program duration also improves the likelihood of completion.

MULTIPLE CAMPUSES AND REGIONAL LABOR MARKETS. For-profits with multiple campuses provide identical programs in multiple locations proximate to and sensitive to changes in regional labor markets. For-profits invest in developing programs that are responsive to labor market demands and then decide which to offer at which campuses. As I detail in the next section, for-profits work with local and national employer advisory groups as they formulate their plans. They add programs to (and drop them from) campuses based on their market performance. In contrast to traditional, usually single-campus institutions, these for-profits tend to behave in a way that is much more sensitive to changes in the labor demands of local employers. They can move their programs into and out of regional labor markets much more nimbly than can traditional institutions. This advantage is particularly characteristic of the large, publicly traded for-profits, and explains in part why they are growing more rapidly than for-profits as a whole and much more rapidly than traditional colleges.

Table 6.1 shows the wide distribution of campuses of some of the larger for-profits, which illustrates the prevalence of nine of these firms in the fifty largest urban areas, in the two hundred fifty largest U.S. cities, and internationally. Those nine for-profits operate a total of 842 campuses across these locales, an average of over ninety campuses per institution. The distribution of campuses inserts for-profits into a large number of local labor markets. From this vantage point, they can ascertain local and national employment–related trends in their industries of interest, including job demand changes, job content changes, and program effectiveness.

Employers in high-demand markets value the ability and willingness of for-profits to bring programs into those markets. Those who manage them and those who invest in them see their ability and willingness to exit markets where demand has dropped as an advantage. Consider the example of Universal Technical Institute (UTI), which announced in late

TABLE 6.1

Campus distribution of nine for-profits

	Number of campuses			
	Largest 50 cities in the U.S	**Largest 250 cities (population 100,000+)**	**International**	**Total locations**
Apollo Group	45	87	9	260
Career Education	26	35	7	75
Corinthian Colleges	28	54	17	106
DeVry	32	46	2	91
Education Management	24	40	2	88
ITT Educational Services	38	72	0	102
Lincoln Education Services	13	20	0	35
Strayer Education	9	26	0	57
Universal Technical Institute	4	6	0	28
Total	**219**	**386**	**37**	**842**
Average per company	24	43	4	94
Average per city	4.4	1.5		

Source: Michael Moe, NeXt Knowledge Factbook 2010, http://www.nextupresearch.com/, 119.

2009 that due to the economic problems plaguing the auto industry and the downturn in demand for trained automotive technicians, it was closing its programs at campuses in Avondale, Arizona; Exton, Pennsylvania; and Rancho Cucamonga, California. These programs, paid for by several automakers whose need for automotive technicians had plummeted, were no longer profitable. They accounted for less than one percent of UTI's revenues, and the move to eliminate those programs enabled UTI to concentrate on larger, more promising areas within its mission.

PRICE POINTS BETWEEN PUBLICS AND NONPROFITS.   Tuition accounts for a very large fraction of for-profit top-line revenues, or about 87.5 percent for for-profits, compared to 17 percent for publics and 29 percent for nonprofits.[23] Factors related to tuition, such as prices, enrollment stability, and financial aid, are centrally important to for-profits, and price setting is a key decision that affects overall organizational performance. Program pricing at for-profits varies considerably and is usually influenced by perceived demand, cost of production, and strategies for penetrating new markets—not unlike other businesses. In general, tuition prices at four-year for-profits tend to be higher than in-state tuition prices at four-year public institutions and less than four-year nonprofit private institutions: $14,692 at for-profits versus $6,319 at publics and $24,692 at privates. Among two-year institutions, for-profit tuitions are significantly higher than in-state tuition at two-year publics and are slightly more than nonprofits: $13,853 versus $2,137 and $12,424.[24]

Analysts of for-profit higher education institutions sometimes suggest that tuition prices at for-profit institutions may be unjustifiably high and that for-profits are profiteering as a result.[25] This perspective is at best incomplete and at worst misleading. While the desire to raise tuition prices above existing levels is both natural and necessary for long-run sustainability (if not profitability), pricing decisions at for-profits take into consideration many of the same variables that traditional institutions factor into price setting, including costs of production and perceived elasticity of demand. Profit also arises from movement on two fronts, not just one—*increased* unit prices and *decreased* unit costs. The same profit incentives that foster tuition increases also foster incentives to create efficiencies in operation.

In fact, when tuition prices and *total* costs to produce programs are compared among for-profits and traditional colleges, the differences between the two kinds of organizations shrink dramatically. For example, if we calculate the total costs for each graduating or transferring student (each positive outcome) from institutions that specialize in two-year-or-less programs, we find that for-profits are actually not much more costly to the taxpayer than public institutions in this sector. Specifically, for-profits spend about $26,700, while traditional colleges spend about $25,300.[26] Much of the price differential is attributable to differences in institutional subsidies. At the end of the day, however, for-profits have to generate *some* level of profitability in order to stay in business. The net income margins of publicly traded for-profits range from about 6 percent to 23 percent and average about 13 percent.[27]

Governance Differences Foster Growth and Innovation

The pursuit of net revenues is *not* uniquely characteristic of for-profits, although the relative importance of margin growth as a measure of success and a greater level of control over organizational strategies explain much of the visible differences between for-profits and traditional colleges and universities. As profit-seeking organizations, for-profits pursue profits through a combination of growth in volume and growth in unit margins. The centralized leadership of the firm formulates and monitors these goals and strategies. Compared to their counterparts in nonprofits, the senior managers at for-profits can more easily: (1) invest personally in their institutions; (2) guide and direct strategies through substantial control of internal operations; (3) guide and direct the strategies through mergers, acquisitions, and by selling off parts of their businesses; and (4) promote growth by attracting added investment capital from private financial markets.

OWNING PART OF THE ORGANIZATION.   Senior managers at for-profits tend to have equity stakes in the organizations they manage; some of their personal wealth is attached to the fortunes of the organization. In many of the smaller, privately held for-profits, senior managers *are* the major investors. Because this practice tends to align the incentives of senior management with those of its investors, investors generally approve it. As a consequence, senior managers in for-profits have enhanced incentives to improve the long-run performance and profitability of the organization in ways above and beyond the incentives of annual salaries and raises that traditional institutions provide to senior managers. Sometimes senior management's share is substantial, even to the point of enabling it to be able to make private its publicly traded college.[28]

GREATER OPERATIONAL CONTROL.   Relative to their nonprofit counterparts, senior managers in for-profits have enhanced governance rights over their organizations, tend to exert more direct control over internal departments and divisions, and have greater ability to align the incentives of campus and program managers with those of senior management. In contrast, senior managers in traditional institutions operate within an environment of shared governance, which is a "set of practices under which college faculty and staff participate in *significant* decisions concerning the operation of their institutions" [emphasis added].[29] In traditional institutions, committees of faculty members within programs carry out core organizational decisions, such as those involving program and course development, evaluation, marketing, and faculty hiring, deployment, compensation, and promotion. These programs are nested within departments, which are in turn within the schools, such as business or arts and sciences, of a traditional university. Senior managers at traditional institutions, then, share these and other decisions in a highly decentralized environment.

Senior management in for-profits has much more direct responsibility in each of these decision areas. For instance, one large for-profit's governing relationships between its corporate-level management group and its campus-level executives are significantly more hands-on than managerial relations between provosts and deans at traditional colleges and universities. This particular for-profit, despite its dozens and dozens of campuses dispersed across the country, conducts weekly two-hour phone meetings of all campus presidents, where it makes the performance data of *all* campuses (including breakdowns by program) available to *all* campus presidents. While campus presidents have substantial decision rights over the instructional programs they can bring into or eliminate from their campuses, their performance is also subject to the continual review by all relevant peers and superiors. The metrics of volume, growth, and margins at the campus level are analogous to those that govern the performance of the for-profit institution at the corporate level, including changes in enrollments, revenues, expenditures, and margins by program. The information and incentives of faculty committees in traditional institutions are not so well aligned with those of senior managers, and direct communication between the two on matters of organizational performance is infrequent.

BUYING AND SELLING PARTS OF THE ORGANIZATION.   Senior managers of for-profits can dramatically focus and enhance their organizational strategies in ways that senior management of traditional institutions cannot. They can sell off divisions that, in their opinion, are not working well enough. They can merge with other organizations when they deem it in their institution's interest to do so. They can acquire new divisions that they believe will enhance their overall performance. According to Mark DeFusco, an investment banker with personal experience in dozens of for-profit college and university transactions, for-profits pursue transactions for one or more of three reasons: they want to enter a geographical market that would otherwise be difficult to penetrate; they want to acquire new programs that they can distribute more effectively than by building them on their own; and they want to acquire senior management talent when it is easier and quicker than developing it in-house.[30]

Through the process of buying, selling, and merging, some for-profits grow and flourish, while others fade or go out of existence. Not all for-profits succeed, but those that do have greater capacity as a result. In 2007, Corinthian Colleges sold twelve of its schools in Canada because they were too remote to manage effectively. The resulting sale enabled Corinthian to concentrate its efforts on its remaining Canadian schools in the province of Ontario.[31] More recently, Apollo Group's purchase of U.K.-based BPP Holdings provided Apollo with access to lifelong learning programs in the U.K.'s professional education sector, established a significant U.K. and pan-European platform, and expanded the range of advanced degrees and cross-border educational opportunities available to its students.[32] DeVry University's purchase of a leading medical and veterinary school enabled it to expand its education platform into medicine and health sciences.[33] For-profits have purchased other for-profits operating in New York, Texas, and

California in part because they could thus avoid the inherent difficulties as a start-up firm in penetrating the regulatory barriers to entry in those states.

For-profits also frequently buy and sell buildings, but for slightly different reasons. Unlike traditional institutions that are based in a particular place and heavily invested in physical plant infrastructure, usually in one location, for-profits tend to own buildings only when other options are unavailable. They pursue a lease strategy for three reasons: purchasing does not yield a competitive return; it retards the firm's ability to be nimble and shift locations; and they are reluctant to mass all fixed assets in one place. The willingness and ability of for-profits to buy and sell both academic units and facilities add to their ability to pursue growth and differentiate themselves from traditional, place-based institutions.

GOING PUBLIC.   Senior managers of for-profits can attract capital in ways that their counterparts in traditional institutions cannot. Senior managers of traditional institutions have several options for raising capital to grow, but most often these are limited to debt instruments such as loans and bonds. Those same instruments are available to for-profits, but they also have the option of selling pieces of the for-profit institution in exchange for needed cash. Often this takes the form of a small group of investors who buy into the institution at a mutually agreeable price. If, on the other hand, the institution has already grown to a substantial size and plans on growing even more, then another option it has is to go public by making an initial public offering of shares available to a much larger number of investors.

The ability to raise capital quickly facilitates high growth rates among for-profit institutions. The average size of for-profit institutions is increasing, in part because a few firms are growing rapidly through mergers and acquisitions and by going public. A number of the smaller institutions are being acquired or are merging. Between 2006 and 2009, several U.S. for-profits have gone public, including Capella University; American Public Education, Inc.; Grand Canyon Education, Inc.; and Bridgepoint Education). Lest we think that this is a uniquely American phenomenon, at least an equal number of for-profit higher education institutions went public at the same time in other countries, including China (New Oriental Education & Technology Group, ChinaEdu Corp., ATA Inc., CIBT Education Group, and China Distance Education Holdings, Ltd.) and Brazil (Anhanguera Educacional Participacoes SA, Estacio Participacoes SA, Kroton Educacional SA, and Sistema Educacional Brasileiro).

Although going public provides a means to gain access to additional capital, there are a number of drawbacks that often accompany the decision to go public, over and above the cost of making the public offering. Future profits must be shared with outsiders (if dividends are offered). Added reporting and transparency requirements lead to a loss of confidentiality and to an inherent increase in liability for any false and misleading information in company reports. Under certain conditions, outside stockholders can even wrest control from senior management. Despite these problems, the majority of the largest for-profits have elected to go public.

In brief, the features of for-profit governance of greatest consequence vis-à-vis traditional colleges are their combination of access to added sources of capital and increased incentives to employ capital in order to grow capacity. Given the differences in governance and incentives of for-profits, their relatively high rates of growth are neither unexpected nor unusual. For-profit colleges and universities are further set apart from their traditional counterparts by organizational practices that *flow from* these governance differences. Though less visible, these organizational practices have greater direct impact on the educational services that for-profits provide.

ORGANIZATIONAL PRACTICES REFLECT GOVERNANCE DIFFERENCES

As I suggested earlier, for-profit colleges and universities, especially regionally accredited ones, are governed differently from traditional colleges and universities, and those differences are largely, but not totally, associated with their profit motive. Differences in governance and incentives in turn lead to differences between for-profits and traditional colleges and universities in educational practices. Three practices, in combination, distinguish most for-profits from most traditional colleges and universities: (1) centralized program, curriculum, and human resource development in for-profits versus decentralized decisions by departmental faculty in traditionals; (2) curricular programs designed to attract *employers* such as local businesses and national or international industry groups versus programs designed solely to attract students; and (3) integrated systems of student recruiting, program advising, and academic support versus functionally specialized departments. These three distinctions are largely between traditional colleges and the larger, often regionally accredited for-profit institutions. These distinctions tend *not* to apply to the large number of nationally accredited vocational schools and to the small, mom-and-pop haircutting or truck driving schools.

Centralized Development of Programs, Curricula, and Human Resources

Traditional colleges and universities are organized by disciplines and schools, which are further segmented by departments and programs, each with smaller groupings of specialized faculty. Decisions involving courses, programs, admissions, and faculty are decentralized, several levels below the office of the university president, although permission to fill faculty vacancies usually is passed down from above. After the work is done, approvals are then secured up through the hierarchy. These practices in traditional colleges are undertaken by departmental or programmatic faculty, but in for-profits, the programs, courses, and human resource decisions tend to be the responsibility of senior management. Senior managers make decisions at the top and then roll them out through the for-profits' ranks; they are personally responsible for determining what programs to create and offer. Much of the intelligence that feeds into these decisions comes from its campuses, but the decisions about creation and implementation are made centrally. Senior management assembles curriculum working groups of internal instructors and external experts who design complete programs, including, but not limited to, the formal courses.

Although local for-profit campuses recruit and hire faculty, their human resource policies and practices, as well as categorical staffing levels, are fundamentally shaped at the corporate level. The larger for-profits, despite having a larger number of campuses, have developed more formal systems of faculty quality control than have smaller for-profits and, arguably, more than most traditional institutions. At traditional institutions, faculty hiring and evaluation take place at the department level. Left to individual departments, quality control and evaluation procedures at traditional institutions vary significantly from the formal and professional to the informal and political. In contrast, hiring, deployment, and quality-control processes are formulaic and predictable at most of the larger for-profits. A description of the University of Phoenix's faculty certification process provides one illustration of a centrally operated process for recruiting, vetting, selecting, deploying, and evaluating faculty that is common among for-profit colleges and universities.

Faculty certification is Phoenix's process through which faculty candidates have the opportunity to learn about the university's teaching and learning model, acquire teaching skills, understand the university's policies, and learn about the university's expectations of its faculty members. The process employs a multi-workshop course, augmented by Web-based readings and training modules.

The procedures for faculty certification are described here in some detail to portray the extensive degree to which the University of Phoenix has institutionalized instructional quality control:

> The . . . Faculty Certification process . . . begins with a Faculty Candidate who has been thoroughly screened by the Faculty Recruiter through a series of interviews and an examination of educational and professional credentials. Faculty Recruiters notify the Certification Team when a Faculty Candidate is ready to begin the Certification process. The Certification process has two phases: The first phase is Certification which is an intensive four week training process that is administered as two modules: Core Certification and Specialized Certification. All Faculty Candidates complete the Core module.

After completing the Core module, Faculty Candidates complete either the [Program A] Specialization or the [Program B] Specialization. The Online Faculty Certification is conducted in an online classroom and is structured to model a typical class, where the candidate is an active participant in a classroom. Candidates are assessed weekly by the Certification Trainers on their skills demonstration and provided suggestions for improvement, using a standardized evaluation form provided by the Certification Team.

When a candidate successfully completes the first phase, in the second phase the Faculty Recruiter notifies the Mentorship Team that the candidate is ready to move on to the second phase, Mentorship. In the Mentorship phase, the candidate works with a mentor before the class, during the class, and after the class to submit final grades. The candidate teaches the class and the mentor remains behind the scenes.

Candidates are evaluated each week by the mentor during the mentorship class using a standardized evaluation form provided by the Mentorship Team. Candidates are provided with helpful advice and areas to improve. At the end of the class, the mentor makes a recommendation to the Mentorship Team as to the preparedness of the faculty candidate to remove the candidate status and join the faculty of the University. On occasion, faculty candidates may be asked to complete a second mentorship or the candidate may be terminated. Inputs to the process are: faculty candidates; [our institution's] Colleges; Deans' offices; Legal and Compliance departments; Certification Trainers and Mentors; and Faculty Candidates. Outputs are trained faculty. Formally established process feedback points are the following: weekly and final Certification Trainer reports, weekly and final Mentor reports, candidate end-of-course surveys, mentee end-of-mentorship surveys, and student surveys in a mentorship course. Informal process feedback points are Certification Trainer and Mentor feedback on the training materials and processes.[34]

The faculty certification process has been in effect since the early 1990s.[35] It would be difficult to find as comprehensive and formal a process for monitoring faculty quality in most traditional institutions. More fundamentally, at most for-profit institutions, human resource development is a senior management, rather than a faculty, responsibility.

Develop Programs for Employers, Not Students

One of the performance metrics for-profits use that prepare students for employment is, naturally, the occupational placement of program graduates. The quality and relevance of their programs, as perceived by employers, is of the utmost importance to for-profits, even beyond their need to successfully place graduates.

As such, ongoing communication links with regional employers are a critical component of the intelligence-gathering and marketing strategies of for-profit institutions. Given the importance attached to the employability of their graduates, for-profits create and interact regularly with local, industry-specific employer advisory boards (EABs) or industry advisory councils (IACs), which are composed of representatives from firms and regional industry trade associations. IACs are widely recognized as important functional components for high-quality career-oriented programs and are required by some of their (national) accrediting agencies.

For-profits nurture the development and functioning of these advisory boards for at least four, mutually reinforcing reasons, beyond being required by some for accreditation: to gain feedback on the performance of recently placed graduates, to gain insights into changing industry and employer skill requirements, to market current programs, and to test the feasibility of new and modified programs. The experience that DeVry University has had in working with several engineering-related industries illustrates the degree of interaction between IACs and career-oriented for-profits.[36]

John Giancola, DeVry's dean of engineering and information sciences, works with about ninety local IACs across the country, with each council representing at least one campus and also with six regional industry advisory boards (IABs). IABs are regional aggregations of IACs and meet with senior managers once a year, where they identify and consider national industry-related trends. In forming these bodies, DeVry seeks employers who hire a lot of graduates and those firms that might contribute to new DeVry initiatives, such as those involving career services, faculty and subject matter experts, and line managers with extensive supervisory responsibilities. In preparation for these board meetings, DeVry provides members with descriptions of curricula and a set of questions about DeVry's offerings and graduates. The one-day meeting is structured into three unequal parts: (1) DeVry's presentation of the issues it is addressing, (2) candid participant responses to the questions DeVry raised, and (3) a summary of the meeting. The meetings often focus on pressing industry issues of the day. For instance, one of the central issues at a recent session involved how green technology might affect the curriculum and the nature of work of DeVry graduates. The value of the intelligence that can be gathered with these industry-representatives depends a lot on the qualities of the individuals invited to participate. Senior management seeks to secure the best possible members on these committees.

DeVry experiences the value of these bodies as much on its local campuses as it does nationally. Major employers in Phoenix, Arizona, such as Motorola, for example, may emphasize different problems and opportunities than Intel does in Austin, Texas. These bodies also play a central role in DeVry's strategies for developing and rolling out new programs. Finally, through these bodies, DeVry finds firms that are willing and sometimes even eager to take on students in practicum and intern roles, a critical component of many DeVry programs.

Employers, on the other hand, are willing to participate in these advisory boards for similar reasons: more direct access to trained graduates, ability to influence the focus and content of preparation programs for current and future employees, and opportunities for their firm's employees to learn more about industry trends, earn extra income as faculty members, and work directly with new entrants into the industry. Participation on advisory boards is usually nonexclusive in that employers participate on the boards of multiple for-profits, and for-profits engage multiple employers on their boards. American Public University's relationship with Wal-Mart is unusual in this regard. After considering eighty-one institutions of higher education, Wal-Mart chose APU, a publicly traded for-profit, as a partner—to date, exclusive—to provide higher education courses to its more than 1.4 million U.S. employees. Currently APU offers a wide range of programs, all online, to over seventy thousand students. Wal-Mart is providing $50 million in scholarship support, and APU is reducing tuition by 15 percent for Wal-Mart employees. When the discounts are applied, undergraduate tuition will be $212.50 per credit hour for undergraduates and $255.00 per credit hour for graduate education. [37]

Working relationships between for-profit institutions and the workplace, whether in the form of employee advisory bodies like DeVry's or the partnership of APU and Wal-Mart, are in marked contrast to practices in traditional institutions. Traditional institutions rely on faculty members in specialized program fields to evaluate, refashion, and create their own instructional programs. The presumption is that specialized faculty talent is the most logical and best available resource for addressing issues of program and course development in that specialization. Those who created the program then approve faculty-led development of program objectives and curriculum. The functional relationship between the traditional university and the relevant industry is completely decentralized and fragmented. For example, the most direct link between traditional colleges and the workplaces of their graduates is through their career services offices, where the staff has little functional relationship with the faculty who teach in particular career areas or with employers, other than with their human resources departments. This is not necessarily problematic, especially if the traditional institution is offering programs that are not intended to prepare students for specific industries and positions. But, for purposes of linking education and the workplace, EABs appear to function for the benefit of both for-profits and for employers.

Client-Centered Versus Functionally Organized Student Services

The internal organization of for-profits, compared to traditional institutions, is structured more around *clients* or, in this case, students, than it is around *functions,* such as marketing, recruiting, admissions, advising, teaching, financial aid, student affairs, and academic support services. This arrangement translates into fewer for-profit staff people needing to interact with each student, because these staff members have broader responsibilities for fostering student success and are assigned greater responsibility for seeing that their students succeed. In most traditional colleges and universities, on the other hand, these functions operate as separate and independent departments. Further, it falls more on the students to self-diagnose any problems they are having and then self-select into the appropriate office for services. For example, specialists in financial aid tend to operate separately from specialists in academic advising. But student problems do not parse so neatly. When a currently enrolled student who is also employed full-time loses her job, for example, it affects both her academic program and her financial circumstances. In general, for-profits recognize this kind of dilemma and organize themselves accordingly. These kinds of student problems may be less common at some traditional institutions, so the need to rethink these fragmentation issues may be less compelling for them.

Though there is great variation among all colleges and universities in the extent to which educators are held accountable for student success, for-profit educators tend to be more personally and directly responsible and accountable for the success of individual students than are educators in traditional institutions.[38] Rather than students finding a variety of offices and services on their own as they feel a need to, students in for-profits more often have a single person or group of individuals assigned to them throughout their academic career to monitor their progress; look for academic, financial, social, and personal problems; and, where feasible, bring resources to bear to address those problems.

In turn, for-profit educators, especially those in large-scale firms, and their nontraditional students have access to a wider array of learning support services than do their counterparts at traditional institutions. These range from supports for writing papers and doing math to counseling about financial planning and organizing for success. The larger for-profits tend to have more formal, systematic processes in place to achieve these functions. Consider, for example, some of the services at the University of Phoenix that are designed to support student academic progress.

Like all colleges and universities, the University of Phoenix provides a variety of student services, defined as processes, systems, procedures, and programs that are intended to increase the likelihood of student persistence and ultimately completion of a program of study. One difference between University of Phoenix and many public two- and four-year institutions involves how it deals with entering students with known and unknown academic weaknesses. Most student services programs at traditional institutions—especially publics—focus heavily on identifying basic math and literacy deficiencies of entering students only. After testing into or out of one or more basic skills courses at those institutions, students are presumed to be academically proficient and proceed on their own. If they subsequently falter academically, it is up to them to seek further academic assistance.

In contrast, student services at University of Phoenix are comprised of a wide array of academic services that are extended throughout the student's enrollment. Perhaps more significantly, *faculty members* have responsibility to both identify and help remedy student problems that the faculty identify in their classes. This is University of Phoenix's early alert system. Faculty use the system to identify, track, and remediate student learning challenges. The model consolidates three different functional systems—financial aid, academic advising, and program planning—for the purpose of identifying a student's deficiencies or problems and proactively offering him or her solutions to promote success. Once a faculty member identifies a problem, he or she sends a notification to the classroom issues tracking system, where the designated academic affairs staff members will create a file for the academic adviser. The academic adviser seeks out and addresses the areas of concern with the student, while providing guidance and information about available resources. The approach at many traditional institutions places more responsibility on the student to self-diagnose and pursue remedies among different institutional resources. The early alert system places much of this responsibility on the institution.

Of course, the University of Phoenix and other for-profits also make available a large battery of customized tutorials, work samples, guides, and study aids, all of which students are encouraged to access at no additional cost. For instance, Phoenix makes two writing support services available—WritePoint and Tutor Review—throughout a student's program, over and above the support faculty provide in classes. WritePoint gives feedback on basic grammar and usage. It processes a paper quickly—usually in less than two hours—and is available twenty-four hours, seven days a week.[39] Tutor Review is more involved and gives students detailed feedback on academic papers on overall format and organization, as well as grammar, punctuation, and usage.

I suggested earlier that, more than governance differences, these operating differences—how programs are developed, how school is linked to employment, and how students are supported—are more closely associated with what students actually experience at these institutions. It is premature to assert with certainty that, all else equal, for-profits support student success more effectively than do traditional institutions. However, we *do* know that, in comparison to traditional colleges, for-profits have proportionately more dependent students in the lowest income quartile, more students with parents with a high school education or less, more students who have no parental support, more students who are married, more students who are single parents, and fewer students who are high school graduates.[40] Even though for-profits serve disproportionate numbers of students who are considered high risk, on average, they graduate higher proportions of students (certificates and degrees combined) than do traditional two-year-or-less public institutions—44 percent at publics and 65 percent at for-profits.[41] A more certain conclusion awaits more detailed comparisons of what students with similar backgrounds in similar programs actually experience at these and other types of colleges and universities. At the very least, the for-profit models for program development, faculty training, and student support represent a definite break with the way traditional institutions organize these processes.

Do the differences between for-profits and traditional colleges and universities in operating processes constitute innovations on the part of for-profits? Perhaps they do, but deciding that here may not be critically important. Suffice it to say that such operational differences do appear to be closely associated with the sector in which a school resides. At the same time, it is possible that these newer features may also reflect directions that *all* traditional and for-profit institutions pursuing expanded nontraditional student markets must pursue as well.

PROGRAM INNOVATION AS PURSUIT OF "MARGINAL" STUDENT MARKETS

All of the previous discussion, and much of what follows, runs the risk of portraying for-profits as a monolith—all behaving similarly, if not identically. That is not the case, and is even less so in the portraits of innovative practices that follow. The three program innovations detailed here are anecdotal and by no means widespread. Rather, they reflect the pursuits of individual for-profits, each of which is seeking simultaneously to build on its historic strengths, to exploit its comparative advantages, and to pursue its path to distinctiveness as the go-to educational institution for particular kinds of programs and students.

These innovations may be better understood as sustaining rather than disruptive, in that they reflect more of a natural extension of their current business model.[42] Nevertheless, all move beyond the norm of traditional programs for nontraditional students to pursue relatively untapped segments of the broad and growing nontraditional or marginal student market. *Marginal* here has two intended meanings: marginal in a student characteristic sense, as in students who have characteristics not typically associated with success in higher education; and marginal in the economic sense, as in the next incremental cohort of new entrants into higher education. The following three programs illustrate the kinds of innovations in business models some for-profits are developing to better serve nontraditional students.

Creating Joint Ventures with Traditional Institutions

Joint-venture relationships entail a for-profit and a traditional institution co-creating a single program for a common pool of students, where the comparative advantages of each organization benefit the other and they share risks. With participation in a joint venture, often an organization may potentially be able to postpone start-up costs, penetrate otherwise inaccessible markets, and gain access to otherwise unavailable technical and financial capital—all at the expense of sharing any anticipated future revenues that accrue from new, heretofore untapped sources of students. In one example, a public community college and a for-profit formed an agreement wherein successful completion of the AA degree leads to automatic admission to the BA program of the for-profit, and the admission charges to the for-profit are waived. See, for example, the arrangement between Long Beach Community College (LBCC) and the University of Phoenix.[43] This is more than an articulation agreement; it constitutes a joint recruiting initiative for students just out of high school to a BA degree program via a public community college. The new increment of students is composed of those who complete the new program, but would not have completed LBCC and then applied to and completed the University of Phoenix bachelor's degree.

In another joint venture, the for-profit recruits international students into its college readiness program, and this program then automatically feeds into the four-year public institution's bachelor's degree program. Oregon State University's arrangement with Australian for-profit Navitas provides a pathway or transition-year program for international students into Oregon State's undergraduate program. Navitas has similar arrangements with twenty-two universities worldwide, including Western Kentucky. Typically, the for-profit incurs the marketing, recruitment, and operational costs of the transitional program, while the traditional university provides classroom and office space. Students pay tuition to the for-profit, which in turn provides the university a cut of 20 percent to 30 percent, depending on the course of study.[44] Kaplan, Inc., has similar partnership arrangements with five traditional British universities.

2tor, Inc., a new for-profit created by Princeton Review's John Katzman, operates a joint venture with the University of Southern California's Rossier School of Education to develop, market, and operate an online master's in teaching degree. 2tor provides the online and marketing expertise, and USC provides the program, staffing, and the branded degree. Each incurs development and operating costs and shares subsequent revenues. Another joint venture, between Middlebury College and for-profit K12 Inc. (a well-known provider of online learning at the K–12 level), is intended to create online language programs aimed at middle and high school students.[45] In joint-venture arrangements between for-profits and traditional institutions such as these, both parties share the costs and risks as well as any rewards that may accrue.

Reaching Further Down into the High School Pipeline

The largest gap or leak in the U.S. educational system pipeline is between high school and college. Some new for-profit programs seek to bridge that gap and amount to a new form of the traditional dual-enrollment programs between high schools and community colleges—with one difference. These new forms are geared to more average and below students and their entry into career programs beyond high school, whereas earlier dual-enrollment programs targeted higher achieving students.

Other for-profits are acquiring and opening up virtual high schools to grow more formal feeder patterns. Kaplan and Princeton Review have both purchased online high schools, similar to the Apollo Group's purchase of Portland-based Insight High Schools.[46] Corinthian is also pursuing the secondary school market, but in a different way. It is developing its instructional programming to provide students who haven't graduated from high school with *simultaneous* entry-level career preparation and GED completion.[47]

Transferring More Prior Learning into Degree Programs

The American education system runs on accumulated courses that lead to degrees. Unfortunately, increasing numbers of higher education students are moving across more and more institutions as they seek to educate themselves, while institutions generally remain conservative in the amount of prior course work that they allow students to transfer into their institution's programs. The aggregate costs in student time to degree, student financial aid, and foregone earnings are significant, approaching $30 billion per year.[48] Nontraditional students in particular often find that they can't apply much of their previous course work to their next degree or certificate. Some for-profits provide classic degree programs, but their degree can be made up of a greater proportion of prior student course work from multiple institutions, multiple programs, and a growing variety of prior learning experiences such as work experience, nondegree training, and military service. They can evaluate prior learning experiences through a variety of tests or by prior program approval.

Recent research suggests that students who are able to transfer more courses through assessment of their prior learning are more likely to successfully complete their degree programs.[49] These institutions pursue students who are from low-income backgrounds and are at risk of noncompletion, in spite of (or perhaps because of) the fact that they have acquired prior course work at an excessive number of institutions. Some for-profits are now granting significantly more prior credits to incoming students than has typically been the case. Further, they are making it possible for individual students to transfer *simultaneously* into online as well as in-seat programs, enabling them to take their course of study with them wherever they go in the future. In combination, these innovative practices combine to allow students to start a program farther ahead than would otherwise be the case and to improve their likelihood of completion. When these for-profits also price their services at the low end of the for-profit spectrum, they are even more attractive to nontraditional students.

Bridgepoint Education's (BPE) business model is illustrative. Its two campuses—Ashford University and University of the Rockies—deliver their programs online as well as at traditional campuses located in Clinton, Iowa, and Colorado Springs, Colorado. These regionally accredited institutions accept an unusually high number of transfer credits from other institutions—up to ninety units for transfer into a one-hundred-twenty-unit bachelor's degree program. BPE recently raised the minimum student age to twenty-two years from eighteen years at Ashford, which now has over forty articulation agreements representing over a hundred-thirty colleges, accepting high proportions of previously earned units from other institutions into either its on-campus or online versions of its programs. As the director of articulation agreements at participating Barstow Community College, California, said, "We wanted to collaborate with Ashford because they offer students flexibility and convenience when pursuing their education. Many of our students are working adults, so this is essential."

In pushing up the historical limits on transferable credits and prior experiences into a degree program, these institutions raise two broader questions about their higher education degrees. What skills, knowledge, and aptitudes do their degree holders possess, and what proportion of this learning did they acquire at that institution? Although the second question is more directly at issue with increased transfer activity, the first question is more important, more difficult to objectively ascertain, and applies to all higher education institutions. In the APU–Wal-Mart partnership discussed earlier, Wal-Mart employees can earn college credits in areas such as retail management, logistics, pricing, inventory management, and ethics for performing their regular jobs.[50] Whether APU bachelor's degree holders learned retail management largely on the job or in class is less important to future students, past graduates, and current employers than having some objective sense of what APU bachelor's degree holders who learned retail management actually learned.

These three innovations—into joint venturing, secondary education, and expanded course transfer—are all variations on the theme of pursuing incremental additions to the non-traditional student marketplace. As such, they align more with the historical trajectory of for-profits vis-à-vis nontraditional student markets than they do with any departure from it. However, some for-profits are migrating toward more traditional markets. While governance differences between for-profits and traditional institutions seem to be quite distinct, as are differences in some educational practices, for-profits are not the only institutions serving growing proportions of nontraditional students. Nonetheless, for-profits *are* developing new and different ways to pursue marginal students, and they continue to grow disproportionately compared to traditional institutions.

It is not clear whether any of these or other innovations in higher education will be of consequence for traditional public and nonprofit institutions at any degree level. If we *are* witnessing a truly disruptive innovation in higher education, it may well be in the growing utilization of the for-profit form of organization to provide educational services rather than any individual innovative element within that model. That is the presumption around which I base the following conclusions.

CONCLUSION: GOVERNANCE, GROWTH, INNOVATION— AND FOR-PROFIT HIGHER EDUCATION

For-profits appear to be structured, governed, and incentivized to grow through innovation in the programs and services that they offer. Unlike traditional institutions that admit the most eligible students up to a capacity constraint, for-profits tend to focus on an acceptable minimum level of admissions qualifications and then grow their institutional capacity as quickly as is feasible in order to respond to demand for their services. Innovation is important to for-profits, especially when it fuels demand. When they succeed and grow, for-profits have ways to raise more capital and to grow even further. In this sense, for-profit higher education institutions are not materially different from for-profit businesses in other fields, and, like other for-profit businesses, the regulatory environment—broadly construed to include legislative, judicial, and industry-specific oversight—that it faces fundamentally shapes its long-term behavior.

Some for-profit colleges and universities have been accused of practices that are harmful both to students and to society at large, essentially driving up enrollments and profits without providing corresponding value to the students who enroll or to the taxpayers who subsidize the tuition bill.

Many more for-profit colleges and universities have not. Either way, the regulatory environment within which they all operate has shaped and will continue to shape their behavior and, as a consequence, their contribution to American higher education. The differences between for-profit and traditional higher education discussed in this chapter raise three issues of regulatory oversight that have been implied, but not directly addressed in depth here: certification, transparency, and consumer protection. Although raised in reference to for-profit higher education, these issues of oversight apply in varying degrees to all higher education institutions.

Certification

How can the quality of an institution's degrees be objectively certified? This is a particularly problematic issue if we seek to separate the quality of the student from the quality of what the student learned in the program. For instance, how much is the quality of a bachelor's in history from Harvard different from the quality of a bachelor's in history from Bridgepoint, and how much is relatively due to the program and to the selectivity of the students? Both the supporters and the detractors of for-profit higher education base their arguments on presumptions of program quality, and the current system of accreditation and regulation in the United States does not adequately address this issue. It does not address it, because current certification processes do not reflect the value *added by the institution* to the education of the individual. Princeton may have added little value to its students, whereas Bridgepoint may have added a lot. We do not know either way, and certification does not tell us.

Transparency

Can education services be made more transparent? To the extent that instructional processes and practices are made transparent to students, sponsors, and regulatory bodies, the mystery behind service quality can be removed. That's easier said that done. Publicly traded for-profits already face extensive reporting requirements through the Securities and Exchange Commission, over and above those required by the U.S. Department of Education and by various accreditation bodies. Those reporting requirements focus extensively on financial measures of relevance to investors, and, more to the point, the vast majority of for-profits are privately held and *not* subject to those requirements. Nonprofit and public higher education institutions have historically been required to produce annual reports, but their value in revealing factual, comparative quality in contrast to aspirational quality is low.

Consumer Protection

What degrees and kinds of consumer protection should apply to the sale of higher education services? Because students in all sectors of higher education are bearing increasing proportions of the cost of higher education, the issues surrounding truth in advertising are growing. The problems associated with extensive student debt, plus high dropout and loan default rates, are less easily addressed in higher education than in many other industries. The worthy goal of providing credit to students to enable them to invest in their education ultimately pushes against the problem of unwitting students becoming inextricably mired in personal debt. Strategies for promoting the former without exacerbating the latter—and strategies for mitigating the latter without dampening the former—are not immediately evident, although individual institutions seek to address these countervailing forces as best they can.

Regulatory oversight applied to for-profits (indeed, to all educational institutions) clearly influences their behavior for better or worse. The regulatory rules of the game under which they play can either enhance their demonstrated virtues—like growth and responsiveness to changing labor market demands—or foster other, less desirable behaviors. Whether for-profits become more widely recognized as net contributors to the public good of postsecondary education will depend in part on the regulatory environment (and changes in that environment) that they face. As with other fields such as health care, financial services, social services, and compulsory education, regulation both shapes organizational behavior and is a reaction to it. In postsecondary education, for-profits have demonstrated a disproportionate willingness and capacity to provide more educational services to nontraditional students at scale. Absent major changes in its regulatory environment, for-profits are likely to have an increasing impact on the shape of higher education in the future, certainly for nontraditional students and perhaps for traditional students and institutions as well.

What Online Learning Can Teach Us about Higher Education

Peter Stokes

INNOVATION TEACHES US THINGS we didn't know about ourselves. It disrupts our feelings of familiarity with the day to day. It forces us to raise questions about the value of long-held traditions. It is often, as a result, freighted with aspects of the messianic and the heretical simultaneously. It draws the attention of acolytes and reactionaries while leaving a great many of us wondering which point of view will eventually prove the more reasonable. Done well, innovation can stir up a good deal of trouble. Small wonder then that inventing, say, movable type might eventually lead to the burning of a few choice books, or that plugging in an electric guitar at a folk festival might take a relatively staid art form into a bold, new direction.

Within the field of higher education, online learning has had a no less conflicted reception. Consider these contrasting positions on the effects of this new technology within the academy.

> "The Internet is the biggest technological change in education and learning since the advent of the printed book some 500 years ago," claims William Draves.[1] "It is destroying the traditional classroom and replacing it with an even better way to learn and teach."

"[T]he new technology of education, like the automation of other industries," counters David Noble, "robs faculty of their knowledge and skills, their control over their working lives, the product of their labor, and, ultimately, their means of livelihood."[2]

For innovation, it is always the best of times and the worst of times. For one observer, online learning improves the educational experience. For another, online learning destroys it.

In this chapter, I argue that the trouble caused by an innovation like online learning is itself instructive. Debates over the last fifteen years about the efficacy of this new way of teaching and learning have taught us important things about higher education, particularly with respect to our understanding of the relationships between learning environments and learning, cost and quality, profit and mission, and the needs of faculty and the needs of students. One of the benefits resulting from the online learning phenomenon, in my view, has been the extent to which it has forced us to reconsider what we know about the traditional classroom and the traditional institution—and that can only be a good thing. Not only does reflection of this sort help us to recognize and incorporate promising new practices into the work of higher education, it also helps us to better recognize and reinvigorate the critical traditions that have made our system of higher education so successful up to now.

The traditional and virtual classrooms are, after all, only a means to an end, and that end is education. As someone who has studied and taught in the traditional as well as the online classroom, I find the more extreme rhetoric regarding online learning—both at the pro- and anti-online ends of the spectrum—to be largely confusing means with ends. The fact is that, today, one in four students within higher education is enrolled in at least one online course.[3] Nearly one in ten is enrolled in a fully online degree program.[4] I think it's fair to say that our colleges and universities have not been destroyed as a result, but neither have they been changed utterly for the better.

So what has online learning accomplished? And what has it taught us about higher education? To better understand the strengths and limits of online learning, we first need a way of judging the extent to which online learning is in fact innovative. For that reason, I begin this examination of the effects of online learning on higher education by looking at a framework for recognizing innovation. I then provide a brief history of online learning, from its roots in centuries-old correspondence programs up to the present moment when nearly all institutions offer some online courses. Next, I explore some of the critical challenges associated with online higher education today. I then close with a look into the near future and consider how online learning might further change higher education.

WHAT IS INNOVATION?

Given the tremendous growth in online learning over the last decade and a half, we might comfortably hypothesize that this new form of learning has been both disruptive and innovative. But if we're serious about this proposition, we would still need a means of testing the hypothesis. Clayton Christensen's theory of disruptive innovation comes in handy here. In 1997, Christensen authored *The Innovator's Dilemma: When New Technologies Cause Great Firms to Fail*, a business book that first introduced his now-famous concept. More recently, in 2008, Christensen, along with colleagues Michael Horn and Curtis Johnson, adapted the concept to the field of K–12 and higher education in *Disrupting Class: How Disruptive Innovation Will Change the Way the World Learns*.

A "disruptive innovation is *not* a breakthrough improvement," Christensen and his colleagues argue, but one that brings to market "a product or service that actually is not as good as what companies historically had been selling."[5] This new product is by and large inferior to what has traditionally been offered, but it is "affordable and simple to use," and—most importantly—serves new customers. As an example, the authors point to mainframe computers from companies such as IBM, which were expensive and entrenched in the computer market of the late 1970s. Soon, however, companies like Apple came along with relatively inexpensive and inferior computers for a different set of customers altogether—customers who previously had not been in the market for a mainframe computer. It is the interest of these new customers that makes a paradigm-shifting innovation such as the personal computer truly disruptive. The difficulty for firms like IBM under these changing market conditions is that their traditional products are—initially at least—much more profitable than these newer products, and thus it is difficult for leading firms to embrace such innovations. They are too busy trying to serve their current customers and meet their needs for bigger, more powerful computers. They don't have the incentive to make less expensive and easier-to-use products, at least, not until someone else has. By then, it's often already too late. At that point, the inferior product has improved dramatically, and the customers of the older product line begin to switch to the newer product line themselves.

Something similar may have begun unfolding within higher education in the late 1990s, when a number of universities—many of them for-profit—jumped into the online learning market, while other universities hesitated or turned their backs. No doubt this early entrance into the online market helps explain why for-profits, a class of institutions that accounts for approximately 9 percent of all higher education enrollments today, account for a disproportionate 42 percent share of fully online enrollments.[6] Have for-profit universities managed to create a new market? Possibly. Enrollments within a number of the leading for-profit institutions skew heavily toward low-income, minority populations that are often poorly represented within traditional institutions. Indeed, one of the great debates of the online learning era has been whether the technology is creating a new market or cannibalizing an old one. What Christensen and his colleagues argue, however, is that all disruptive innovations start out doing the former and end up doing the latter. Insofar as for-profit institutions were early leaders in online higher education, it may well be that they not only have brought new customers into higher education, but have done so in large measure on the back of a disruptive innovation, a technology that is arguably cheaper to scale and easier for certain students to use than the traditional classroom. Certainly the for-profits have focused on developing a simpler offering, one focused on career utility, and largely unencumbered by amenities such as dormitories, sports stadia, or the recently much maligned rock-climbing wall. The fact is that greater numbers of students than ever before report that they are willing to consider earning a degree online. Perhaps online learning is on its way to becoming a truly disruptive innovation, as its history might suggest.

A BRIEF HISTORY OF ONLINE LEARNING

Web-based online higher education has been with us for a good fifteen years, but it can trace its genealogical roots back many decades through a variety of distance education media—with video, CD-ROM, television, radio, film, and correspondence instruction representing key branches in the distance-delivery family tree.

As with so many things historical and educational in the United States, the city of Boston has a claim to playing a foundational role in distance education—the great-great-grandfather of today's online learning. One Caleb Phillips is reported to have advertised correspondence lessons for mastering the art of shorthand as early as 1728 in the *Boston Gazette*.[7] By 1873, another Boston resident, Anna Ticknor, reportedly established a society dedicated to correspondence instruction for women, which served some ten thousand students over more than two decades.[8] In *Universities in the Marketplace*, former Harvard University president Derek Bok notes that the University of Chicago created its own correspondence school in 1892.[9] (In fact, a number of well-known universities within the United States—the University of Minnesota and the University of Kansas, among them—continue to offer traditional correspondence programs to this day.) By the early twentieth century, however, new technologies, such as film, had entered the field. According to Michael Jeffries, instructional films had proliferated in such great numbers in the first decade of that century that it was possible to put together a catalog of these films as early as 1910.[10]

Each of these media had its evangelists. As Jeffries notes, in 1913, no less a personage than Thomas Edison remarked, "Our school system will be completely changed in the next ten years" as a result of the invention of film. Similarly enthusiastic forecasts have, of course, greeted the introduction of each successive new technology in the early and latter halves of the twentieth century, from radio to video, and all points in between. As we've already seen, the Internet has provided only the latest opportunity for some to foretell the complete revolution of our education system.

Prognostications such as these seem hyperbolic, mostly in retrospect. But they may well nurture the skepticism of some contemporary observers, such as Robert Zemsky and William Massy, who, in 2004, wrote in, "Thwarted Innovation: What Happened to e-learning and Why," that when it comes to online instruction, "the reality never matched the promise—not by a long shot."[11] It is still fair to question whether or not online learning has lived up to its promise, but there can be little doubt that its reach and impact far exceed those of earlier technologies adapted for the purposes of education.

By Eduventures's estimates, fewer than seven thousand students were pursuing degrees via fully online instruction in 1995, that is, earning their degrees exclusively through online learning, without taking any courses in the traditional classroom.[12] By 2008, that number had soared to 1.8 million.[13] According to the Sloan Consortium, a professional association of distance educators and administrators that tracks data on a wider variety of online learning activities, by 2008 more than 4.6 million students were enrolled in at least one online course—a figure that amounts to 25 percent of the total higher education student head count.[14] The Sloan figures look not only at students who are pursuing degrees entirely online, but also at individual course enrollments among students who might be taking the bulk of their courses via the traditional classroom. No other technological advance has extended so widely, so quickly. The growth in online learning has been swift and steep, and along the way it has helped to create some very large institutions.

By the fall of 2009, the for-profit University of Phoenix was enrolling 364,000 students in its online division alone.[15] That's more students than eight NYUs put together. Many of the other leading providers of online-degree programs are likewise for-profit institutions, such as Kaplan University with fifty-seven thousand students, and Walden University with forty thousand students. The nonprofit institution with the greatest number of online students is Liberty University, a private evangelical Christian institution founded by Rev. Jerry Falwell, with approximately forty-five thousand fully online degree seekers—up from approximately three thousand as recently as 2002. The nonprofit public institution with the greatest number of online students is Rio Salado College, a community college with thirty-five thousand fully online students. Of the fifteen institutions with the largest numbers of fully online students, eleven are for-profit.

This level of growth might not have been possible without the help of a small number of pioneers who brought online learning out of the margins and into the mainstream, people like Frank Mayadas of the Sloan Foundation, who has provided seed funding to help institutions such as the University of Illinois, the University of Massachusetts, and many others, go online; Carol Twigg of the National Center for Academic Transformation (NCAT), who has conducted important research on the costs and benefits of online instruction; and academic scholars like Harvard's Chris Dede, who has examined the pedagogical implications of moving teaching and learning online. Institutional decision makers have been further helped by the emergence of professional associations, periodicals, scholarship, new job titles, new institutional departments, and a host of businesses dedicated to helping colleges and universities deliver programs and courses online—from course management systems to enrollment management services to assessment tools. Today, online learning is both big business and a serious academic endeavor. Nearly three hundred years from the emergence of correspondence instruction, we now have far more compelling ways of helping students to learn at a distance, whether the distance be near or far.

For some, however, all this growth is symptomatic of everything that is wrong with online learning. The recently deceased York University social scientist and historian of automation David Noble, writing in his 1998 essay "Digital Diploma Mills, Part II," argues that, "In the wake of the online education gold-rush, many have begun to wonder, will the content of education be shaped by scholars and educators or by media businessmen, by the dictates of experienced pedagogy or a quick profit? Will people enroll in higher educational institutions only to discover that they might just as well have stayed home watching television?"[16]

Despite its title, Noble's influential essay does not actually address the matter of diploma mills. But he is not the only observer of the online learning phenomenon to fail to differentiate fraudulent credentials, online learning, and for-profit institutions—a conflation that has certainly confused the public discourse about online higher education. Diploma mills are typically thought of as organizations that offer degrees in exchange for money rather than as institutions that award diplomas based on demonstrated achievement of learning or the completion of accredited degree programs. While many of the largest providers of online instruction are for-profit, that does not make them diploma mills. Nor does the fact that nonprofit institutions such as Harvard University, NYU, UCLA, or the University of Texas system offer online programs make them diploma mills. Furthermore, as Bok notes, continuing education or extension divisions such as Harvard's "are usually operated on a for-profit basis, especially in private universities where some programs manage to earn millions of dollars each year for their parent institutions."[17] They earn some of those millions by enrolling students online. Does this mean that schools such as Harvard are diploma mills? Surely not.

It is worth noting, furthermore, that diploma mills have a long history themselves and are by no means limited to online institutions. At least as far back as 1876, there was a proliferation of fraudulent degree providers seeking to meet the growing demand for credentials fostered by the Morrill Act of 1862.[18] In more recent times, regulators have worked to set standards for institutions that would prevent such instances of fraud. One key regulation that has had a bearing on the growth of online learning is "the 50 percent rule," a federal statute from 1992 that prevented students enrolled at universities providing more than 50 percent of their courses online from qualifying for Title IV loans. In the later 1990s and early 2000s, under the U.S. Department of Education's Distance Education Demonstration Program, a select set of institutions—including the University of

Phoenix and the North Dakota University System, among others—was allowed to exceed the 50 percent rule, provided those schools submitted to additional regulatory oversight. In 2006, Congress struck down the 50 percent rule, allowing students at institutions with as much as 100 percent of their courses delivered online to access Title IV funds. As a result, some schools, such as Liberty University, grew rapidly. Prior to 2006, the institution's online student head count might have stalled at ten thousand—or at roughly half the school's total size. By 2007, however, one year after the elimination of the regulation, Liberty University had approximately seventeen thousand online students. Just three years further on, that figure had grown nearly threefold to forty-five thousand in the spring of 2010.

In spite of these additional regulatory burdens, strong critiques, and sometimes overinflated expectations, online learning has taken root within U.S. higher education over the last fifteen years, to the point where it is now hard to imagine the future of higher education completely absent of online learning.

A TAXONOMY OF ONLINE LEARNING

There are, of course, many kinds of online learning. In its simplest form, online learning might refer to "lecture capture"—videotaping classroom lectures and posting them on a course Web site so that students might review them after class. In other cases, it might refer to self-paced online courses where students progress through Web site materials on their own, without the aid of any instructor or classmates, typically completing each unit by taking a competency exam. In other cases, online learning refers to cohorts of students going through an online course together, but in an asynchronous fashion, meaning that students can log into the course when it suits them and participate in Web discussions by posting messages at all hours of the day, though they generally have to meet weekly deadlines to stay current with the rest of the group. In more rare cases, online learning can refer to Web-based course experiences that are synchronous—where groups of people log into a Webinar at the same time and participate in live instruction and group interaction, sometimes incorporating elements of two-way video. And there are also cases where Web and classroom components are mixed together, in what is sometimes called "blended" or "hybrid" learning. All of these modes can be applied to a wide variety of educational contexts—from non-credit courses to certificates to undergraduate and graduate degree programs.

Though many typologies have been developed to describe these different forms of online instruction, perhaps the most frequently referenced rubric is that of the Sloan Consortium. In its nomenclature, there are four kinds of course delivery: "traditional," which features no online component; "Web facilitated," in which courses taught in classrooms are augmented by online syllabi and other resources; "blended/hybrid," in which one delivery mode—classroom or online—predominates but where there is a substantial amount of online delivery; and "online," where most of the course is delivered online and there are no face-to-face class meetings.[19]

WHAT THE HIGHER EDUCATION ONLINE LEARNING MARKET LOOKS LIKE TODAY

There is a further important distinction to make among the many varieties of online learning, however. In some cases, students enroll in online courses. In other cases, they enroll in fully online programs. Sloan's figures on the participation rates for online learning encompass both sorts of online learning experiences—courses and programs. Eduventures tracks participation rates within fully online programs only. For many years, the Sloan and Eduventures figures have tracked at a relatively consistent ratio, with roughly equal numbers of students studying in either mode, via individual courses, which predominate slightly, or in fully online degree programs. Because the Sloan numbers include both modes of learning, consistently they are roughly twice the size of the Eduventures numbers.

The estimated Fall 2009 enrollment for fully online programs is over 2.1 million, on the back of a 20 percent year-over-year growth rate.[20] While growth is not as rapid as it was in the late 1990s, when it topped 100 percent annually, it is still significant, and double-digit growth is expected to continue for at least the next several years. By Eduventures's estimates, 20 percent of all students will be in fully online programs by 2014. Today, the top online degree programs are much the same as the top classroom-based degree programs: business, education, information technology, and health care. Disciplines such as nursing and criminal justice were among the fastest growing in 2009—at 45 percent and 41 percent, respectively.[21] In the fall of 2009, there were 835,000 students enrolled in fully online bachelor's programs—representing 8 percent of the overall bachelor's degree market. In the same period, there were 510,000 students enrolled in fully online master's degree programs—representing 24 percent of the overall master's degree market.[22] Thus, while the absolute numbers of bachelor's students studying fully online is larger, the number of students pursuing master's degrees represents a comparatively larger share of the market for that credential.

At the same time, the number of institutions participating in online learning continues to grow, with many colleges and universities moving from dabbling in to scaling up their online efforts. In addition to leading for-profits like the University of Phoenix and niche private, nonprofit institutions like Liberty University, many well-known nonprofit institutions and state systems now have sizable numbers of online students. For example, the estimated online head count for Fall 2009 was thirty-two thousand at University of Maryland University College, the adult learner–focused institution within the Maryland university system; eighteen thousand at UMassOnline; and fifteen thousand at Western Governors University, an online institution developed in collaboration with nineteen western states and launched in 1999 to deliver competency-based bachelor's and master's degrees. Western Governors serves more than fifteen thousand students with programs in business, education, information technology, and health care.

The typical online learner is a white female in her late thirties, married, often with children, employed, and with an annual household income of approximately $65,000. Her primary motivations for study are to prepare for a change of career or to improve skills in order to advance in her current field.[23] There is of course a great variety of online students, from all ethnic and economic groups, of nearly all ages, and with diverse motivations for studying, but this composite profile reflects the most common characteristics of online learners.[24]

When we talk about online learning, we are talking about many kinds of learning and many kinds of students. Yet, as with any instructional mode—whether correspondence, classroom, or otherwise—the many varieties of online learning have their strengths and weaknesses.

CHALLENGES IN ONLINE LEARNING

One of the reasons online learning is often rightly criticized is that it has struggled with the problem of student retention. On the one hand, there is some anecdotal evidence to suggest that successful online learners possess higher levels of self-discipline and drive than those students who don't succeed online. It does, after all, take a certain amount of focus and determination to study after work, once the children are in bed, isolated from your classmates and instructor. On the other, not everybody overcomes these challenges equally successfully, and not all students possess equal amounts of self-discipline and drive.

Although data are hard to come by, it isn't difficult to see the extent of the problem with online retention. For example, a 2004 survey conducted by the Distance Education and Training Council, a national accreditor of distance learning institutions, reported an average graduation rate of 69 percent among the "highest enrollment" programs among its accredited institutions—suggesting that 31 percent of students are not graduating.[25] There are many caveats that we should note with respect to this figure: it averages results across a number of delivery modes and credential levels and omits lower enrollment programs from its analysis, among other issues. But when almost a third of students are not graduating, that's clearly a problem, whatever the nuances of the statistics.

Of course, those who focus on this weakness of online programs often miss the point that retention rates in traditional classrooms are nearly as dismal. According to a 2006 study from the National Center for Education Statistics, the average graduation rate for traditional bachelor's programs was 57 percent—after *six* years.[26] Some argue that this attrition rate has held constant for more than a hundred years.[27]

Critics of online learning also frequently point to quality issues with online programs. This is certainly true along a number of dimensions: not all students are equally prepared to study online; not all institutions task their strongest faculty with delivering courses online; and not every institution enters the online learning market for the right reasons. Some institutions may see it as a cash cow and little more. But one can make a number of the same arguments with respect to the traditional classroom, and one hardly needs statistics to substantiate the claim. As any of us who have ever studied in traditional classrooms can undoubtedly attest, not all faculty are equally capable or motivated, not all institutions are equally resourced, and not all curricula are equally responsive to the needs of the marketplace.

To truly understand what online learning makes possible today and what it may make possible in the future, we need to move beyond the sort of false dichotomy that asserts that one delivery modality is tried and tested and that another is reckless and ineffective. We actually know very little about how well the traditional classroom works as a mode of delivery. In fact, there are many academic leaders, Bok among them, who recognize the potential for online learning to reinvigorate faculty thinking about what does and doesn't work, pedagogically speaking, in both the traditional and online classrooms. As Bok puts it, "The collaborative work of such a team [of faculty, designers, and technicians] in creating a finished product [or online course] will itself provoke more discussion about pedagogical methods than teachers in a university normally experience."[28]

Bok's assertion implies that there is generally too little reflection on pedagogy within the university. Many supporters of online learning agree, arguing that our comfort with the traditional classroom may be based on a romantic rather than realistic view of what transpires there. Edward Goldberg and David Seldin, writing in "The Future of Higher Education in an Internet World," put it this way, "[E]xamples of Internet-based online delivery show great promise in matching and surpassing the quality of traditional face-to-face higher education. If we don't romanticize what really occurs in many of our traditional classrooms, we are faced with some unpleasant realities."[29]

In the spring of 2009, the U.S. Department of Education released a meta-analysis of earlier studies on the quality of online learning in order to assess how students performed in that medium relative to the traditional classroom. Among the report's key findings was the observation that "students who took all or part of their class online performed better, on average, than those taking the same course through traditional face to face instruction."[30] Remarkably, the study received very little press and, less remarkably, hardly ended the debates about the quality of online learning. In fact, just months later, the Association of Public and Land-grant Universities (APLU, formerly known as NASULGC) released a study of its own on faculty perceptions of online learning that illustrates just how unsettled debates about the quality of online courses really are. According to the APLU study, "Over 80 percent of faculty with no online teaching or development experience believe that the learning outcomes for online are 'inferior' or 'somewhat inferior' to those for face-to-face instruction."[31] Given their lack of experience, it's hard to understand what qualifies this group of respondents to judge the efficacy of online learning. Certainly, this must be considered an important bias. A full two-thirds of the faculty surveyed for the study had never taught an online course, so we can only assume they are judging the outcomes of other instructors' students. "Among faculty with online teaching or development experience," the study goes on to explain, "a majority believe that the learning outcomes are as good or better than face-to-face instruction."[32] Here, at least, we have a sample with firsthand experience with online learning, and some basis on which to compare the effects of the two forms on learning.

The study itself is subtitled "The Paradox of Faculty Voices," and thus it is not entirely surprising when, in spite of the doubts some faculty raise about the quality of online outcomes, especially those who have never taught online, a majority of respondents (56 percent) indicate that they have recommended online courses to their students.[33] Why would faculty who claim to believe that online is inferior to classroom instruction actually recommend online courses to their students? It is paradoxical indeed.

The U.S. Department of Education's meta-analysis also found that "instruction combining online and face-to-face elements had a larger advantage relative to pure face-to-face instruction than did purely online instruction"—suggesting that hybrid programs may ultimately achieve some of the best results, perhaps by bringing together the best elements of both modes of delivery: the dynamic interaction and relationship-building benefits of the traditional classroom with the reflective and participatory written dialogue of the online classroom.[34]

Notwithstanding the decade and a half of experience we now have in developing and delivering online learning, the debate about quality is still in some measure a debate between those who haven't taught online, who think it's inferior, and those who have taught online, who think it isn't. And rarely does the debate about quality in online programs encompass a thoughtful discussion about quality in the traditional classroom. Perhaps the growing interest in hybrid delivery can gradually help to bring about something closer to a consensus view on the value of online learning among these—for the moment—still disparate groups of faculty.

The Cost of Online Learning

Another area of continued concern for schools looking to go online, or seeking to scale their online operations, is cost. Some of the earliest and strongest supporters of online learning proclaimed that it would be much cheaper than traditional instruction. But those early promoters of online learning might have supposed that it would replace traditional instruction altogether. Back in the middle and late 1990s, as course management systems became more common on college campuses, many individuals—both on campus and within the business world—believed that online learning would quickly and radically reshape higher education. At the time, one would often hear the claim, for example, that for every Chinese student studying within the

United States, there were four more back in China who wanted to but could not afford the expense of moving overseas. The implication was that online learning would permit U.S. colleges to vastly expand their reach to students in distant markets. Of course, that didn't happen as quickly as some people might have imagined. Furthermore, online learning still has not replaced the traditional classroom, nor has a low-cost online delivery model supplanted a relatively higher-cost classroom delivery model. What has happened, of course, is that all the varieties of course delivery continue to sit side by side, and thus many colleges and universities find themselves adding costs rather than replacing them. Impatience for realizing these promised cost efficiencies is understandable, especially since the conversation about costs has been underway for some time and still continues to raise doubts, for some at least, about the potential for online learning.

A decade ago, the American Council on Education published a volume of essays devoted to this topic—*Dollars, Distance, and Online Education*. One of the volume's authors, Judith Boettcher, works out some not unreasonable estimates for designing Web courses ($40,500 per course) and delivering them over the course of a semester ($184,000 per course).[35] Allowing for some inflation, those numbers in today's dollars would be significant and may well be large enough to keep certain institutions waiting on the sidelines, especially if the investments amount to additional costs on institutional budgets rather than replacement costs.

There is some evidence, however, to suggest that real cost savings are possible via online learning. Twigg's NCAT has provided $200,000 grants to thirty institutions to redesign courses with the aid of technology. The goal is to change what Twigg characterizes as "an outmoded, labor intensive delivery model coupled with an outmoded set of assumptions about the relationship between cost and quality."[36] Among the thirty schools participating in these projects, an average cost savings of 37 percent was realized, Twigg claims.[37] Furthermore, twenty-five of the thirty institutions "showed significant increases in student learning with the remaining five showing learning equivalent to traditional formats."[38] Twigg suggests that colleges and universities can realize the biggest savings and best results by redesigning those courses that touch the most students: "In order to have a significant impact on large numbers of students, an institution should concentrate on redesigning the 25 courses in which most students are enrolled instead of putting a lot of energy into improving quality or cutting costs in disparate small-enrollment courses."[39]

Among the key drivers of cost savings, Twigg points to course management systems, automated assessments, online tutorials, shared resources, staffing substitutions, reduced space requirements, and the consolidation of courses and sections.[40] These cost-reduction strategies can be applied to fully online courses as well as hybrid courses and Web-facilitated courses. As with most things managerial, however, the degree of success depends in many respects on the quality of execution. Of course, not all institutions are equally gifted in this regard.

The Role of Faculty in the Online Classroom

As challenging as these questions of quality and cost may be, they are not necessarily the thorniest issues related to online learning. There are a host of issues related to faculty labor, promotion, tenure, compensation, and ultimately motivation that must continue to be examined. Certainly one of the sources of faculty resistance to online learning is the perceived threat to the autonomy of professors' intellectual work. At the root of this anxiety, however, may be the even more worrying prospect of being cut out of the academic equation altogether.

Noble has been a consistent and outspoken defender of faculty interests and, for that reason, has been one of the most widely cited critics of online learning. Writing in 1998, Noble argues that "universities have acknowledged that faculty, as the authors of courses, have owned their course materials and hence course development . . . But universities are now undertaking to usurp such traditional faculty rights in order to capitalize on the online instruction marketplace . . ."[41] In a subsequent installment of his essay, published in 1999, Noble even considers the possibility that one day actors will replace faculty in online learning.[42]

The thrust of Noble's argument is that faculty are at risk of being made redundant in the online revolution. Bok, writing four years later, observes that Noble's prediction "seems plausible only in universities where the administration is indifferent to whether its professors stay or leave."[43] Still, as the APLU study suggests, faculty in great numbers are still unconvinced of the benefits of online learning, and if many of them have been reluctant to get involved in online learning themselves, the fault is not entirely their own.

Bringing courses online may provide opportunities to think more deeply about pedagogy than usual, but precisely for that reason the work takes time, and many faculty may quite reasonably feel that this work takes them off-task and is poorly aligned with the traditional faculty reward systems. While schools have experimented with numerous forms of incentives, including incremental pay increases, revenue sharing with academic departments, release time, and so on, there are no clear standards for motivating and rewarding faculty to make the necessary investment of time in online learning. And as with most things faculty related, if the investment of time does not contribute to obtaining tenure, then it may not be an investment many tenure-track faculty are likely to make.

HOW INNOVATIVE IS ONLINE HIGHER EDUCATION?

Is online learning a disruptive innovation or just a disruption? By taking another look at Christensen's theory of disruptive innovation, we can try to arrive at an answer. Again, a disruptive innovation involves bringing a simpler and less expensive product to market to serve a new set of customers. Eventually, the disruptive innovation improves in quality and begins attracting customers away from more traditional products until it becomes the leading product category in the market.

Is online learning simpler to use? Yes, in the sense that it is more limited than traditional classroom learning. Few would argue that the traditional classroom doesn't permit great spontaneity, direct personal interaction, and the opportunity to incorporate many modes of instruction at once.

But it also requires students to arrive at campus on time to meet with their classmates and instructors. Online learning is simpler and more limited in the same sense as the personal computer was, relative to the mainframe.

Is online learning less expensive? For some institutions and for many students, it may well be. The ability to study anytime, from anywhere, to continue to work, and to study from home, has a number of economic advantages for students, from avoidance of lost income to reduced travel expenses. Of course, students still have lots of options with respect to tuition pricing at competing institutions, and the mode of education delivery is not the most important determinant of price. Some online programs have premium pricing, while other programs are comparatively affordable. The variation is no different from what we see across a range of traditional campus settings—from community colleges to elite, private universities. It seems reasonable enough to assert that online learning can help students reduce the cost of study. Whether online instruction is less expensive—or more profitable—for many institutions than the traditional classroom is another matter. But then Christensen's theory anticipates that disruptive innovations will produce fewer profits than more mature products, until, that is, the products improve and attract greater numbers of customers. What we have seen already, however, is that for-profit universities, which were among the early leaders in online learning, do not make the same investments in amenities and physical plants as traditional universities, and thus the total cost of operations relative to income can be lower. For virtual universities, like the entirely online Capella University, this is true in the extreme. There is very little physical plant to manage at an entirely online institution.

Does online learning create new customers? This is the most difficult question to answer. A common argument against online learning is that it will draw students away from traditional instruction, rather than attract a new group of students. The closest we may get to answering this question with available data is via proxy. We do know that for-profit universities have growing enrollments and a disproportionate share of online students. If we can accurately assert that for-profit universities have attracted a new group of students, then we might reasonably infer that they have done so, in part at least, with the aid of online learning. That in turn might suggest that online learning has attracted a new set of customers.

Between 1997 and 2007, the United States experienced a net gain of more than 660,000 undergraduate students over the age of twenty-five.[44] For-profit colleges and universities saw an increase of more than four hundred thousand in these students over the same period—or a 77 percent share of the total net gain. According to my Eduventures colleague Richard Garrett, a senior researcher on adult learning and online higher education, the combination of a slight decline over the past decade in the population of twenty-five- to forty-four-year-olds in the United States, along with a 16 percent enrollment growth rate among students aged twenty-five and older in undergraduate programs over the same period, points to new market expansion. "The fact that 77 percent of undergraduate growth among older students took place at for-profit schools, where growth has been primarily online," Garrett argues, "highlights nontraditional institutions and delivery modes as key drivers of expansion."[45] If Garrett is correct, then in online learning we may, in part, be witnessing the creation of a new set of customers. It remains an open question, of course, just how big online learning can become, and whether it will grow sizable enough not only to disrupt but also to supplant traditional forms of learning as the new standard. I noted earlier that by Eduventures's forecasts, we can expect 20 percent of students to be enrolled in fully online programs by 2014. Keeping in mind the consistent ratio between Eduventures's figures for fully online students, and Sloan's figures for fully online and individual course enrollments, it's conceivable that in a few short years as many as four in ten students could be enrolled in some form of online learning.

For their part, Christensen, Horn, and Johnson do not venture a guess as to the future online market share within higher education. They do, however, conjecture that "by 2019, about 50 percent of high school courses will be delivered online"—up from a percentage in the extremely low single digits today.[46] If Christensen and his colleagues are right, then we might well assume that higher education online enrollments over the next ten years will be truly explosive, since higher education is the more mature online learning market.

For the moment, though, it is fair to say that the case for online learning being a truly disruptive innovation in higher education is still somewhat equivocal. This form of learning may be simpler to use and less expensive, at least for some parties. But there is still potential for online learning to push farther in both of these directions. It may also be creating a new set of customers for colleges and universities, but the size of this new customer set is still far smaller than the traditional customer set. It is possible that in the space of a few short years, online learning may come to dominate the way higher education is delivered, but it is difficult for a bystander watching the online learning debate to come away convinced just yet that this new mode of education will inevitably dominate the future of higher education.

This uncertainty about the future of online learning, which permits doubters and believers to talk right past one another, only adds fuel to the occasionally overheated rhetoric about the future of higher education and the place of online learning in it. But while the debates continue, the market is evolving in ways that may point to still more disruptive changes in the way higher education is delivered in the years ahead, both here at home and abroad.

THE UNMAKING OF THE UNIVERSITY?

Let's consider for a moment some potentially game-changing activities currently taking place at the margins of the higher education landscape that might one day affect even more radical change with respect to how students learn and acquire education credentials. In a very simple sense, a college or university is, at its core, three things in combination: faculty, curriculum, and credentials. Students are the consumers of the services resulting from the combination of these three core elements of the institution. At the most basic level, students attend a college or university in order to study curricula with experienced faculty en route to earning credentials. Together, these three elements comprise a value chain, or set of interlocking services and products that are transacted in such a ways as to provide more value in combination than they might independently. Recent and potentially disruptive innovations within higher education, however, suggest that new forms of value might be emerging that could undo the traditional higher education value chain.

Take, for example, MIT's OpenCourseWare initiative (OCW), nearly a decade old, which has brought materials from more than nineteen hundred MIT courses to the Web in the form of syllabi, readings, lecture notes, video, tests, and more. OCW allows individuals from around the world to view these online materials free of charge. Current or prospective students can use these materials as reference tools for exploring new professional opportunities, preparing for courses of study, reviewing basic concepts from a variety of disciplines, and more. Note also the growing interest in competency-based credentials, such as those Western Governors University offers. Western Governors measures the success of its students not in credit hours but by demonstrated mastery of subject matter through competency exams or papers. Finally, look at StraighterLine, a recently launched subscription service that offers self-paced, online general education courses for $99 a month, along with some modest per-course fees. Through its relationship with the American Council on Education's transcript services, Straighter-Line offers a still very small number of customers access to college credits at a fraction of the cost of traditional colleges and universities. Interestingly, StraighterLine emerged as a stand-alone enterprise after being incubated within the online higher education tutoring company SMARTHINKING, suggesting that the establishment of a curriculum company was a natural outgrowth of what is essentially a kind of teaching organization.

Now imagine a scenario in which an individual (the student) somewhere in the world hires an online tutor (the faculty) somewhere else in the world to guide her through freely available online course materials (the curriculum), which might be available anywhere in the world, before taking an online competency-based exam (the credential) that has recognized market value in one or another profession. Would there even be a need for traditional universities in such a scenario?

The answer, in both the near term and the long term, is assuredly yes. But the scale of the need for traditional universities might well diminish over time as growing numbers of students seek more control over the ways they access education and demonstrate their competency in particular disciplines. While such a scenario is, of course, highly speculative, it is not inconceivable.

In fact, in some respects, it is already beginning to happen on a very modest scale. Consider the University of the People, based in Pasadena, California, and founded in 2009 by Shai Reshef, formerly chairman of the Israeli for-profit education company Kidum. University of the People proclaims itself to be "the world's first tuition free online academic institution dedicated to the global advancement and democratization of higher education."[47] According to its Web site, the institution is setting out to provide "universal access to quality, online post-secondary education to qualified students."[48] It takes its name quite literally; it is by design very much of the people, by the people, and for the people insofar as students learn in a peer-to-peer manner or, in other words, largely from one another. The institution draws on open courseware projects from around the world, including MIT's, for its syllabi and course materials, and currently offers unaccredited, nondegree programs in business administration and computer science to 380 students.[49] That is a modest number, to be sure, but University of the People's admissions criteria have recently been characterized as "rigorous" by one reputable higher education news publication.[50] The institution employs five faculty, while another eight hundred volunteers facilitate the courses under the oversight of these few faculty. University of the People is not yet accredited, but it is currently seeking accreditation in the United States, and looking at becoming licensed in the state of California to award degrees.[51]

While actors have not been installed in place of faculty at University of the People, the institution looks not altogether unlike Noble's dark vision for the future of higher education. But where Noble sees faculty losing control over the means of their livelihood, others see increased access to learning and pedagogical improvements that produce better outcomes for students. For example, Christensen and his colleagues point out that one of the pedagogical benefits of the trend toward a more student-centered approach to learning is that "assessments and individualized assistance can be interactively and interdependently woven into the content-delivery stage, rather than tacked on as a test at the end of the process."[52] Perhaps decentering the faculty member as the key means of educating students is not an entirely bad thing.

Still, we should not overlook the power of teachers, and many faculty are unlikely to accept this sort of marginalization without a fight. Christensen anticipates this problem and acknowledges that—particularly in the K–12 environment—teacher unions wield considerable power. But he and his colleagues argue that "when disruptive innovators begin forming user networks through which professionals and amateurs—students, parents, teachers—circumvent the existing value chain and instead market their products directly to each other . . . the balance of power in education will shift."[53] This might well be an apt description of University of the People, which works around the traditional university business model and puts professionals and amateurs in conversation with one another to meet the needs of an emerging set of new customers.

Clearly, higher education innovations such as online learning promise or threaten, depending upon your point of view, to create new winners and losers in the marketplace. And while the unmaking of the traditional university may pose problems for institutions that resist innovation, it will also create opportunities for those institutions that embrace these new developments. It remains to be seen who precisely the winners and losers will be, but some observers believe that traditional universities may fall into the latter camp. In their book *New Players, Different Game*, William Tierney and Guilbert Hentschke (both authors elsewhere in this volume) ask, "Who is better situated to take advantage of a disruptive technology—the traditional organization with a defined system for how to conduct activities, with a significant portion of the organization believing how it operates is satisfactory, or the investor-backed start-up company that has no set procedures and whose leadership seeks to expand markets in as aggressive manner as possible?"[54] The question, in this case, is largely rhetorical. While the authors admit that customers might not inevitably find the product of the investor-backed start-up palatable, they note that "so far the opposite seems to have been the case."[55] For this reason, they anticipate a scenario in which for-profit institutions are better equipped to maintain and increase their leadership position in the online learning market.

By the same token, Bok argues that traditional universities will do themselves no favors by sitting out the game altogether. "If universities do not enter the field, refusing to cater to consumer and vocational tastes," he writes, "other providers, such as the University of Phoenix, will do the job for them . . . On the other hand, if universities compete, any profits they earn can presumably go to finance precisely those precious forms of teaching and research that cannot be supported by the marketplace alone."[56]

Of course, by conceiving of online learning as being responsive to "vocational tastes," Bok may be missing a larger and deeply academic opportunity. Online learning futurist William Draves makes the case, in his book *Nine Shift*, that far from narrowing the curriculum to a slim band of vocationally oriented programs, online learning might actually resuscitate interest in once-obscure fields of study. A typical university today might teach as many as two thousand subjects (think of MIT's nineteen hundred OCW courses), but there is an opportunity through online learning to vastly increase access to learning materials by syndicating courses across institutions. "The result will be that the number of subjects offered will dramatically increase to 10,000 or so subjects," Draves writes. "Courses that have too little interest on a single campus, or no expert faculty, will be able to be offered. The religion of the Druids, seventeenth century French poetry, the life of Adlai Stevenson, the care of mango trees, and thousands of other legitimate academic subjects will become available."[57] In Draves's view, online learning will succeed in dominating the market not because of the convenience it offers, but simply because it has the potential to offer a better way of learning, one that is cognitively richer and more intellectually expansive than the typical college or university campus experience of today. In the long run, it could be that the unmaking of the contemporary university will result in the establishment of something even better.

LOOKING AHEAD

Innovation is troubling. It promises new benefits, but threatens our security and challenges our traditions. As such, it can provoke pessimism and optimism in equal measure. Disruptive innovations change the way we get things done and along the way can force us to undergo a process of defamiliarization, where the well understood becomes strange and uncertain. That's why many organizations fail in the face of innovation. They can't adapt quickly enough to the new values of the changing market. Their worldview becomes calcified, and they miss the signs of change. But defamiliarization has a positive aspect as well. In the world of online learning, the challenges of bringing the classroom online force us to rethink matters of pedagogy we may have begun to take for granted. Online learning can teach us a lot about higher education, such as the assumptions we in the higher education community make about the relation between cost and quality, as Twigg points out, or the assumptions we make about the relation between the profit motive and the work of educating, as Bok points out, or the assumptions we make about the values of faculty and the values of students, as Rob Jenkins points out.

Who is Rob Jenkins? He's an associate professor of English at Georgia Perimeter College. In a recent issue of the *Chronicle of Higher Education*, Jenkins authored a commentary called "A Technophobe's Guide to Managing Online Courses." Jenkins admits to disliking online learning, even though his administrative responsibilities have tasked him with managing his institution's online programs. Like many faculty who are skeptical of online learning, Jenkins has never taught online. "I've never gone bungee jumping, either," he observes wryly, "but I'm pretty sure I wouldn't like it."[58] At the start of his work managing online programs, Jenkins did what he could to slow the growth of these courses. "I became a chair in the mid

1990s, at the onset of what we might call the online revolution," he writes. "Back then I argued not against distance learning—that would have been career suicide—but at least for a more measured approach, as my campus (like every other) raced to offer more and more online courses, mostly for financial, not pedagogical, reasons." Jenkins felt pushed to operate in a world he did not personally want to live in—one in which he was "expected not only to function," as he puts it, "but lead. Since then," he adds, "I've learned a great deal, not least of which is that I might have been wrong about online courses." Why? Because colleagues he respects have embraced online learning, and because, as he himself observes, "whatever I might think of online courses, they are loved by lots of students."

There's an old saying that elementary teachers teach out of love for their students, high school teachers teach out of love for their subjects, and college and university teachers teach out of love for themselves. Certainly, online learning has exacerbated the long-standing tensions between faculty-centric and student-centric views of the purpose of the institution. But it is a tension that will be resolved when more faculty like Jenkins realize that the choice is constructed less as an either/or proposition than as a both/and proposition. Until then, higher education institutions will continue to struggle with these fundamental tensions: whether they must contain all of the basic components of the educational value chain or need only specialize in one or a few of them; whether they should turn their backs on commercialization or take a more market-driven (some would say market responsive) approach to their customers; and whether they will limit growth or pursue a mission of access.

It pays to be skeptical of dichotomies such as these. Profound advances can be made by combining the best of the old and the new ways. "So far technology has hardly changed formal education at all," wrote Bill Gates recently. "But a lot of people, including me, think this is the next place where the Internet will surprise people in how it can improve things—especially in combination with face-to-face learning."[59]

Useful innovations, disruptive innovations, teach us not only about our habits and routines, but about our capacities to invent and improve, as well as our capacities to take advantage of the opportunities presented by the new, while being guided by the values of the past and the present. I have taught in traditional classrooms, computer labs, and online classrooms. I have earned academic credentials the old-fashioned way, over semesters sitting in classrooms, and the newfangled way, over weeks studying online. Both modes of teaching and learning have much to offer, and each mode has its limitations and challenges. In the years ahead, it may well be that the most effective form of higher education for a great many students will be the one that combines the best elements of the traditional classroom with the innovations of online learning. Like everyone else, I'm interested in seeing what the future of higher education looks like, and I'm curious to see what we learn along the way.

8

The Mayo Clinic of Higher Ed

Kevin Carey

ON A COLD FRIDAY AFTERNOON in February, Chelsea Griffin walked through the fading winter light of downtown Rochester, Minnesota, past old-style restaurants and stores filled with balloons and flowers, into the marble-clad halls of the Mayo Clinic.

An elevator and staircase led her to a windowless laboratory, with a stainless steel sink on her left and cabinets filled with medical equipment on her right. In the center of the room, lying prone on a table, was the corpse of a middle-aged man. His chest was split open and his ribs were splayed to either side. Griffin put on a white laboratory coat and pulled a pair of blue latex gloves over her hands. As a group of students watched, she reached into the cavity and pulled out the heart, feeling the weight of it in her wrist and arm. Her index finger traced a path to a spot just above the right ventricle. She knew this part of the internal human anatomy better than any other. Twice, she had undergone surgery to repair a hole there that threatened her life.

The thought of it brought her up short, and her eyes welled with tears. For a moment, her perspective shifted up and out. She saw herself, standing in a lab coat with a stranger's heart in her hands. This, she thought, is where I'm meant to be.

And yet, if it were up to the norms and conventions of American higher education, Griffin wouldn't have been there. She is not a doctor or a nurse, or an intern or a researcher or even an upperclassman studying pre-med.

She's an eighteen-year-old college freshman. Instead of sitting bored in the back of a cavernous lecture hall or starting another weekend bacchanal, she's been getting the kind of education that most undergraduates only dream about: modern facilities, small classes taught by tenure-track professors, a cutting-edge interdisciplinary curriculum, and access to the best minds of science and industry. Instead of reading about human anatomy, Griffin sees it firsthand.

A GROUNDBREAKING APPROACH

In a competitive economy, many students need an education like this. Unfortunately, most people like Griffin aren't getting one. The small colleges that specialize in high-quality teaching tend to be exclusive and cripplingly expensive. Meanwhile, the public universities that educate most students are in crisis. Rocked by steep budget cuts, they're increasing class sizes, cutting faculty salaries, and turning away tens of thousands of qualified students. Many of those universities offered a mediocre, impersonal education to begin with. Now they're getting worse, and nobody seems to know how to stop the bleeding.

But here's the thing about Griffin: she isn't enrolled at an ancient private liberal arts college or an exclusive, wealthy university. Her institution admitted its first undergraduates less than a year ago. And while nearly every other public university in America is retrenching, Griffin's university is expanding, under exactly the same financial conditions. And what will the taxpayer cost of this expansion be? Nothing at all.

Griffin's school has an unremarkable-sounding name but a groundbreaking approach to education. She is a student at the University of Minnesota–Rochester (UMR), a campus based on the idea that most of what we know about how a public university should operate is wrong, and that it can be done better, for modest amounts of money, right away. States across the nation could solve many of their higher education problems by replicating this effort, if they can overcome the entrenched interests of existing colleges and their own failure of imagination.

Understanding what UMR is requires first understanding what it is not: an institution built in the classic mold. That model was established in the late nineteenth century, based on the German research university, and revolves around the individual scholar. In the mind's eye, we still see men like Newton, hunched over a desk in the stone aeries of Trinity College, revealing the universe through sheer force of cognition. That kind of individuality goes hand in hand with autonomy. And autonomy, more than anything else, has defined the way higher education works today.

Ideas like these were on Stephen Lehmkuhle's mind when he first arrived in Rochester in 2007. Tall and balding with a genial affect and a neat moustache, Lehmkuhle was then a senior administrator in the University of Missouri system. He was also, crucially, a trained experimental psychologist. He had thought deeply about the human brain and the vast web of neural links that turn a mass of individual cells into glorious, high-functioning complexity. Yet when he looked around his university, he saw instance after instance of unmade connections between the autonomous components of organizations that were far more atomized than they needed to be.

Lehmkuhle was competing to be the first chancellor of UMR. While the University of Minnesota had offered classes to Rochester's hundred thousand residents since the 1960s, a blue-ribbon commission convened by Governor Tim Pawlenty recommended in 2006 to expand those operations into an official fourth branch of the university, joining branches Duluth, Morris, Crookston, and the flagship campus in the Twin Cities of Minneapolis and St. Paul.

The commiion envisioned that UMR would focus exclusively on graduate programs in health, taking advantage of the world-famous Mayo Clinic's expertise. But Lehmkuhle wanted to do more. He proposed adding a new bachelor's degree of health sciences, a novel program that would operate unlike anything else in the system. In September 2007, he got the job.

Lehmkuhle's first challenge was deciding where to put the university. College campuses tend to evolve over time into miniature city-states, with their own churches, police forces, concert halls, and security walls, cut off from surrounding communities. Lehmkuhle wanted his campus to be an integral part of Rochester. Plus, he didn't have a lot of money to work with. Fortunately, Rochester was eager for a new university to create jobs and liven up a city center whose restaurants and stores mostly served elderly visitors to Mayo. Lehmkuhle set up shop on the third and fourth floors of a shopping center in the heart of downtown, where a food court used to be. The city kicked in $11 million to help him build offices, classrooms, and laboratories.

Lehmkuhle then struck up a partnership with the city's biggest employer. Under the terms of an unusual agreement between UMR and Mayo, the clinic's doctors and researchers are guest lecturers in UMR health science classes. UMR students have access to research laboratories, a ten-thousand-square-foot medical simulation center complete with robotic surgical mannequins, and other facilities—including Mayo's cadaver lab. That's how Griffin and a small class of fellow students ended up spending time with dead people on a Friday afternoon.

Next, Lehmkuhle had to hire professors and decide how to organize their work. Traditional universities isolate their faculty in academic departments that often view one another as strange denizens of another planet at best, outright enemies at worst. Departments also accumulate administrative structures—chairs, vice chairs, and so on—over time. Lehmkuhle didn't have enough money to pay for vice chairs, and, anyway, he wanted professors from different disciplines to work together. The solution: no departments.

Traditional universities also separate teaching from research. These functions are not just disconnected, but often antagonistic as well. Many professors vying for tenure in the publish-or-perish system are openly encouraged to neglect their students in favor of scholarship. Lehmkuhle resolved this tension by making tenure at UMR contingent on three factors: teaching, research in the academic disciplines, and research *about teaching*. For UMR professors, applying their analytic powers to their own teaching practice would be a standard part of the job.

Having connected the university to the community, disciplines to disciplines, and teaching to research, Lehmkuhle also wanted to connect students to one another. Decades of academic studies have found that sticking freshmen in passive, impersonal lectures is educational malpractice. Most students learn best when they're actively engaged in dialogue and collaboration with faculty and fellow students. UMR classrooms were to be small and intimate, with no "front" from which professors could lecture. Instead of facing a teacher, students would face one another, around tables in teams of four or five.

UMR AND THE MAYO WAY OF MEDICINE

Rochester turned out to be a particularly hospitable place for Lehmkuhle's vision. The brothers William and Charles Mayo, who founded their clinic in the late nineteenth century, pioneered the concept of group practice, where doctors collaborate with an emphasis on diagnosis and prevention. The clinic also has a thriving medical school with a focus on hands-on education. When Lehmkuhle looks out his office window at the glass skyways that link the university to the Mayo Clinic buildings two blocks away, he sees the physical manifestation of a philosophical connection between the two institutions.

UMR began offering graduate health sciences programs in 2008. But getting final approval for the undergraduate program took time, leaving UMR with only a matter of months to scramble and recruit candidates for the 2009–2010 school year. It tracked down students who had already been accepted to the main Twin Cities campus and offered them the chance to be both subjects and co-designers of a novel higher education experiment. To Lehmkuhle's relief, a healthy crop of students were up for the challenge. Last fall, fifty-seven enrolled in the inaugural class.

To oversee academics, Lehmkuhle brought in Claudia Neuhauser, an applied mathematician with a PhD from Cornell. The author of papers such as "An Explicitly Spatial Version of the Lotka-Volterra Model with Interspecific Competition," Neuhauser might have seemed like an unusual choice to guide students only a few months removed from high school. But she is also the author of *Calculus for Biology and Medicine*, a well-known undergraduate textbook designed precisely to help health science majors learn complex math. She understands the importance of building connections between disciplines.

I met Neuhauser on a Monday morning in early March, after crossing a skyway from my hotel and riding an escalator near a LensCrafters and a knitting supply shop. She explained the parallels between the UMR educational philosophy and the Mayo way of medicine. "They call it personalized health care," she said. "We call it personalized learning." Both processes require diagnosis. Who is this person, exactly? What makes them tick? And diagnosis is only as good as the information to which it's applied.

At traditional universities, nearly all of the information generated about teaching and learning is discarded. Tests, papers, homework, class projects, and the record of day-to-day interaction between students and teachers disappear; only course syllabi and final grades remain. Lehmkuhle calls this the Las Vegas approach to higher education: "What happens in the classroom stays in the classroom."

UMR captures much of that information. It begins by breaking each course into two- to three-week segments called "learning objects," which are electronically tagged in a way that allows them to be matched in a database to student records, course materials, group assignments, draft papers, and exams. (The UMR campus was designed as a paperless environment, and students are issued identical Lenovo ThinkPad laptops, which they seem to keep two feet in front of their faces at all times.) This information will be stored in an electronic database that professors will analyze in conducting the learning research they need to get tenure. That research, in turn, will improve their ability to refine new teaching strategies. By analyzing the relationship between historical student learning patterns and specific educational techniqes, UMR may discover that students who struggle with certain concepts benefit from some learning environments but not others. Such insights will allow UMR to personalize the college experience for each student.

There are strong parallels in the health care industry, where Mayo and the Veterans Health Administration have led the way in using electronic medical records to help doctors work together and analyze huge archives of medical data. Neuhauser also oversees UMR's graduate biomedical informatics and computational biology program, where students apply large-scale statistical analysis to medical data, working in partnership with Mayo and Rochester's second-biggest employer, IBM.

LEARNING AT UMR

For the next few hours, I hopped from one class to the next: first writing, then organic chemistry, then biology. As the day wore on, something unusual started to become clear. Each professor came from a different academic background and ostensibly taught a different subject. But they were all, in different ways, talking about the same thing.

For instance, during a writing seminar I attended, the term *creatine* came up. Creatine is a naturally occurring organic acid that athletes take in extra doses to build muscle. Later that day, the term showed up a biology class, in which Professor Rob Dunbar noted that there are reasons to believe that ingesting large amounts of creatine can reduce muscle fatigue. But how might experiments testing the proposition be designed, he asked? The class proceeded to work this out as a group.

Everyone at UMR, it turns out, was talking about creatine. Students synthesized it in chemistry, studied its effects on muscle fatigue in biology, learned how to interpret those studies in statistics, pondered the ethics of using artificial performance-enhancing substances in philosophy, and developed papers combining these perspectives in writing. Nobody worked alone, because every student at UMR takes the same structured curriculum for their first two years.

While Griffin wants to be a cardiologist, other UMR students will be able to use their health science degrees to enter a range of jobs: research scientist, hospital administrator, small-town doc with a general practice. People don't need to know much about creatine to succeed in those careers. What they need is to be able to understand things *like* creatine from the perspective of biology, chemistry, statistics, and philosophy, all at once. They need to be able to develop and improve those ideas within small, close-knit teams of other people. And they need to be able to communicate that knowledge, in writing, to the rest of the world.

This represents perhaps the most foundational of all the connections that Lehmkuhle and his colleagues have been steadily knitting together in Rochester: that between facts and ideas. Traditional college instruction—the lecture—is largely a process of orally transmitting facts from the brain of a teacher to a student. It's a tremendously inefficient method—even harmful. UMR chemistry professor Rajeev Muthyala points to research finding that undergraduates often finish lecture-based introductory science classes with less expertise than when they started. They get *worse*.

That's because there is a crucial difference between the way novices and experts learn. Experts have a much greater ability to retain information, because they incorporate new facts into complex structures of interconnecting concepts and ideas. For an expert wrestling with large questions of, say, political economy, a data point like the failure of the Smoot-Hawley Tariff Act of 1930 is interesting and significant for suggesting how protectionism can backfire. But a novice often doesn't know what do with new facts, where to put them, or how to connect them to other facts. Something like Smoot-Hawley is nothing more than a name and a date. Simply put, a lot of new information bounces off a novice's brain for want of a place to fit.

This is the reason that so many sophomores at traditional universities fail organic chemistry, says Muthyala, who teaches the class at UMR. Organic chemistry is usually taught "as if it's completely disconnected from other disciplines," he says, and in many schools it's notoriously used to cull weak students in their sophomore year.[1] But UMR students, who enroll with solid but not earth-shattering ACT scores (typically around 24, or 1100 on the SAT), all take organic chemistry as freshmen and are passing at unusually high (85 percent to 90 percent) rates.

I saw Muthyala's approach to teaching in action when I attended one of his classes. For more than an hour, Muthyala stayed in motion, moving in a 270-degree arc around the room, alternating between short explanations of the material and friendly interrogation. Questions and diagrams popped up on wall-mounted projection screens as students used their laptops to examine data on spreadsheets and flip back and forth between charts on PowerPoint slides. Some pulled portable whiteboards down from racks and began scrawling out equations with green markers as other members of their team pointed and offered suggestions. "Can we rule out an ester unambiguously?" Muthyala asked at one point. "No, we cannot. Make sure you read up on proton NMR spectroscopy before you come to the next class." This went over my head, but the students seemed to understand completely. And I did understand the term *creatine* when it was mentioned. After all, it had come up in another class already.

THE UMR MODEL

The UMR experience is highly structured at the beginning, a marked contrast to universities that hand freshmen a huge course catalog and expect them to fend for themselves. UMR faculty from different disciplines carefully map out the sequences of their courses together, coordinating topic areas week by week. But the curriculum is much *less* structured at the end. The plan is for these undergraduates to have a senior year devoted entirely to a personalized "capstone experience" like getting an allied health certificate at Mayo, taking graduate classes, or working with professors on new research.

The groundbreaking UMR model could not have been created at an established college or university. Lehmukuhle was only able to make all the right connections, hire all the right people, and build the right organizational culture by starting a new university from scratch.

Traditional research universities defend their departments, vice chairs, and classically tenured professors on the grounds that autonomy is vital for research. The point is arguable, but also largely irrelevant. According to the Carnegie Foundation, there are only 167 public research universities in America, out of nearly seventeen hundred public colleges and universities nationwide. Only sixty-three qualify as top-tier research institutions. The vast majority of students enroll somewhere else.

State lawmakers don't think much about creating new universities, because they can barely afford the existing ones. But new universities are expensive only if you build them using the old model. When the Minnesota legislature signed off on the new Rochester campus, it increased the University of Minnesota's annual budget by $6.3 million. Otherwise, it has provided no additional funding for UMR, and it doesn't intend to. The cost of UMR's planned expansion to fifteen hundred students by 2015 will come entirely from student tuition, which is currently the standard University of Minnesota rate of $11,200 per year.

Five years from now UMR is scheduled to receive a little over $5,000 per student from the taxpayer, which is roughly one-third of what the flagship Twin Cities campus receives today. Even after discounting spending on research, the flagship is still two to three times costlier than UMR. And, if UMR eventually grows to a modest size of three thousand to five thousand students, it will be the most cost-effective public university in the state, by far. That's because existing universities have to pay for things and ideas from an earlier time.

Take Winona State University, which is fifty-three miles due east of Rochester on the shores of the Mississippi River. Although it's not a research university, it has dutifully divided its faculty among five colleges and scores of departments, seventeen in the College of Liberal Arts alone. It also takes a traditional approach to buildings. In the late 1990s, Winona decided to erect a handsome new brick and stone library on the corner of the central quad. The facility holds two hundred twenty thousand volumes, employs seventeen people, and sports a terrazzo floor inlaid with images of the Mississippi River and quotes from Bob Dylan. In a nod to information technology, Winona added wi-fi and included a bank of computer terminals and comfortable chairs. The cost to Minnesota taxpayers: $17.7 million, plus annual expenses for maintenance and the seventeen people.

UMR took more or less the same approach in building its library, except without the brick, stone, floors, tile, books, engravings, people, or $17.7 million. UMR's library consists of wi-fi, one librarian, a bank of computer terminals, and comfortable chairs. Students who need to borrow physical books get them through the University of Minnesota's interlibrary loan.

UMR's entire print collection fits in a small metal bookcase, the type you can buy at Office Depot for $129. The bottom two shelves are empty.

Instead of living in subsidized dorms, UMR students rent privately owned apartments at a group rate negotiated by the university. Instead of working out at the kind of elaborate fitness center that many universities have built in recent years, students go to the YMCA, which organizes intramural sports. UMR is exclusively in the teaching and learning business. It turns out that if that's the only business you're in, you can do it very well for relatively small amounts of money.

Traditional universities complain that they need expensive amenities to compete for today's entitled, hedonistic student. But the example of UMR suggests that students are quite happy to have something more modest. While UMR students have parties and take part in extracurricular activities—including a competitive ballroom dance team and something called "boot hockey," which involves boots instead of skates and brooms instead of sticks—the students take their work seriously and stay busy. I asked every student I could find how much they work on academics outside of class. The typical answer: thirty to thirty-five hours a week. According to the nonprofit National Survey of Student Engagement, only 6 percent of freshmen at the biggest, most prestigious research universities work that hard. Nearly a third work ten hours or less. Eighteen-year-olds are highly sensitive to expectations and organizational culture. If you give them a lot of work and commensurate support, they'll do it. If you give them little work, a lot of free time, and an elaborate social infrastructure centered on alcohol consumption, they'll react accordingly.

A NEED FOR INNOVATIVE LOW-COST PUBLIC UNIVERSITIES

We need more schools like UMR, public universities dedicated to teaching and designed from the ground up with the latest technological developments and research findings in mind. Existing universities cannot and will not provide this. They won't be bulldozing their libraries, disbanding the champion basketball team, radically overhauling tenure, or demoting department chairs anytime soon. Most are doing something vaguely UMR-like—some interdisciplinary courses here, some professors experimenting with technology there. But this is a case where half measures are all but indistinguishable from no measures. Only new universities will do. Therefore, states should start building large numbers of new, innovative, highly focused, low-cost public universities.

Every state has at least one public research institution with a well-known brand name and the accreditation needed to open new branches right away. University systems can also provide support services cheaply using existing infrastructure. For instance, UMR contracts with the main Twin Cities campus to handle student financial aid applications, purchasing, and other administrative tasks.

Like Rochester, local governments will be eager to lend a financial hand. Municipalities routinely spend millions subsidizing shopping malls and condo developments. Why not subsidize universities, which bring culture, status, and prestigious jobs? A city the size of New York could easily build ten or fifteen new UMR-sized universities throughout the five boroughs, each focusing on academic specialties that match the city's economic strengths in medicine, finance, media, culture, manufacturing, and international trade. Cities like Chicago could provide better options for students mired in chronically failing public universities such as Chicago State.

Big cities aren't the only potential location for such schools, either. Archer Daniels Midland, based in Decatur, Illinois, ranks twenty-seventh on the *Fortune* 500 and employs legions of scientists, chemists, and genetic engineers. Yet the only public higher education institution in Decatur is a community college. Many cities and towns across the country have economic and cultural strengths around which they could design new public universities.

Students and faculty will flock to these institutions. Lehmkuhle was initially worried about recruiting students to an unknown university in a flat, cold city filled with people who eat dinner at 4:30 in the afternoon. Instead, nearly four hundred students applied for a hundred twenty-five slots in the 2010 entering class. He was also concerned about finding good faculty, particularly given the unusually high expectations for teaching. Instead, it turns out that a lot of people *like* teaching and are frustrated by traditional universities that care only about research.

The only real barrier to creating new public universities will be the objections of the existing ones. One reason it took so long to take the obvious step of opening a health-focused university in Rochester was push back from existing southeastern Minnesota universities like Winona and Minnesota State University, Mankato. Many existing universities see a threat from efficient, high-value institutions like UMR. And they should. Schools like UMR will put pressure on traditional institutions with bloated cost structures that have contributed to decades of skyrocketing tuition.

Indeed, there is plenty of ferment in higher education right now. It's just all happening in the for-profit sector. Venture capitalists are buying up bankrupt private colleges and turning them into for-profit money machines. Corporate giants like the University of Phoenix now serve hundreds of thousands of students online. While many for-profits are at the cutting edge of higher education innovation, others are shamelessly ripping students off. New public universities would combine the best of both worlds—the kind of innovation happening in the private sector wedded to public values and purpose.

PERSONALIZED LEARNING

At the end of his chemistry class, Muthyala was telling me about "personalized learning," when a young woman with spiky black hair and a small pink nose stud walked past us, an open laptop cradled in her elbow, and said, "Ooh, *personalized learning*," with a smile as she walked out. I waited a moment until she'd left. "Do you think she doesn't buy it?" I asked. "I'd be surprised," Muthyala replied, with a look of concern. "She's one of my best students."

Her name, I later learned, is Jessica Gascoigne, and she likes personalized learning just fine. She doesn't have the natural self-confidence of young people who attend famous universities as a matter of birthright, but she's humming through organic chemistry and is one of only three freshmen who tested out of calculus before starting college. She's wanted to be a doctor ever since she and her father, a dairy equipment salesman, began sitting on the couch together Thursday nights to watch *ER*.

For Gascoigne, the flagship University of Minnesota campus in the Twin Cities seemed monstrously large, and private St. Olaf College was far too expensive. So she commutes twenty-four miles each way to UMR from her three-thousand-citizen hometown of Zumbrota (motto: "The only Zumbrota in the world"). She describes her typical weekend as "studying, and cleaning my apartment," which she shares with her roommate, a hairdresser. This explains the spiky hair.

America's system of old universities has always done a good job of educating a small percentage of talented and well-off students. But the old system is ill-equipped for Gascoigne and Griffin and hundreds of thousands of other students who need universities that are designed to help them in the way that UMR helps its students. For now, the University of Minnesota's new Rochester campus is an interesting outlier. If more people can see the true potential of its newness, it will be much more.

Conclusion

Ben Wildavsky, Andrew P. Kelly, and Kevin Carey

MUST UNIVERSITIES CHANGE? How might they change? Can they change in significant ways on a broad scale? The chapters in this volume have offered a range of answers to these questions, not identical by any means. But their consistent thrust is this: change is necessary, at least for many institutions. Change is also inevitable, and plenty of examples show that it's possible. Yet change is difficult and complicated, especially at scale. The real challenge ahead will be how to overcome the ubiquitous disincentives for change outlined in the previous pages. Only then can innovation begin to take hold in American universities—and spread.

In the first chapter, Dominic Brewer and William Tierney succinctly laid out the imperative for innovation in U.S. higher education, a mixture of demographic, economic, and technological forces. Yet Brewer and Tierney set a less-than-encouraging tone about prospects for reform, citing an array of obstacles. Many colleges and universities have failed to learn from innovations that have become routine in other service industries: these range from intelligent use of new information technology and re-thinking of rigid labor roles to focusing on a central educational goal, thus avoiding the mission creep that has too often characterized postsecondary institutions. Throughout U.S. higher education, it seems, incentives to innovate vary enormously and—often because of public policy barriers—are frequently too weak to induce colleges and universities to break out of the straitjacket of standardization.

Still, despite all the barriers to innovation that exist, these chapters reveal many examples of creative practices that have emerged within traditional universities, in brand-new postsecondary institutions, and through an array of new providers that have entered the higher education market. Indeed, some of the most promising initiatives are cited in multiple chapters. Several authors point to the work of the National Center for Academic Transformation (NCAT), which relies on technology and peer instruction to redesign introductory college courses, lowering their cost and improving academic outcomes. Carnegie Mellon's Open Learning Initiative has become similarly influential; it creates online courses that draw on cognitive psychology to tailor lessons to individual learners, both independent students and those studying in traditional institutions.

Perhaps unsurprisingly, innovation has also thrived at universities that were designed from scratch as test beds for serving students in new ways. One oft-cited example: Western Governors University, created by nineteen mostly Western states, which has attempted a paradigm shift. Moving away from the model of granting credit for seat-time in traditional classrooms, it tests students to see which subjects they have already mastered, then offers targeted online classes that allow them to complete degrees (typically in career-oriented subjects) on an accelerated timetable. Another brand-new university, the Harrisburg University of Science and Technology, is highlighted by Jon Marcus as a promising exception to universities' historical resistance to change. The central Pennsylvania college is emphatically student-centered, with no traditional academic departments and no tenure for professors.

Similarly, in his discussion of how to improve teaching productivity, William Massy cites the University of Minnesota–Rochester (UMR), which employs a large number of instructors devoted to teaching and applies cognitive and behavior science, together with a heavy dose of technology, to its pedagogical mission in the health sciences. In a full-length study of UMR, Kevin Carey suggests that it provides even broader lessons for the entire postsecondary sector, arguing that the new college's ability to serve students much more effectively at a relatively lower cost is paradigmatic of the possibilities for reinvention of public universities.

Guilbert Hentschke and Peter Stokes provide still more examples of fresh approaches to postsecondary learning in their chapters on the extraordinary growth of for-profit and online learning. The two are often intertwined, of course, because industry leaders like the University of Phoenix and Kaplan University offer some or all of their degrees online. Moreover, beyond the for-profit sector, traditional universities are beginning to include some online learning in their menu of course options. It would surely not have been imaginable as recently as forty years ago that more than one out of every four students would have taken at least one class delivered through distance learning. Indeed, Stokes suggests that online education likely meets Harvard School of Business professor Clayton Christensen's definition of disruptive innovation—both creating new markets and cannibalizing old ones.

Despite all this activity, however, the question the authors address both implicitly and explicitly remains: why have these frequently discussed innovations failed to spread more widely and quickly within the traditional sector where most students are still enrolled? As Brewer and Tierney declare at the outset of their chapter, "In order for successful innovations to drive gains in productivity, they not only must be created, but must be adopted by others." But from using new technology to reshaping course offerings to rethinking how professors are deployed, traditional universities have been slow to experiment with new ideas and slower still to adopt them. Even the well-regarded course-redesign work of an organization such as NCAT remains limited to about sixty universities around the United States.

Notwithstanding the willingness of new institutions to innovate, brand-new campuses just aren't established very often. And while the universe of for-profit postsecondary institutions is expanding rapidly (despite growing regulatory scrutiny), the sector's top-down management and curriculum design, coupled with a strong outcomes-focus, remains alien to most traditional universities. Online learning, too, is frequently discussed but less frequently relied on as more than an adjunct to, or transmission vehicle for, conventional instruction. Hybrid models show promise, as with the partnership between the University of Southern California's school of education and 2tor, Inc., the online institution created by Princeton Review founder John Katzman. For now, though, such arrangements remain rare.

How might innovation spread more quickly? Most fundamentally, institutions must have incentives to actively seek out promising innovations, and then invest the time and resources necessary to experiment with them. This is partly a question of providing colleges with practical tools—like the productivity measures Massy describes—to assess what they are currently doing and how they might do it better. But Massy reminds us that such guidance is unlikely to drive real change without the support and encouragement of campus leaders. Presidents, provosts, and other senior administrators must encourage professors and departments to innovate. That's difficult when fundamental barriers persist, such as the practice of tying government funding to enrollment rather than to graduation and learning outcomes. Moreover, regional accreditors, while more attuned to outcome measures than in the past, still tend to foster uniformity across institutions that would do better to pursue new and more effective ways of teaching undergraduates.

More broadly, political support is crucial. There have recently been encouraging signs on this front. Former West Virginia Governor Joe Manchin, the 2010 chair of the National Governors Association, placed higher education reform at the top of his policy agenda, calling on his fellow governors to focus on improving higher education productivity, defining it in terms of improving enrollment, persistence, and graduation rates. Still, as Paul Osterman points out in his analysis of barriers to community college improvement, lawmakers themselves must persist. More than half of the twenty-six states that adopted incentive-based funding schemes for community colleges in recent decades later discontinued their schemes, which were typically never well funded or particularly effective. In the wake of the 2010 midterm elections, many higher education reform initiatives will fall under the control of new political leadership. Whether incoming governors and state legislators will continue their predecessors' higher education work or choose to strike off in a different direction could fundamentally alter the incentives for innovation.

Even with the encouragement of policy makers, universities can make little progress unless they are well informed about successful innovations—which ideas have been successfully piloted and which are the best candidates for widespread adoption. Despite islands of excellence and fresh thinking, higher education has yet to develop the kind of research and development network that emerged during the nation's decades-long K–12 reform movement. Readers of the *Chronicle of Higher Education* and *Inside Higher Ed* may keep abreast of innovative practices that have blossomed on a piecemeal basis on campuses across the country, but this knowledge often fails to accumulate, limiting the extent to which promising experiments can spread.

We cannot realistically expect unanimity on these matters, of course. Thoughtful analysts such as Ronald Ehrenberg see the changing role of the faculty less as a desirable imperative than as an inevitability that ought to be managed carefully by improving the selection, evaluation, and training of instructors. Here, too, even reluctant innovators need guidance. Perhaps the top-down governing structure of for-profits, which Hentschke highlights, has lessons for institutions in which faculty governance, including decisions over curriculum, is a long-cherished prerogative that has not always met students' needs.

Perhaps wide-reaching higher education reform will be driven only by external forces, as Marcus suggests. There are some signs that this is beginning to happen. In the spring of 2010, the financially beleaguered University of California (UC) proposed to reach more students at lower cost to UC (although not necessarily to students) by piloting an online learning program that backers say could eventually lead to high-quality online bachelor's degrees. There is even evidence that some opinion leaders in the higher education trade associations are beginning to recognize the need for innovation. In July 2010, the American Association of State Colleges and Universities' vice president for academic leadership and change, George Mehaffy, argued:

"It is past time to think in profoundly new ways about how we organize and deliver instruction, structure and sequence the curriculum, design and assess learning environments. In short, we can use the current economic crisis to re-imagine the entire undergraduate experience."

But many faculty members remain dubious about such fundamental changes. At the University of California–Berkeley, for example, while the systemwide faculty senate approved the pilot classes, UC–Berkeley's faculty association and graduate student union have expressed serious concerns about the proposed online program; similar opposition scuttled an online degree program at the University of Illinois several years ago. As Marcus points out, comparable sentiments have frustrated change for centuries. Put simply, many universities remain institutionally conservative places. Previous economic downturns have often led to a batten-down-the-hatches approach, in which universities cut back existing programs, freeze or postpone hiring, and put plans for new facilities on hold. There has been little of the fundamental rethinking—of faculty roles, use of technology, student-learning measurement, even collaboration with for-profits—that should be the hallmark of serious campus reform efforts.

Obstacles to innovation in American higher education certainly remain formidable. Yet, on balance, there is reason for cautious optimism. New practices may not be ubiquitous, but enough efforts have emerged on traditional campuses, in start-up institutions, and in the burgeoning worlds of for-profit and online learning, to offer plenty of models for effective change. Moreover, the appetite for considering such models seems to be growing, thanks not only to budget pressures, but to public demand for expanded college opportunities and reduced costs, together with an increasing willingness among policy makers to confront the shortcomings of too many postsecondary institutions. These pressures are only likely to increase in the years to come.

As the analysts whose work is collected in this volume suggest, there is no single blueprint for reinventing American universities. Indeed, we can make a case that some of our very best institutions don't need major changes. In the many places where fundamental reforms are needed, however, the best chances for innovation lie in taking a range of actions: developing and disseminating promising reforms more systematically; providing greater regulatory flexibility; improving institutional and financial incentives for raising academic productivity; making more creative use of fast-changing technology; and insisting on a much clearer focus on measuring what students really learn in college. Much will be lost if the United States squanders the opportunity provided by today's economic and political environment to rethink important aspects of U.S. higher education. And much will be gained if universities and policy makers seize on the promise educational innovation holds for students, institutions, and the nation.

Notes

Introduction

1. Richard Arum and Josipa Roksa, "Are Undergraduates Actually Learning Anything?" *Chronicle of Higher Education*, January 18, 2011, http://chronicle.com/article/Are-Undergraduates-Actually/125979/.

2 U.S. Department of Education, *A Test of Leadership: Charting the Future of U.S. Higher Education, A Report of the Commission Appointed by Secretary of Education Margaret Spellings* (September 2006), www.ed.gov/about/bdscomm/list/hiedfuture/reports/final-report.pdf.

Chapter 1

1 Harold Enarson, "Innovation in Higher Education," *Journal of Higher Education* 31 (1960): 495.

2 Dominic J. Brewer, Susan M. Gates, and Charles A. Goldman, *In Pursuit of Prestige: Strategy and Competition in U.S. Higher Education* (Edison, NJ: Transaction Publisher, 2002).

3 Thomas D. Snyder and Sally A. Dillow, *Digest of Education Statistics 2009* (Washington, DC: U.S. Department of Education, National Center for Education Statistics, April 2010).

4. William G. Tierney and Guilbert C. Hentschke, *New Players, Different Game: Understanding the Rise of For-profit Colleges and Universities* (Baltimore: Johns Hopkins University Press, 2007).

5. Edwin Mansfield and Jeong-Yeong Lee, "The Modern University: Contributor to Industrial Innovation and Recipient of Industrial R&D Support," *Research Policy* 25 (1996): 1047–58; Richard Florida, "The Role of the University: Leveraging Talent, Not Technology," *Issues in Science and Technology* 15, no. 4 (1999): 67–73; Richard Florida, *The Rise of the Creative Class* (New York: Basic Books, 2002).

6. Roger Benjamin and Steve Carroll, "The Implications of the Changed Environment for Governance in Higher Education," in *The Responsive University: Restructuring for High Performance,* ed. William G. Tierney (Baltimore: Johns Hopkins University Press, 1998), 92–119.

7. Organisation for Economic Co-operation and Development, *Education at a Glance 2009: OECD Indicators* (Paris: Organisation for Economic Co-operation and Development, 2009).

8. Laura Palmer-Noone, "Perceived Barriers to Innovation: First Report from a Study on Innovation in Higher Education," *Assessment and Accountability Forum* (Summer 2000): 1.

9. U.S. Department of Education, Commission on the Future of Higher Education, "A Test of Leadership: Charting the Future of U.S. Higher Education: A Report of the Commission Appointed by Secretary of Education Margaret Spellings" (Washington, DC: U.S. Department of Education, 2006), http://ed.gov/about/bdscomm/list/hiedfuture/index.html.

10. U.S. Department of Education, National Center for Education Statistics, "Fast Facts" (Washington, DC: National Center for Education Statistics, 2009).

11. Dominic J. Brewer, Eric Eide, and Ronald G. Ehrenberg, "Does It Pay to Attend an Elite Private College? Evidence on the Effects of College Type on Earnings," *Journal of Human Resources* 34 (1999): 104–23.

12. Sarah R. Crissey, "Educational Attainment in the United States: 2007: Population Characteristics" (Current Population Report P20–560) (Washington, DC: Department of Commerce, Census Bureau, 2009), www.census.gov/prod/2009pubs/p20-560.pdf.

13. University of California, Office of the President, "The UC Budget Myths and Facts" (Sacramento, CA: University of California Office of the President, August 2009), http://ucfuture.universityofcalifornia.edu/documents/budget_mythsfacts.pdf.

14. Kevin O'Leary, "California's Crisis Hits Its Prized Universities," *Time*, July 18, 2009, www.time.com/time/nation/article/0,8599,1911455,00.html.

15. Ronald G. Ehrenberg, *Tuition Rising: Why College Costs So Much* (Cambridge, MA: Harvard University Press, 2000); U.S. Department of Education, National Center for Education Statistics, *Digest of Education Statistics* (Washington, DC: U.S. Department of Education, National Center for Education Statistics, 2008).

16. U.S. Department of Education, Commission on the Future of Higher Education, "A Test of Leadership: Charting the Future of U.S. Higher Education."

17. Gene I. Maeroff, *A Classroom of One: How Online Learning is Changing Our Schools and Colleges* (New York: Palgrave MacMillan, 2004).

18. Martha Markward, "Do Accreditation Requirements Deter Curricular Innovation? Yes!" *Journal of Social Work Education* 35 (1999): 183–94; John W. Prados, George D. Peterson, and Lisa R. Lattuca, "Quality Assurance of Engineering Education Through Accreditation: The Impact of Engineering Criteria 2000 and Its Global Influence," *Journal of Engineering Education* 94 (2005): 165–84.

19. Richard Luecke and Ralph Katz, *Managing Creativity and Innovation* (Boston: Harvard Business School Press, 2003).

20. Calculations based on Thomas D. Snyder and Sally A. Dillow, "Digest of Education Statistics 2009" (Washington, DC: U.S. Department of Education, National Center for Education Statistics, April 2010), table 221.

21. For examples, see Wesley M. Cohen and Daniel A. Levinthal, "Innovation and Learning: The Two Faces of R&D," *Economic Journal* 99 (1989): 569–96; Wesley M. Cohen and Daniel A. Levinthal, "Absorptive Capacity: A New Perspective on Learning and Innovation," *Administrative Sciences Quarterly* 35 (1990): 128–52; Fariborz Damanour, "Organizational Innovation: A Meta-analysis of Effects of Determinants and Moderators," *Academy of Management Review* 34 (1991): 555–90; Joseph Farrell and Garth Saloner, "Standardization, Compatibility, and Innovation," *Rand Journal of Economics* 15 (1985): 70–83; Ikujiro Nonanka, "A Dynamic Theory of Organizational Knowledge Creation," *Organization Science* 5 (1994): 14–37; Gabriel Szulanski, "Exploring Internal Stickiness: Impediments to the Transfer of Best Practice within the Firm," *Strategic Management Journal* 17 (1996): 27–43.

22. Malcolm Getz, John J. Siegfried, and Kathryn H. Anderson, "Adoption of Innovations in Higher Education," *Quarterly Review of Economics and Finance* 37 (1997): 605–31.

23. Clayton M. Christensen, Michael B. Horn, and Curtis W. Johnson, *Disrupting Class: How Disruptive Innovation Will Change the Way the World Learns* (New York: McGraw-Hill, 2008).

24. This section is based in part on Hill and Roza (see note 27) to which one of us (Brewer) contributed. We thank them for sharing this review of research related to Baumol's cost disease.

25. Modern technology has actually altered this example. Since a string quartet's performance can be distributed to millions via CDs, online, etc., productivity gains can be realized at a scale that was not possible in the past.

26. Getz, Siegfried, and Anderson, "Adoption of Innovations in Higher Education," 605.

27. Paul Hill and Marguerite Roza, *Curing Baumol's Disease: In Search of Productivity Gains in K–12 Schooling* (Seattle, WA: Center on Reinventing Public Education, 2010). Much of the material in the following discussion draws on their analysis.

28. John M. Budd, "Academic Library Data from the United States: An Examination of Trends," *LIBRES Library and Information Science Research Electronic Journal* 19 (2002): 1–21.

29. Margaret W. Sallee and William G. Tierney, "The Transformation of Professors of Education," *Journal of the Professoriate* (in press).

30. Tierney and Hentschke, *New Players, Different Game*; Guilbert C. Hentschke, Vincente M. Lechuga, and William G. Tierney, *For-profit Colleges and Universities: Schools or Businesses? Their Markets, Regulation, Performance, and Place in Higher Education* (Sterling, VA: Stylus, 2010).

31. Dominic J. Brewer, Susan M. Gates, and Charles A. Goldman, *In Pursuit of Prestige: Strategy and Competition in U.S. Higher Education* (Edison, NJ: Transaction Publisher, 2002); Dominic J. Brewer and Maryann Jacobi Gray, "Do Faculty Connect School to Work? Evidence from Community Colleges," *Educational Evaluation and Policy Analysis* 21 (1999): 405–16.

32. Kenneth N. Daniels, Dogan Tirtiroglu, and Ercan Tirtiroglu, "Deregulation, Intensity of Competition, Industry Evolution and the Productivity Growth of U.S. Commercial Banks," *Journal of Money, Credit, and Banking* 37 (2005): 339–60.

33. Dominic J. Brewer and Guilbert C. Hentschke, "An International Perspective on Publically-Operated, Privately-Financed Schools," in *Handbook of Research on School Choice*, eds. Mark Berends, Matthew G. Springer, Dale Ballou, and Herbert J. Walberg (New York: Routledge, 2009): 227–46.

34. Tierney and Hentschke, *New Players, Different Game*.

35. Roberto Rodriguez Gomez, "Entre lo Publico y Privado: La Polemica de las Universidades 'Patito' en 2003," in *Anuario Educativo Mexicano: Visión Retrospectiva*, ed. Guadelupe Teresinha Bertussi (Mexico: Universidad Pedagogica Nacional, 2004): 431–67; Francisco Lopez Segrera, "El Estado del Arte Educación Superior en América Latina y el Caribe en el Contexto Mundial Globalización" (presentation, Universidad Autónoma de Occidente, Cali, Columbia, n.d.), http://dali.uao.edu.co:7777/pls/portal/docs/PAGE/UNIAUTONOMA_INVESTIGACIONES/_OF_DI%2001/GRUPGR/CATEDRA/DOCUMENTOS/II_12_SEPT_EST_ARTE_ES_ALC_MUNDIAL.PDF; Roberto Miranda, "Una Cronica de la Politica del Campo Intersticial de la Educacion Superior," *Noesis: Revista de Ciencias Sociales y Humanidades* 15 (2006): 127–63.

36. Joseph Farrell and Garth Saloner, "Standardization, Compatibility, and Innovation," *Rand Journal of Economics* 15 (1985): 70–83; John W. Prados, George D. Peterson, and Lisa R. Lattuca, "Quality Assurance of Engineering Education Through Accreditation: The Impact of Engineering Criteria 2000 and Its Global Influence," *Journal of Engineering Education* 94 (2005): 165–84.

Chapter 2

1. All interviews with Harrisburg University administrators, faculty, and students were conducted by author in person on March 31 and April 1, 2010, except with Mel Schiavelli, president, who was interviewed on March 24, 2010.

2. Interview with Arthur Levine, May 12, 2010.

3. Robert Zemsky, *Making Reform Work: The Case for Transforming American Higher Education* (New Brunswick, NJ: Rutgers University Press, 2009), 17.

4. Ibid., 174.

5. Ibid., 210.

6. W. H. Cowley and Don Williams, *International and Historical Roots of American Higher Education* (New York: Garland Publishing, 1991), 71.

7. Ibid., 91.

8. Ibid., 74.

9. Ibid., 72.

10. Ibid., 78.

11. Ibid., 83.

12. Ibid., 74.

13. Ibid., 82.

14. Ibid., 92.

15. Ibid., 82.

16. Schiavelli.

17. Ibid., 117.

18. Susan Tyler Hitchcock and Jennings Wagoner, "Short History of U.VA," *A Short History of the University of Virginia*, www.virginia.edu/uvatours/shorthistory/first.html.

19. Cowley and Williams, *International and Historical Roots of American Higher Education,* 116.

20. Harvard College Observatory, "HCO: The Great Refractor," www.cfa.harvard.edu/hco/grref.html.

21. Cowley and Williams, *International and Historical Roots of American Higher Education*, 108.

22. Levine.

23. Donald G. Tewksbury, *The Founding of American Colleges and Universities Before the Civil War* (New York: Teachers College, Columbia University), 15.

24. Cowley and Williams, *International and Historical Roots of American Higher Education*, 87.

25. Rensselaer Polytechnic Institute Hall of Fame, http://128.113.2.9/about/hof/vanrensselaer.html

26. Ibid., 115.

27. Indiana State Constitution of 1816, Article IX, Section 2, www.in.gov/history/2460.htm.

28. Cowley and Williams, *International and Historical Roots of American Higher Education*, 121.

29. The Morrill Act, 7 U.S.C. § 304, 1862.

30. Cowley and Williams, *International and Historical Roots of American Higher Education*, 109.

31. Derek Bok, *Our Underachieving Colleges: A Candid Look at How Much Students Learn and Why They Should be Learning More* (Princeton, NJ: Princeton University Press, 2006), 14.

32. Henry Adams, *The Education of Henry Adams: An Autobiography* (Boston: Houghton & Mifflin Company, 1918), 54–55.

33. Cowley and Williams, *International and Historical Roots of American Higher Education*, 121.

34. Ibid., 140.

35. *New Century Magazine* 28, no. 2 (June 1884): 203.

36. Bok, *Our Underachieving Colleges*, 15.

37. Ibid., 16.

38. Cowley and Williams, *International and Historical Roots of American Higher Education*, 138.

39. Bok, *Our Underachieving Colleges*, 16.

40. Levine.

41. Ibid.

42. Ibid., 23.

43. Christopher J. Lucas, *American Higher Education: A History* (New York: Palgrave Mac-Millan, 2006), 224.

44. Ibid., 226.

45. *Time* magazine, June 24, 1935; also, Tim Murphy, "Failure to Launch," *Washington Monthly*, September/October 2009.

46. Institute of International Education, http://iie.org/en/Who-We-Are/History.

47. Bok, *Our Underachieving Colleges*, 236.

48. Levine.

49. Cowley and Williams, *International and Historical Roots of American Higher Education*, 188.

50. *Science: The Endless Frontier, A Report to the President by Vannevar Bush, Director of the Office of Scientific Research and Development* (U.S. Government Printing Office, July 1945); Zemsky, *Making Reform Work*, 2.

51. Cowley and Williams, *International and Historical Roots of American Higher Education*, 189.

52. Lester F. Goodchild and Harold S. Wechsler, eds., *The History of Higher Education* (Boston: Pearson Custom Publishing, 2008).

53. Ibid., 590.

54. Ibid., 596.

55. Ibid.

56. Ibid., 597.

57. Statement by the president upon signing the National Defense Education Act, September 2, 1958.

58. Bok, *Our Underachieving Colleges*, 24.

59. Alexander Meiklejohn, *The Experimental College* (Madison: University of Wisconsin Press, 1932), x.

60. Ibid., xi.

61. Ibid., xv.

62. Tufts University Experimental College, www.excollege.tufts.edu/.

63. Interview, February 4, 2010.

64. Interview, February 8, 2010.

65. Interview, May 4, 2010.

66. Ibid.

67. Ibid.

68. Interview, March 31, 2010.

69. Lucas, *American Higher Education*, 333.

70. Ibid., 332.

71. Darr.

72. Levine.

73. Richard H. Hersh and John Morrow, eds., *Declining by Degrees: Higher Education at Risk* (New York: Palgrave Macmillan, 2005), 9.

74. Zemsky, *Making Reform Work*, 111.

75. Ibid., 109.

76. Interview, April 1, 2010.

77. Ibid.

78. Interview, March 30, 2010.

79. Ibid.

80. Schiavelli.

81. Darr.

82. Schiavelli.

83. Interview, April 22, 2010.

84. Ibid.

85. Ibid.

Chapter 3

1. Harry Brighouse, a philosophy professor at the University of Wisconsin–Madison, considers efficiency in university teaching and learning to be *intrinsically* valuable, and that inefficiency in pursuing this mission *harms* moral stakeholders. Harry Brighouse, "Ethical Leadership in Hard (and easy) Times: A Partial Audit" (paper presented to the Forum for the Future of Higher Education, Aspen, CO, June 16, 2009).

2. *Random House Dictionary of the English Language, The Unabridged Edition* (New York: Random House, 1973).

3. William F. Massy, *Honoring the Trust: Quality and Cost Containment in Higher Education* (San Francisco: Jossey-Bass, 2003), 87.

4. William F. Massy, "Collegium Economicum: Why Institutions Do What They Do," *Change* 36, no. 4 (July-August 2004): 26; and William F. Massy, "Academic Values and the Marketplace," *Higher Education Management and Policy* 21 no. 3 (2009): 51.

5. Dominic J. Brewer, Susan M. Gates, and Charles A. Goldman, *In Pursuit of Prestige: Strategy and Competition in US Higher Education* (New Brunswick, NJ: Transaction Press, 2001).

6. Massy, *Honoring the Trust*, 191.

7. William F. Massy, Stephen W. Graham, and Paula Myrick Short, *Academic Quality Work: A Handbook for Improvement* (San Francisco: Jossey-Bass, 2007).

8. Ernest L. Boyer, *Scholarship Reconsidered: Priorities of the Professorate* (Princeton, NJ: Carnegie Foundation for the Advancement of Teaching, 1991).

9. Michael Hammer and James Champy, *Reengineering the Corporation: A Manifesto for Business Revolution* (New York: Harper, 2003).

10. Jack M. Wilson, "Reengineering the Undergraduate Curriculum," in *The Learning Revolution: The Challenge of Information Technology in the Academy*, eds. Diana G. Oblinger and Sean C. Rush (San Francisco: Jossey-Bass, 1996), 107–28.

11. See, for example, Carl Weiman and Katherine Perkins, "Transforming Physics Education," *Physics Today* 58 (November 2005): 36–41.

12. Robert Zemsky and I described the approach at an early conference on instructional productivity held at Wingspread (Racine, WI). See William F. Massy and Robert Zemsky, "Using Information Technology to Enhance Academic Productivity" (Washington, DC: Educom, 1995).

13. David S. P. Hopkins and William F. Massy, *Planning Models for Colleges and Universities* (Stanford, CA: Stanford University Press, 1981), 208–20.

14. Carol A. Twigg, "Improving Quality and Reducing Costs: the Case for Redesign" (Lumina Foundation, 2005), 46, 48.

15. Michael F. Middaugh, *Understanding Faculty Productivity: Standards and Benchmarks for Colleges and Universities* (San Francisco: Jossey-Bass, 2001). Table 3.3 presents a list of metrics for measuring "productivity," e.g., Credit Hours per Faculty FTE and Direct Expense per FTE Students Taught.

16. Many commentators have identified the proliferation of courses that allow faculty to teach their specialties as a drag on departmental productivity. See, for example, Robert Zemsky, William F. Massy, and Penny Oedel, "On Reversing the Ratchet," *Change* 25, no. 3 (May/June 1993), 56–63.

17. The concept of coherence represents an extension of the more commonly used "student level" (for example, upper and lower division, lower division or graduate). See Robert Zemsky, *Structure and Coherence: Measuring the Undergraduate Curriculum* (Washington, DC: Association of American Colleges, 1989). Middaugh, *Understanding Faculty Productivity*, differentiates credit hours by student level. The idea of coherence, however, is to consider student level as an attribute of *courses*.

18. While not an attribute of any particular course type, faculty teaching loads are an integral part of the model and thus are listed here for completeness. It may also be desirable to assign relative out-of-class workload indices to each class type—for example, teaching a seminar in one's specialty takes considerably less effort than teaching a survey course, even when enrollment differences are taken into account.

19. These variables aren't required to operate the model, but they may prove useful for analyzing student attainment.

20. Faculty unit costs depend on the department's normal teaching load and the treatment of departmental research, and all the unit costs depend on the treatment of overhead. Such issues, while amenable to solution, are beyond the scope of this chapter.

21. Middaugh, *Understanding Faculty Productivity*, walked up to this issue in table 5.1 but does not pursue it.

22. Among other things, the upper critical value for the number of large classes can reflect the number of large classrooms that can be made available to the department. This, in turn, can be incorporated in the goal-seeking analysis described later.

23. The technical term is "optimization analysis," but I'll use the more colloquial "goal seeking." In effect, it automates the process of doing what-ifs. The optimization uses integer programming to minimize the weighted sum of squared deviations of the planning variables from their targets, subject to constraints representing the critical values and applicable constraints based on resources. For targets, we take the midpoint of the variables' normal ranges with the weights (which need only be defined in proportional terms) equaling the widths of the ranges.

24. See Massy, *Honoring the Trust*; William F. Massy, "Academic Audit for Accountability and Improvement," in *Achieving Accountability in Higher Education: Balancing Public, Academic, and Market Demands*, ed. Joseph C. Burke (San Francisco: Jossey-Bass, 2005), 173–97; and Massy, Graham, and Short, *Academic Quality Work*.

25. William F. Massy, "Using the Budget to Fight Fragmentation and Improve Quality," in *Fixing the Fragmented University: Decentralization With Direction*, ed. Joseph C. Burke (San Francisco: Jossey-Bass, 2006).

26. Clayton M. Christensen, *The Innovator's Dilemma: The Revolutionary Book That Will Change the Way You Do Business* (New York: Harper Collins, 2003).

27. See Massy, *Honoring the Trust*, chapter 8.

28. Robert Zemsky, *Making Reform Work: The Case for Transforming American Higher Education* (New Brunswick, NJ: Rutgers University Press, 2009), 157–61. He coined the "Job One" metaphor.

29. "Eberly Center for Teaching Excellence," www.cmu.edu/teaching/eberly.

30. James E. Zull, *The Art of Changing the Brain: Enriching Teaching by Exploring the Biology of Learning* (Sterling, VA: Stylus Publishing, 2002).

31. I had worked with Lehmkuhle to introduce these principles at the University of Missouri (Massy, Graham, and Short, *Academic Quality Work*), which is why I was brought in as a consultant at UMR. Robert Zemsky and Carnegie Mellon University's Joel Smith also participated.

32. "Learning Goes under a New Microscope," *Chronicle of Higher Education* 66, no. 11 (November 6, 2009).

33. A highly encouraging development at the time of this writing is that a group of institutions from the Consortium on Financing Higher Education (COFHE) have begun experimenting with Carnegie Mellon University's learning modules and use of cognitive science.

Chapter 4

1. Ronald G. Ehrenberg, *Tuition Rising: Why College Costs So Much* (Cambridge, MA: Harvard University Press, 2002); Ronald G. Ehrenberg, "The Perfect Storm and the Privatization of Public Higher Education," *Change* 38 (January/February 2006): 46–53.

2. Liang Zhang and Xiangmin Liu, "Faculty Employment at 4-year Colleges and Universities," *Economics of Education Review* 29 (August 2010): 543-552.. Zhang and Liu also show that the employment of full-time nontenure-track faculty is higher when their salaries are lower relative to those of tenured and tenure-track faculty; James Monks, "The Relative Earnings of Contingent Faculty in Higher Education," *Journal of Labor Research* 28 (July 2007): 487–501.

3. John Cross and Edie Goldenberg, *Off Track Profs: Nontenured Teachers in Higher Education* (Cambridge, MA: MIT Press, 2009).

4. The end of mandatory retirement would not have necessarily put pressure on academic institutions to reduce their reliance on tenured and tenure-track faculty if the institutions adopted post-tenure review procedures. However, faced with faculty resistance, post-tenure review procedures have not been widely adopted and, when adopted, typically are at public institutions, often under pressure from state legislatures.

5. Ehrenberg, "The Perfect Storm and the Privatization of Public Higher Education"; Ronald G. Ehrenberg and Liang Zhang, "The Changing Nature of Faculty Employment," in *Recruitment and Retirement in Higher Education: Building and Managing the Faculty of the Future,* eds. Robert Clark and Jennifer Mas (Northampton, MA: Edward Elgar, 2005), 32–52; and Cross and Goldenberg, *Off Track Profs.* Liang Zhang and Ronald G. Ehrenberg show that an increased use of part-time faculty members at research universities is associated with an increase in external research funding per full-time faculty member. See Liang Zhang and Ronald G. Ehrenberg, "Faculty Employment and R&D Expenditures at Research Universities," *Economics of Education Review* 29 (June 2010): 329-337.

6. Ronald G. Ehrenberg and Liang Zhang, "Do Tenured and Tenure-Track Faculty Matter?" *Journal of Human Resources* 40 (Summer 2005): 647–59.

7. Daniel Jacoby, "Effects of Part-Time Faculty Employment on Community College Graduation Rates," *Journal of Higher Education* 77 (November/December 2006): 1081–103; M. Kevin Eagan and Audrey J. Jaeger, "Effects of Exposure to Part-Time Faculty on Community College Transfer," *Research in Higher Education* 50 (March 2009): 168–88; and Audrey J. Jaeger and M. Kevin Eagan, "Unintended Consequences: Examining the Effect of Part-Time Faculty Members on Associate's Degree Completion," *Community College Review* 36 (January 2009): 167–94.

8. Eric P. Bettinger and Bridget Terry Long, "The Increased Use of Adjunct Instructors at Public Institutions: Are We Hurting Students," in *What's Happening to Public Higher Education? The Shifting Financial Burden,* ed. Ronald G. Ehrenberg (Baltimore, MD: Johns Hopkins University Press, 2007), 51–70; Audrey J. Jaeger and M. Kevin Eagan, "Examining Retention and Contingent Faculty use in a State System of Public Higher Education," *Education Policy* (forthcoming); and Eric P. Bettinger and Bridget Terry Long, "Does Cheaper Mean Better? The Impact of Using Adjunct Instructors on Student Outcomes," *Review of Economics and Statistics* 92 (August 2010): 598 – 613. In one recent study for a major Ca-

nadian research university, Florian Hoffman and Philip Oreopoulos found that the tenure or tenure-track status and the full-time or part-time status of faculty in introductory-level classes had no effect, on average, on student outcomes. See Florian Hoffman and Philip Oreopoulos, "Professor Qualities and Student Achievement," *Review of Economics and Statistics* 91 (February 2009): 83–92.

9. Zhang and Liu (2010) show that academic institutions located in urban areas make more use of part-time faculty than other institutions.

10. The data in table 4.3 suggests that only about 40 percent of all of the faculty in American higher education in 2003 had doctoral degrees, although the share of classes taught by faculty with doctoral degrees is higher because full-time faculty are much more likely to have doctoral degrees.

11. See Ronald G. Ehrenberg, "Involving Undergraduate Students in Research to Encourage Them to Undertake PhD Study in Economics," *American Economic Association Papers and Proceedings* 95 (May 2005): 184–88 for a discussion of my own efforts to encourage undergraduates to go on for PhDs in economics by involving them in research.

12. Joan Burrelli, Alan Rapoport, and Rolf Lehming, "Baccalaureate Origins of S&E Doctorate Recipients," *Science Resources Statistics InfoBrief* NSF 08-311 (Washington, DC: National Science Foundation, July 2008).

13. Intellectual integrity requires me to inform the reader that I am a longtime member of the AAUP and have chaired several of its committees.

14. Many of these arguments are discussed in George Stigler, "An Academic Episode" in *The Intellectual and the Marketplace*, ed. George Stigler (Cambridge, MA: Harvard University Press, 1984), 1–9. See, also, Edward Lazear, "Why is there *Mandatory* Retirement?" *Journal of Political Economy* 87 (December 1979): 1261–284; Sherwin Rosen and Edward Lazear, "Rank Order Tournaments as Optimum Labor Contracts," *Journal of Political Economy* 89 (October 1981): 841–64; and Ronald G. Ehrenberg, Paul J. Pieper, and Rachel A. Willis, "Do Economics Departments with Lower Tenure Probabilities Pay Higher Faculty Salaries?" *Review of Economics and Statistics* 80 (November 1999): 503–12.

15. Piper Fogg, "For These Professors, 'Practice' is Perfect," *Chronicle of Higher Education* 50 (April 16, 2004): A12; and Karen Arenson, "Professors Teaching? N.Y.U. President Says It Isn't Such a Novel Idea," *New York Times*, September 3, 2003, B1.

16. Ehrenberg presents data on the growth in faculty salary differences across institution types, as well as between public and private institutions. See Ronald G. Ehrenberg, "Studying Ourselves: The Academic Labor Market," *Journal of Labor Economics* 21 (April 2003): 267–87.

17. The assistant professor and professor figures do not distinguish between tenure-track and nontenure-track faculty.

18. As the last column of table 4.5 indicates, the average salary of lecturers at public doctoral universities is less than the average salary of assistant professors in all categories.

19. The rankings are found in Marvin L. Goldberger and Brendan A. Maher, *Research Doctorate Programs in the United States: Continuity and Change* (Washington, DC: National Academy Press, 1995). I am grateful to Mirinda Martin for collecting the data for this table.

20. Ehrenberg and Zhang, "Do Tenured and Tenure-Track Faculty Matter?"

21. Barbara Means et al., *Evaluation of Evidence-Based Practices in Online Learning: A Meta-Analysis and Review of Online Learning Studies* (Washington, DC: U.S. Department of Education, 2009).

22. Greg von Lehmen, "College Degrees Without Going to Class," *New York Times*, Online Room for Debate, March 3, 2010.

23. More information available at www.thencat.org.

24. In spite of all of its successes, dissemination of NCAT's models within institutions that already have had adopted its approaches in some courses and across institutions to institutions that have not yet adopted any of its approaches has been slow. Ben Miller discusses a number of the factors that limit rapid dissemination of the NCAT models. See Ben Miller, "The Course of Innovation: Using Technology to Transform Higher Education," *Education Sector Reports*, May 2010.

25. More information available at http://oli.web.cmu.edu/openlearning/initiative.

26. Marsha Lovett, Oded Meyer, and Candace Thille, "The Open Learning Initiative: Measuring the Effectiveness of the OLI Statistics Course in Accelerated Student Learning," *JIME* no. 14 (2008), http://jime/open.ac.uk/2008/14.

27. Steve Kolowich, "Hybrid Education 2.0," *InsideHigherEd*, December 28, 2009, www.insidehighered.com/news/2009/12/28/carnegie.

28. Guilbert Hentschke (this volume) discusses for-profit higher education much more extensively.

29. More information available at www.phoenix.edu.

30. University of Phoenix, *2009 Academic Annual Report*, www.phoenix.edu/about_us/publications/academic-annual-report/2009.html; personal communication, Dr. Jorge Klor de Alva.

31. David W. Breneman, "The University of Phoenix: Icon of For-Profit Higher Education" in *Earnings from Learning: The Rise of For-Profit Universities*, eds. David W. Breneman, Brian Pusser, and Sarah E Turner (Albany, NY: SUNY Press, 2006), 71–92; personal communication, Dr. Jorge Klor de Alva.

32. Personal communication, Dr. Jorge Klor de Alva.

33. Breneman, "The University of Phoenix."

34. Personal communication, Dr. Jorge Klor de Alva.

35. University of Phoenix, *2008 Academic Annual Report*, www.phoenix.edu/about_us/publications/academic-annual-report/2008.html; University of Phoenix, *2009 Academic Annual Report*.

36. Doug Lederman, "How Students Fare at For-Profits," *InsideHigherEd*, April 1, 2010, www.insidehighered.com/news/2010/04/01/corinthian.

37. University of Phoenix, *2008 Academic Annual Report*; University of Phoenix, *2009 Academic Annual Report*.

38. I am grateful to Michael Offerman, former President of Capella and now both Vice Chairman for External Initiatives and Interim President for Capella for providing me with insights about and data for the institution. More information can be found at www.capella.edu.

39. These models may be more difficult to apply to younger students.

40. David Moltz, "In the Midnight Hour," *InsideHigherEd,* December 9, 2009, www.inside-highered.com/news/2009/12/09/midnight.

41. David Glenn discusses efforts that have been made to embed student learning outcomes in course evaluations including those of the IDEA Center (www.ideacenter.org) and the Student Assessment of Learning Gains (www.salgsite.org). See David Glenn, "Rating Your Professors: Scholars Test Improved Course Evaluations," *Chronicle of Higher Education* 50 (April 25, 2010).

42. Jeff Young, "Who Needs a Professor When There's A Tutor Available," *Chronicle of Higher Education* 54 (June 17, 2008).

43. Daniel de Vise, "Online Courses Can Reduce the Costly Sting of College," *Washington Post,* February 26, 2010.

44. The material is this paragraph was provided to me by Burck Smith, e-mail, March 25, 2010.

45. Peter Katopes, "Do Professors Matter?" *InsideHigherEd,* October 30, 2009, www .insidehighered.com/views/2009/10/30/katopes.

46. Burck Smith, "Public Policy Barriers to Post-Secondary Cost Control" (forthcoming in a conference volume).

47. StraighterLine is not the only purveyor of individual online classes. For example, Statistics.com (www.statistics.com) teaches more than eighty statistics classes online and currently enrolls about 2,500 primarily adult students. The American Council on Education has supported its members granting transfer credits for these courses, although it has only documented about thirty-eight requests for such credits to date. See Steve Kolowich, "The Specialists," *InsideHigherEd,* April 5, 2010, www.insidehighered.com/news/2010/04/05/statistics.

48. College Board, *The Sixth Annual AP Report to the Nation* (New York: College Board, 2010); Elyse Ashburn, "Study Finds Dual Enrollment Leads to College Success," *Chronicle of Higher Education* 54 (November 2, 2007): A26.

49. See, for example, Philip M. Sadler and Robert H. Tai, "Advanced Placement Exam Scores as Predictors of Performance in Introductory College Biology, Chemistry and Physics Courses," *Science Educator* 16 (Spring 2007):1–18; Kristin Klopfenstein and M. Kathleen Thomas, "The Link Between Advanced Placement Experience and Early College Success," *Southern Economic Journal* 75 (2009): 873–91; and Kirabo Jackson, "A Little Now for a Lot Later; An Evaluation of the Texas Advanced Placement Incentive Program," *Journal of Human Resources* 45 (Summer 2010): 591–639.

50. David Moltz, "Professors and Students Split on AP Credits," *InsideHigherEd,* February 10, 2009, www.insidehighered.com/news/2009/02/10/ap.

51. I say "most likely" because forces may erode tenure-track faculty at them also. The flagship publics will not be immune to the severe financial pressures that public higher education will continue to face and the social pressures that all the selective institutions will face to expand enrollments, to keep tuition increases moderate, and to provide increased grant aid to maintain and expand their accessibility. These trends will likely place substantial pressures on their cost structures.

52. Douglas A. Webber and Ronald G. Ehrenberg, "Do Expenditures Other Than Instructional Expenditures Affect Graduation and Persistence Rates in American Higher Education," *Economics of Education Review* 29 (December 2010): 947–958.

Chapter 5

1. U.S. Department of Education, National Center for Educational Statistics, *Enrollment In Postsecondary Institutions, Fall 2007, First Look* (Washington, DC: U.S. Department of Education, 2009-155), http://nces.ed.gov/programs/coe/2009/section3/table-trc-4.asp.

2. Ibid. There is still a great deal of income stratification in higher education. If we look at percent enrolling (graduating) from four-year schools for the top family income quintile. it is 79% (53%), while for the bottom quintile, it is 34%(11%). Controlling among those with high school senior math scores in the top third for the top family quintile enrollment is 84%, while for the bottom income quintile, it is 68%. For the middle third in test scores for the top income quintile, it is 59%, and for the bottom income quintile, it is 33%. See Ron Haskins, Harry Holzer, and Robert Lerman, *Promoting Economic Mobility by Increasing Postsecondary Education* (Washington, DC: Pew Charitable Trust, Economic Mobility Project, May 2009), 12–13.

3. U.S. Department of Education, National Center for Education Statistics, *Community Colleges: Special Supplement To The Condition of Education* (Washington, DC: U.S. Department of Education, 2008-033), 2.

4. Data on this will be provided later in the chapter.

5. Jessica Laufer and Sian Winship, "Perception v. Reality: Employer Attitudes and Rebranding of Workforce Intermediaries" in *Workforce Intermediaries For the Twenty-First Century*, ed. Robert Giloth (Philadelphia: Temple University Press, 2004), 216–14, 230, and 234.

6. For the number of community colleges, see www.aacc.nche.edu/AboutCC/Pages/fastfacts.aspx. Among community colleges, 17% have enrollment of at least 10,000 and 12% have enrollment of 500 or below. Twenty-three percent of community colleges are in California. See U.S. Department of Education, National Center for Education Statistics, *Community Colleges*, 3.

7. U.S. Department of Education, National Center for Educational Statistics, *Enrollment In Postsecondary Institutions*, table 1.

8. There are many public four-year schools that grant two-year degrees, major examples being South Texas College (formerly known as South Texas Community College) and Miami Dade College.

9. U.S. Department of Education, National Center for Educational Statistics, *Enrollment In Postsecondary Institutions*. Other data sources present slightly different figures. For ex-

ample, in a survey of high school graduates in 2003–2004, 19.9% of seniors went directly into community colleges. See U.S. Department of Education, National Center for Education Statistics, 41.

10. See Richard Kazis, *Community Colleges and Low Income Populations* (Boston: Jobs for the Future, March 2002).

11. Thomas Bailey, Timothy Leinbach, Marc Scott, Mariana Alfonso, Gregory Kienzl, and Benjamin Kennedy, "The Characteristics of Occupational Students In Postsecondary Education," *CCRC Brief No. 21* (New York: Community College Research Center, Teachers College, August 2004).

12. U.S. Department of Education, National Center for Education Statistics, *Community Colleges*, 21.

13. American Association of Community Colleges puts the figure at 5 million; data available at www.aacc.nche.edu/AboutCC/Pages/fastfacts.aspx. By contrast, researchers at Teachers College Community College Research Center, using the National Household Education Survey, put the number somewhat above credit enrollment. See Michelle Van Noy, James Jacobs, Suzanne Korey, Thomas Bailey, and Katherine Hughes, *The Landscape of Noncredit Workforce Education: State Policies and Community College Practices* (New York: Community College Research Center, Teachers College, January 2008), 5.

14. Steven Brint and Jerome Karabel, *The Diverted Dream: Community Colleges and The Promise of Educational Opportunity In America, 1900–1985* (New York: Oxford University Press, 1989); Kevin Dougherty, *The Contradictory College: The Conflicting Origins, Impacts, and Futures of the Community College* (New York: State University of New York Press, 1994).

15. James Rosenbaum, Regina Deil-Amen, and Ann Person, *After Admission: From College Access to College Success* (New York: Russell Sage Foundation, 2006).

16. The sharpest contrast is with Germany, which utilizes the so-called "dual apprenticeship model" at the high school level and therefore has a noticeably lower postsecondary attendance rate than does the United States (22% for 25- to 34-year-olds in Germany versus 39% in the United States), and among those in postsecondary education, it has a smaller percentage following vocational paths. See Gerhard Bosch and Jean Charest, eds. *Vocational Training: International Perspectives* (New York: Routledge, 2010), 9.

17. Aziza Eugenie Agia, "The Role of Biotechnology Training Partnerships in Expanding Local Employment Opportunities for Community College Graduates in California's Biotechnology Industry" (PhD dissertation, MIT Department of Urban Studies and Planning, 2010).

18. Nochola Lowe, Harvey Goldstein, and Mary Donegan, "Patchwork Intermediaries: Challenge and Opportunities for Regionally Coordinated Workforce Development," *Economic Development Quarterly* (forthcoming).

19. Available at www.milwaukee.tec.wi.us/matc_news/2010_Heath_Info_Tech_Grant.html.

20. There is considerable variation state to state in how these noncredit workforce programs are tracked and funded. In some states, credit and noncredit courses are integrated in terms of governance, while in others, they reside in separate bureaucracies within the community college. Only about half of the states provide guidelines for determining what courses should be credit and what noncredit, twelve states do not require community

colleges to provide any reporting on their noncredit courses, and only about half of all states provide any state funding for noncredit courses. See Van Noy et al., *The Landscape of Noncredit Workforce Education*, 5.

21. See Harry Holzer and Robert Lerman, "The Future of Middle Skill Jobs," *CCF Brief Number 41* (Washington, DC: The Brookings Institution, February 2009).

22. T. Alan Lacey and Benjamin Wright, "Occupational Projections To 2018," *Monthly Labor Review*, November 2009, 82–123.

23. The president of Macomb Community College, where President Obama unveiled his initiative, wrote recently that "in areas such as health, business, and information technology which have been mainstays for community college occupational training programs, employers are increasingly favoring graduates with four year degrees." See Thomas Bailey and Jim Jacobs, "Can Community Colleges Rise To The Occasion," *American Prospect* 20, no. 9 (October 26, 2009): A18–A20.

24. The BLS does evaluate its work, and the conclusions are mixed. See Andrew Alpert and Jill Auyer, "Evaluating The BLS 1988-2000 Employment Projections," *Monthly Labor Review*, October 2003, 13–37. For the period 1988–2000, the projections were correct with respect to direction (growth or decline) for eight of the nine major occupational groups. When it came to detailed occupations, the patterns are more complicated. The average error for all occupations was 23.2%, but when weighted by employment, the error fell to 4.4%. This implies that the projections are most accurate for the largest occupations, which is what in fact is the case. For example, for the twenty occupations that were projected to produce the largest job growth, the average error was 9.2%.

25. Thomas Kain and Ceclia Rouse, "Labor Market Returns To Two and Four Year Colleges," *American Economic Review* 85 (1995): 600–14; Dave E Marcotte, Thomas Bailey, Carey Borkoski, Greg S Kienzl, "The Returns of a Community College Education: Evidence From the National Education Longitudinal Survey," *Educational Evaluation and Policy Analysis* 27 (Summer 2005): 157–75. The estimates year 2000 are for wages for students who were in the eighth grade in 1988 and no longer in school when the earnings data were collected. Because the data source—the National Educational Longitudinal Survey—is quite rich, the authors were able to control for high school performance, as well as a wide range of parental characteristics. These controls substantially reduce concerns regarding selection bias in driving the results.

26. U.S. Department of Education, National Center for Educational Statistics, *Enrollment In Postsecondary Institutions*, table 5.

27. U.S. Department of Education, National Center for Education Statistics, *Beginning Postsecondary Students Longitudinal Study, First Follow-up, 2003–04* (Washington, DC: U.S. Department of Education, 2004), http://nces.ed.gov/das/library/tables_listings/showTable2005.asp?popup=true&tableID=3786&rt=p.

28. Paul Attewell, D. Lavin, T. Domina, and T. Leavey, "New Evidence on College Remediation," *Journal of Higher Education* 77, no. 5 (2006): 886–924. Cited in Thomas Bailey, "Rethinking Developmental Education In Community College," *CCRC Brief Number 40* (New York: Community College Research Center, Teachers College, February 2009).

29. Marty Liebowitz and Judith Combs Taylor, *Breaking Through: Helping Low Income Adults Succeed in College and Careers* (Washington, DC: Jobs For The Future and National Council For Workforce Education, November 2004).

30. Thomas Bailey, D. W. Jeong, and S. Cho, "Referral, Enrollment, and Completion in Developmental Education Sequences in Community Colleges" (Community College Research Center Working Paper no. 15: New York: Community College Research Center, Teachers College, 2008).

31. Liebowitz and Taylor, *Breaking Through.*

32. Thomas Bailey, "Rethinking Developmental Education In Community College," *CCRC Brief Number 40* (New York: Community College Research Center, Teachers College, February 2009), 2–3.

33. The program has been replicated in the Rio Grande Valley; Austin; El Paso; Houston; and Tucson.

34. Project QUEST and several of its replications have been evaluated several times. See Brenda Lautsch and Paul Osterman, "Changing the Constraints: A Successful Employment and Training Strategy," in *Jobs and Economic Development*, ed., Robert Giloth (Thousand Oaks, CA: Sage Publications, 1998), 214–233. See also reports provided by the Aspen Institute Workforce Strategies Initiative, www.aspenwsi.org/. For data on outcomes of Year Up, see www.yearup.org/. For the Tennessee Technology Centers, the graduation rate is 75%. See Jamie Merisotis and Stan Jones, "Degrees of Speed: Millions of unemployed Americans need to upgrade their skills, fast. Community colleges aren't up to the task, but with help from Washington, they could be," *Washington Monthly*, May/June 2010, 14–17.

35. Rosenbaum, Deil-Amen, and Person, *After Admission*; Bailey and Jacobs, "Can Community Colleges Rise To The Occasion?"; Liebowitz and Combes Taylor, *Breaking Through*; Brian Bosworth, *Life-Long Learning: New Strategies For The Education of Working Adults* (Washington, DC: Center For American Progress, 2007).

36. An example of a tightly focused pathway is the Arkansas Career Pathways Initiative. See *The Arkansas Career Pathways Initiative: A New Model For Delivering Postsecondary Training To Adults* (Little Rock, AR: Southern Good Faith Fund, February 2008).

37. City University of New York, "A New Community College Concept Paper," August 15, 2008.

38. A recent study examined what happened to high-achieving students from low-income families. High-achieving students are defined as those in the top 25% of national standardized test scores. Of these who managed to graduate from high school (and there is income-correlated attrition all along the way), 16% above-median family income families went to community colleges, while 24% of those below median did so. See Joshua Weiner, John Bridgeland, and John Diulio, *America Is Failing Millions of High Achieving Students From Low Income Families* (Lansdowne, VA: Jack Kent Cook Foundation, 2007).

39. A good example is the MDRC project "Opening Doors." See www.mdrc.org/project_31_2.html.

40. U.S. Government Accounting Office, *Proprietary Schools: Stronger Department of Education Oversight Is Needed To Assure That Only Eligible Students Receive Federal Financial*

Aid (Washington, DC: U.S. Government Accountability Office, August 2009), 17–8. These figures include less-than-two, two-year, and four-year institutions.

41. U.S. Government Accounting Office, *Proprietary Schools*, 6, 17, 18.

42. U.S. Department of Education, National Center for Educational Statistics, *Enrollment In Postsecondary Institutions*, table 5.

43. Rosenbaum, Deil-Amen, and Person, *After Admission*.

44. Jennifer L. Stephan, James E. Rosenbaum, and Ann E. Person, "Stratification In College Entry and Completion," *Social Science Research* 38 (2009): 572–93.

45. U.S. Department of Education, National Center for Educational Statistics, *Enrollment In Postsecondary Institutions*, table 1.

46. U.S. Department of Education, National Center For Education Statistics, *Community Colleges*, 42.

47. Ibid.

48. A recent example was featured in Peter Goodman, "In Hard Times Lured Into Trade School and Debt," *New York Times*, March 13, 2010.

49. Patricia Steele and Sandy Baum, "How Much Are College Students Borrowing?" *College Board Policy Brief*, August 2009, 2–3.

50. U.S. Government Accounting Office, *Proprietary Schools*, 17–8.

51. For an additional expression of concern about the practices of some proprietary schools, see the letter to the Secretary of Education from a coalition of public interest groups in support of stricter regulations on proprietary school eligibility for student financial aid, http://projectonstudentdebt.org/pub_view.php?idx=613.

52. Robert Lerman, *Training Tomorrow's Workforce: Community College and Apprenticeship As Collaborative Routes To Rewarding Careers* (Washington, DC: Center for American Progress, December 2009).

53. Ibid., 13. Lerman cites Kevin Hollenbeck as showing that the rates of return to registered apprenticeships exceed those for community college.

54. Ibid., 18.

55. For reviews of the evaluation literature, see Paul Osterman, "Demand Side Policies To Improve Job Quality," in *A Future of Good Jobs*, eds. Timothy Bartik and Susan Houseman (Kalamazoo, MI: The Upjohn Institute For Employment Policy, 2008), 203–244; Paul Osterman, "Employment and Training Policies: New Directions for Less Skilled Adults," in *Workforce Policies for a Changing Economy*, eds. Harry Holzer and Demetra Nightingale (Washington, DC: Urban Institute, 2006), 119–154. See also evaluations available on Web sites of the Aspen Institute, Public-Private Ventures, and MDRC.

56. See Louis Soares, *Working Learners: Educating Our Entire Workforce For Success In The 21st Century* (Washington, DC: Center For American Progress, June 2009), 11.

57. Project QUEST costs well over $10,000 per student. Year Up's program cost is $24,000 per student with $16,000 from employer internships, so the net program cost is $8,000. By

contrast, as we have seen, community college costs are under $3,000 per student. Of course, as I argue, these lower costs lead to worse results.

58. U.S. Department of Education, National Center for Educational Statistics, *Enrollment In Postsecondary Institutions*, table 1.

59. This description was provided in a personal communication by Stan Jones of Complete College America

60. For a similar argument about the mission of four-year schools, see Kevin Carey, "Community Colleges: To Thine Own Self Be True," *Newsweek* online, September 16, 2009, www.newsweek.com/id/215469.

61. In commenting on these activities, one report noted that "adult education, workforce development, and developmental education practitioners often see themselves as part of separate and unrelated fields . . ." and to this list could also be added the credit faculty in degree programs. See Liebowitz and Combs Taylor, *Breaking Through*, 8.

62. See Rebecca Klein-Collins, *Fueling the Race to Postsecondary Success: A 48-Institution Study of Prior Learning Assessment and Adult Student Outcomes* (Chicago: Council For Adult and Experiential Learning, 2010).

63. Stephen Katsinas and Terence Tollefson, *Funding And Access Issues In Higher Education: A Community College Perspective* (Tuscaloosa, AL: University of Alabama Education Policy Center, 2010).

64. An example is that in El Paso, the community college worked with the local high schools to identify in advance students who may have needed remedial work when they arrived at the college. These students were given additional attention and assistance in preparing for the entrance tests, and the results were that a substantially lower proportion of new entrants were forced into developmental education. See www.achievingthedream.org/ABOUTATD/CASESTUDIES/default.tp. There are certainly many examples like this, but achieving change at scale is a very different matter.

65. U.S. Department of Education, National Center For Education Statistics, *Community Colleges*, 8.

66. A study of faculty development practices in well-performing and poorly performing schools characterized the *well-performing* as follows: "In the past, it gave new adjunct faculty the textbook and said 'go ahead and teach.' Now the college provides more support to adjuncts, including an office, email and internet connections, and a phone number. At the same time adjuncts are watched more carefully and given more guidance than are full-time faculty." A *low-impact* school was characterized as follows: "the college does not seem to have made any efforts to promote faculty development during our study period." See Davis Jenkins, "What Community College Management Practices Are Effective In Promoting Student Success? A Study of High and Low Impact Institutions" (New York: Community College Research Center, Teachers College, October 2006), 66, 98.

67. Bailey and Jacobs, "Can Community Colleges Rise To The Occasion?"

68. Basmat Parsad, Laurie Lewis, and Peter Tice, "Distance Education At Degree Granting Postsecondary Institutions, 2006–2007" (Washington, DC: U.S. Department of Education, 2009-044, December 2008), 10.

69. I. A. Allen and J. Seaman, *Staying the Course: On-Line Education In the United States, 2008* (Babson Park, MA: Babson Survey Research Group and the Sloan Consortium, 2008), cited in Matthew Zeidenberg and Thomas Bailey, "Human Resource Development and Career and Technical Education In the United States"(paper prepared for the APEC Human Resources Development Group Meeting, Chicago, 2009).

70. For example, in New Jersey, an experimental distance learning program that enrolled poor single mothers reported very high retention and satisfaction rates. See Mary Gatta, *Not Just Getting By: The New Era of Flexible Workforce Development* (Lanham, MD: Lexington Books, 2005).

71. For a more extensive discussion of data accountability systems in higher education, see Kevin Carey and Chad Aldeman, *Ready to Assemble: A Model State Higher Education Accountability System* (Washington, DC: Education Sector, December 2008).

72. Kevin Dougherty and Rebecca Natow, "The Demise of Higher Education Performance Systems In Three States," *CCRC Working Paper 17* (New York: Community College Research Center, Teachers College, May 2009).

73. Tennessee state report available on Complete College America Web site, www .completecollege.org/state_data/.

74. Case studies of some of outcomes of this initiative can be found at www .achievingthedream.org/ABOUTATD/CASESTUDIES/default.tp.

Chapter 6

1. See, for example, Dominic J. Brewer, Susan M. Gates, and Charles A. Goldman, *In Pursuit of Prestige: Strategy and Competition in U.S. Higher Education* (New Brunswick, NJ: Transaction Publishers, 2001).

2. Michael Moe, *Next Knowledge Factbook 2009*, 57, www.nextupresearch.com.

3. The College Board. *Trends in College Pricing 2008,* http://professionals.collegeboard. com/datareports-research/trends/college-pricing-2006.

4. U.S. Department of Education, National Center for Education Statistics, "National Postsecondary Student Aid Study 2003-2004 (NPSAS: 2004)," http://nces.ed.gov/dasol/.

5. William Tierney and Guilbert Hentschke, *New Players, Different Game: Understanding the Rise of For-profit Colleges and Universities* (Baltimore: Johns Hopkins University Press, 2007).

6. See Sorena Badway and Patricia J. Gumport, *For-Profit Higher Education and Community Colleges* (Stanford, CA: National Center for Postsecondary Improvement, Stanford University, 2002).

7. Guilbert Hentschke, *U.S. ex rel Hendow v. University of Phoenix,* Case No. CIV S-03-0457-GEB-DAD, United States District Court for the Eastern District of California.

8. See www.ed.gov/news/pressreleases/2001/09/09192001a.html.

9. See www.apollolegal.com/hendowCase.html.

10. See, for example, www.pbs.org/wgbh/pages/frontline/collegeinc/view/; see, for example, http://higheredwatch.newamerica.net/node/33528.

11. "Quick Takes: High-Profile Trader's Harsh Critique of For-Profit Colleges," *Inside Education*, May 27, 2010.

12. See http://chronicle.com/article/Senators-Vow-to-Crack-Down-on/66058/?sid= at&utm_source=at&utm_medium=en. and, for a contradictory analysis, see http://nexusresearch.org/1/NexusStudy9-1-10.pdf.

13. See http://americancollegeofhair.com/.

14. Lawrence Gladieux and Laura Perna, *Borrowers Who Drop Out: A Neglected Aspect of the College Student Loan Trend* (Washington, DC: The National Center for Public Policy and Higher Education, 2005), www.highereducation.org.

15. Christina Wei and C. Dennis Carroll, *Persistence and Attainment of Beginning Students with Pell Grants.* (Washington, DC: National Center for Education Statistics, U.S. Department of Education, 2002), 85.

16. Richard S. Ruch, *Higher Ed, Inc.: The Rise of the for-Profit University* (Baltimore: Johns Hopkins University Press, 2001), 30.

17. Robert Lytle, Roger Brinner, and Chris Ross, *Parthenon Perspectives on Private Sector Post-secondary Schools. Do They Deliver Value to Students and Society?* (Boston: The Parthenon Group, April 2010), http://insidehighered.com/content/download/342079/4271610/version/1/file/ctives-.

18. U.S. Department of Education, National Center for Education Statistics, Integrated Postsecondary Education Data System (IPEDS), "Institutional Characteristics Survey, 2007–2008," http://nces.ed.gov/dasol/.

19. Based on review of CCI Curriculum Guides and interview with CCI Chief Academic Officer, Rick Simpson.

20. Imagine America Foundation, *Economic Impact of America's Career Colleges* (Washington, DC: Imagine America Foundation, 2007).

21. U.S. Department of Education, National Center for Education Statistics, Integrated Postsecondary Education Data System (IPEDS). "Enrollment Survey, Fall 2007," http://nces.ed.gov/dasol/.

22. Imagine American Foundation, *Economic Impact of America's Career Colleges.*

23. Michael Moe, *Next Knowledge Factbook 2009*, 68–70, based on 2005–2006 data, www.nextupresearch.com.

24. Andrew Steinerman and Jeffrey Volshteyn, *J.P. Morgan Business and Education Services* (New York: J.P. Morgan North America Equity Research, May 2010), 15.

25. Jacqueline Raphael and Sheila Tobias, "Profit-Making or Profiteering? Proprietaries Target Teacher Education," *Change* 29, no. 6 (1997): 44–9.

26. Lytle, Brinner, and Ross, *Parthenon Perspectives on Private Sector Post-secondary Schools,* 9, http://insidehighered.com/content/download/342079/4271610/version/1/file/ctives-.

27. Steinerman and Volshteyn, *J.P. Morgan Business and Education Services*, 17.

28. Examples include Laureate University and, at the K–12 level, Edison Schools.

29. Higher Education Program and Policy Council, *Shared Governance in Colleges and Universities* (Washington, DC: American Federal of Teachers, AFL-CIO, 1996), 4.

30. Based on phone interview.

31. "Corinthian selling 12 schools in Canada," *Sacramento Business Journal,* December 2007.

32. Press release, Apollo Group, April 5, 2010.

33. Press release, DeVry, Inc., March 19, 2003.

34. Online Faculty Certification Process, 10.

35. Based on interview with an individual who served as a UOP faculty member in 1991.

36. Based on phone interview.

37. Nick Klopsis, "Wal-Mart, American Public University Partner to Offer Affordable Employee College Plan," *NY Daily News,* June 3, 2010, www.nydailynews.com/money/2010/06/03/2010-06-03_walmart_american_public_university_partner_to_offer_affordable_employee_college_.html.

38. Interviews with officials from DeVry, Corinthian, and University of Phoenix.

39. Extracted from University of Phoenix's student Web site.

40. *2008 Fact Book* (Washington, DC: Imagine American Foundation, 2008), 6, www.imagineamericafoundation.com.

41. Lytle, Brinner, and Ross, *Parthenon Perspectives on Private Sector Post-secondary Schools,* 7.

42. For the distinction between "disruptive" and "sustaining," see the works of Clayton Christensen, *The Innovator's Dilemma* (Boston: Harvard Business School Press, 1997).

43. See www.stateuniversity.com/universities/CA/Long_Beach_City_College.html.

44. Karin Fischer, "Problem: Foreign Students. Solution: Corporate Partner," *Chronicle of Higher Education,* September 5, 2008, http://chronicle.com/article/Problem-Foreign-Students-/26596/.

45. "Middlebury College and K12 Inc. to create online learning business and expand language academies," press release, www.middlebury.edu/mil/release.

46. See www.insidehighered.com/news/2009/10/20/review; See http://phx.corporate-ir.net/phoenix.zhtml?c=79624&p=irol-newsArticle&ID=948937&highlight= .

47. Based on phone interview with Corinthian senior management.

48. Peter Smith, "You Can't Get There from Here: Five Ways to Clear Roadblocks for College Transfer Students," *AEI Education Outlook* (Washington, DC: American Enterprise Institute for Public Policy Research, May 2010).

49. Rebecca Klein-Collins, *Fueling the Race to Post-Secondary Success: A 48-Institution Study of Prior Learning Assessment and Adult Learning Outcomes* (Chicago: The Council for Adult and Experiential Learning, 2010).

50. See www.changinghighereducation.com/2010/06/walmart-brings-higher-ed-to-its-employees.html.

Chapter 7

1. William A. Draves and Julie Coates, *Nine Shift: Work, Life and Education in the 21st Century* (River Falls, WI: LERN Books, 2004), 229.

2. David F. Noble, "Digital Diploma Mills Part I: The Automation of Higher Education," October 1997, http://communication.ucsd.edu/dl/ddm1.html.

3. I. Elaine Allen and Jeff Seaman, *Learning on Demand: Online Education in the United States, 2009* (Babson Park, MA: Babson Survey Research Group, 2010), 5.

4. Richard Garrett, "The Big Picture 2009: Online Higher Education Market Update," *Eduventures*, October 2009.

5. Clayton M. Christensen, Michael B. Horn, and Curtis W. Johnson, *Disrupting Class: How Disruptive Innovation Will Change the Way the World Learns* (New York: McGraw-Hill, 2008), 47.

6. Richard Garrett, "The Big Picture 2009."

7. Börje Holmberg, *The Evolution, Principles and Practices of Distance Education* (Oldenburg: BIS-Verlag der Carl von Ossietzky Universität Oldenburg, 2005), 13, www.mde.uni-oldenburg.de/download/asfvolume11_eBook.pdf.

8. Bizhan Nasseh, "A Brief History of Distance Education," *Adult Education in the News*, 1997.

9. Derek Bok, *Universities in the Marketplace: The Commercialization of Higher Education* (Princeton, NJ: Princeton University Press, 2003), 81.

10. Michael Jeffries, "The History of Distance Education," www.digitalschool.net/edu/DL_history_mJeffries.html.

11. Robert Zemsky and William F. Massy, "Thwarted Innovation: What Happened to e-learning and Why," The Learning Alliance for Higher Education, 2004.

12. Richard Garrett, "The Big Picture 2009: Online Higher Education Market Update."

13. Ibid.

14. Allen and Seaman, *Learning on Demand*.

15. Author's own research for Eduventures, unpublished.

16. David F. Noble, "Digital Diploma Mills Part II: The Coming Battle Over Online Instruction," March 1998, http://communication.ucsd.edu/dl/ddm2.html.

17. Bok, *Universities in the Marketplace*.

18. Council for Higher Education Accreditation, "Degree Mills: An Old Problem and a New Threat," http://chea.org/degreemills/frmPaper.htm.

19. Allen and Seaman, *Learning on Demand*, 4.

20. Garrett, "The Big Picture 2009."

21. Ibid.

22. Ibid.

23. Eduventures, "Deepening Our Understanding of the Adult Learner's Decision-Making Process," March 2009.

24. Ibid.

25. Distance Education and Training Council, "2004 Distance Education Survey: A Report on Course Structure and Educational Services in Distance Education and Training Council Member Institutions," June 2004, www.eric.ed.gov/PDFS/ED483321.pdf.

26. Laura Horn and C. Dennis Carroll, "Placing Graduation Rates in Context," National Center for Education Statistics, U.S. Department of Education, October 2006.

27. Vincent Tinto, "Limits of Theory & Practice in Student Attrition," *Journal of Higher Education* 53, no. 6 (1982), 687–700.

28. Bok, *Universities in the Marketplace*, 92.

29. Edward D. Goldberg and David M. Seldin, "The Future of Higher Education in an Internet World: Twilight or Dawn?" in *Dollars, Distance, and Online Education: The New Economics of College Teaching and Learning,* eds. Martin J. Finkelstein et al. (Phoenix, AZ: Oryx Press for the American Council on Education, 2000).

30. U.S. Department of Education, Office of Planning, Evaluation, and Policy Development, *Evaluation of Evidence-Based Practices in Online Learning: A Meta-Analysis and Review of Online Learning Studies,* (Washington, DC, 2010), xiv, http://www2.ed.gov/rschstat/eval/tech/evidence-based-practices/finalreport.pdf .

31. Jeff Seaman, "Online Learning as a Strategic Asset: Volume II: The Paradox of Faculty Voices: Views and Experiences with Online Learning," Association of Public and Land-grant Universities, August 2009, 6, www.aplu.org/NetCommunity/Document.Doc?id=1879.

32. Ibid., 7.

33. Ibid.

34. U.S. Department of Education, *Evaluation of Evidence-Based Practices in Online Learning.*

35. Judith V. Boettcher, "How Much Does It Cost to Put a Course Online? It All Depends," in *Dollars, Distance, and Online Education: The New Economics of College Teaching and Learning,* eds. Martin J. Finkelstein et al. (Phoenix, AZ: Oryx Press for the American Council on Education, 2000), 191, 194.

36. A National Dialogue: The Secretary of Education's Commission on the Future of Higher Education, *Testimony of Dr. Carol A. Twigg,* April 6, 2006, 1, http://www2.ed.gov/about/bdscomm/list/hiedfuture/4th-meeting/twigg.pdf.

37. Ibid., 3.

38. Ibid., 2.

39. Ibid., 3.

40. Ibid., 11–14.

41. Noble, "Digital Diploma Mills Part II."

42. David F. Noble, "Digital Diploma Mills Part IV: Rehearsal for the Revolution," November 1999, http://communication.ucsd.edu/dl/ddm4.html.

43. Bok, *Universities in the Marketplace*, 95.

44. Garrett, "The Big Picture 2009."

45. Richard Garrett, conversation, March 24, 2010.

46. Christensen, Horn, and Johnson, *Disrupting Class*, 97–98.

47. University of the People Web site, www.uopeople.org; Note: University of the People's Provost, David H. Cohen, and former provost at Northwestern and vice president of arts and sciences at Columbia University, is on the Eduventures, Inc., board of directors.

48. Ibid.

49. Steve Kolowich, "A Great Experiment," *Inside Higher Ed*, February 22, 2010, www .insidehighered.com/news/2010/02/22/uopeople.

50. Ibid.

51. Ibid.

52. Christensen, Horn, and Johnson, *Disrupting Class*, 111.

53. Ibid., 142.

54. William G. Tierney and Guilbert C. Hentschke, *New Players, Different Game: Understanding the Rise of For-Profit Colleges and Universities* (Baltimore: Johns Hopkins University Press, 2007), 195.

55. Ibid.

56. Bok, *Universities in the Marketplace*, 97.

57. Draves and Coates, *Nine Shift*, 268.

58. Rob Jenkins, "A Technophobe's Guide to Managing Online Courses," *Chronicle of Higher Education*, March 11, 2010, http://chronicle.com/article/A-Technophobes-Guide-to/64549/.

59. Bill Gates, "2010 Annual Letter from Bill Gates," Bill & Melinda Gates Foundation, January 2010.

Chapter 8

1. Interview conducted with the author via telephone on March 9, 2010.

About the Editors

Kevin Carey is the policy director at Education Sector. In addition to managing Education Sector's policy team, he regularly contributes to the Quick and the Ed blog and has published Education Sector reports on topics including a blueprint for a new system of college rankings, how states inflate educational progress under No Child Left Behind, and improving minority college graduation rates. He has published magazine articles and op-eds in publications including *Washington Monthly*, *The American Prospect*, *Phi Delta Kappan*, *Change*, *Education Week*, the *Washington Post*, the *Los Angeles Times*, the *New York Daily News*, and *Christian Science Monitor*. He also writes a monthly column on higher education policy for *Chronicle of Higher Education*. In 1995, Carey worked as an education finance analyst for the state of Indiana, where he developed a new formula for setting local property taxes and distributing state education aid. He subsequently served as a senior analyst for the Indiana Senate Finance Committee, writing legislation and advising the Democratic caucus on fiscal policy. From 1999 to 2001, he served as Indiana's assistant state budget director for education, where he advised the governor on finance and policy issues in K–12 and higher education. In 2001, Carey became an analyst for the Center on Budget and Policy Priorities, a nonprofit research organization focused on policies that serve low- and moderate-income families. There he published new research on state poverty-based education funding programs. Carey subsequently worked at the Education Trust, where he was director of policy research.

Andrew P. Kelly is a research fellow in education policy studies at AEI and a doctoral candidate in political science at the University of California–Berkeley. His research focuses on education policy, congressional policy making, and public opinion. As a graduate student, Kelly was a National Science Foundation interdisciplinary training fellow and graduate student instructor. Previously, he was a research assistant at AEI, where his work focused on the preparation of school leaders, collective bargaining in public schools, and the politics of education. His research has appeared in *Teachers College Record*, *Educational Policy*, *Policy Studies Journal*, *Education Next*, *Education Week*, *Forbes*, and various edited volumes. He is a coauthor of the AEI reports "Diplomas and Dropouts: Which Schools Actually Graduate Their Students (and Which Don't)" and "Rising to the Challenge: Hispanic College Graduation Rates as a National Priority."

Ben Wildavsky is a senior fellow in research and policy at the Kauffman Foundation and author of *The Great Brain Race: How Global Universities Are Reshaping the World* (Princeton University Press, 2010). He joined the Kauffman Foundation following an eighteen-year career as a writer and editor specializing in education and public policy. Most recently, he was education editor of *U.S. News & World Report*. Previously, Wildavsky was budget, tax, and trade correspondent for *National Journal*, higher education reporter for the *San Francisco Chronicle*, and executive editor of the *Public Interest*. A guest scholar at the Brookings Institution, he has also written for the *Washington Post*, the *Wall Street Journal*, the *Washington Monthly*, the *New Republic*, and other publications, and blogs for the *Chronicle of Higher Education*'s new global edition. As a consultant to national education reformers, he has written and edited several influential reports, including the 2006 report of the Secretary of Education's Commission on the Future of Higher Education. In addition to numerous media appearances, he has spoken at Google, Harvard, the London School of Economics, the Association of American Universities, the National Academies, and many other organizations.

About the Contributors

Dominic J. Brewer is associate dean for research and faculty affairs and the Clifford H. and Betty C. Allen Professor in Urban Leadership at the Rossier School of Education at the University of Southern California (USC). He holds courtesy appointments in the USC Department of Economics and in the School of Policy Planning and Development. He is also a codirector of Policy Analysis for California Education, a policy research collaboration of USC, the University of California–Berkeley, and Stanford University. Brewer is a labor economist specializing in the economics of education and education policy. Before joining USC in 2005, he was a vice president at RAND Corporation. Brewer has overseen major projects focusing on educational productivity and teacher issues in both K–12 and higher education. He is the author of *In Pursuit of Prestige* (Transaction Press, 2001). Brewer is a coeditor of *Educational Evaluation and Policy Analysis* for 2010–2012.

Ronald G. Ehrenberg is the Irving M. Ives Professor of Industrial and Labor Relations and Economics and a Stephen H. Weiss Presidential Fellow at Cornell University, as well as the director of the Cornell Higher Education Research Institute. He served as Cornell's vice president for academic programs, planning, and budgeting from July 1995 to June 1998 and was an elected member of Cornell's board of trustees from July 2006 to June 2010.

He currently is a member of the board of trustees of the State University of New York (SUNY). Ehrenberg's most recent coauthored book is *Educating Scholars: Doctoral Education in the Humanities* (Princeton University Press, 2010). He has served as chair of several American Association of University Professors committees and of the National Research Council's Board on Higher Education. He is a member of the National Academy of Education and a fellow of the Society of Labor Economists, the American Educational Research Association, and the TIAA-CREF Institute.

Guilbert C. Hentschke is the Cooper Chair in Education at the University of Southern California's (USC) Rossier School of Education, where he served as dean from 1988 to 2000. At USC, he is faculty adviser of the MBA–EdD program and serves as senior adviser to the National Resource Center for Charter School Finance and Governance. His recent publications (solely and jointly produced) include *New Players, Different Game: Understanding the Rise of For-Profit Colleges and Universities* (Johns Hopkins University Press, 2007); *For-Profit Colleges and Universities: Their Markets, Regulation, Performance, and Place in Higher Education* (Stylus Publishing, 2010); "The Business of Education: Social Purposes, Market Forces and the Changing Organisation of Schools" (in *Handbook of Educational Leadership and Management*, Pearson Education, 2003); and "Characteristics of Growth in the Education Industry: Illustrations from U.S. Education Businesses" (in *New Arenas of Education Politics*, Palgrave Macmillan, 2007). Hentschke's current board directorships include WestEd Regional Education Laboratory, Education Industry Foundation, California Credit Union, Excellent Education Development, Giraffe Charter Schools, and Mercury Online Academies.

Jon Marcus is the U.S. correspondent for the *Times Higher Education* magazine (U.K.) and has written about higher education for *CrossTalk*, the journal of the National Center for Public Policy and Higher Education; *Change: The Magazine of Higher Learning*; *Washington Monthly*; *U.S. News & World Report*; the *Boston Globe Magazine*; and other publications. The former editor of *Boston Magazine*, he also is an author, freelance writer, and investigative journalist. Marcus holds a master's degree from the Graduate School of Journalism at Columbia University and a bachelor's degree from Bates College, attended Oxford University, and teaches journalism at Boston College and Boston University.

William F. Massy is a self-employed consultant to higher education and an emeritus professor and former vice president of Stanford University. He has been active as a professor, consultant, and university administrator for more than forty years. Massy earned tenure as a professor in the Stanford Graduate School of Business, where he also served as director of the doctoral program and associate dean. He then moved to Stanford's central administration as vice provost and dean of research, acting provost, and vice president for business and finance, during which time he developed and pioneered financial planning and management tools that have become standard in the field. For example, his book with David Hopkins, *Planning Models for Colleges and Universities*, received the Operations Research Society of America's Frederick W. Lanchester Prize for 1981, and in 1995 he received the Society for College and University Planning's annual career award for outstanding contributions to college and university planning.

Paul Osterman is the Nanyang Technological University Professor of Human Resources and Management at the MIT Sloan School of Management. His books include *The Truth about Middle Managers: Who They Are, How They Work, Why They Matter* (Harvard Business School Press, 2008); *Gathering Power: The Future of Progressive Politics in America* (Beacon Press, 2003); *Securing Prosperity: How the American Labor Market Has Changed and What to Do about It* (Princeton University Press, 1999); *Employment Futures: Reorganization, Dislocation, and Public Policy* (Oxford University Press, 1988) and *Getting Started: The Youth Labor Market* (MIT Press, 1978). He is also the coauthor of *Working in America: A Blueprint for the New Labor Market* (MIT Press, 2002); *The Mutual Gains Enterprise: Forging a Winning Partnership among Labor, Management, and Government*

(Harvard Business Press, 1994); and *Change at Work* (Oxford University Press, 1997), and the editor of two books, *Internal Labor Markets* (MIT Press, 1984) and *Broken Ladders: Managerial Careers in the New Economy* (Oxford University Press, 1996). In addition, he has written numerous academic journal articles and policy issue papers on topics such as the organization of work within firms, labor-market policy, and economic development. Osterman has been a senior administrator of job training programs for the Commonwealth of Massachusetts and consulted widely to firms, government agencies, and foundations.

Peter Stokes is the executive vice president and chief research officer for Eduventures. In the twelve years that he has been with Eduventures, his work has focused on helping colleges and universities serve adult learners, grow online enrollments, educate future teachers, and demonstrate meaningful outcomes. In 2005, he was recognized as one of "higher education's new generation of thinkers" by *Chronicle of Higher Education*. He provided testimony to then-U.S. secretary of education Margaret Spellings's Commission on the Future of Higher Education and later served as an adviser to the commission in the development of its final report, *A Test of Leadership*. Stokes was a member of the Council for Higher Education Accreditation Tenth Anniversary Commission, which sought to support the strengthening of higher education accreditation. He also worked on Governor Deval Patrick's Commonwealth Readiness Commission to support the development of a ten-year strategy for education in Massachusetts. Previously, he was manager of the industry research group at Daratech, Inc.

William G. Tierney is the director of the Center for Higher Education Policy Analysis, University Professor, and Wilbur-Kieffer Professor of Higher Education at the Rossier School of Education at the University of Southern California (USC). Former president of the USC Academic Senate, he chaired the PhD program for the USC Rossier School of Education and chaired the University Committee on Academic Review. He also served as president of the Association for the Study of Higher Education. His research interests pertain to organizational performance, equity, and faculty roles and rewards. His recent publications include *The Impact of Culture on Organizational Decision-Making* (Stylus Publishing, 2008); *New Players, Different Game: Understanding the Rise of For-Profit Colleges and Universities* (with Guilbert Hentschke, John Hopkins University Press, 2007); *Trust and the Public Good: Examining the Cultural Conditions of Academic Work* (Peter Lang Publishing Group, 2006); *Urban High School Students and the Challenge of Access: Many Routes, Difficult Paths* (Peter Lang Publishing Group, 2006); and *Building the Responsive Campus: Creating High Performance Colleges and Universities* (Sage, 1999).

Index